EXPLORING ISRAEL'S HISTORY

God's Chosen People—
Their Past, Present, and Future

ROBERT T. BOYD

BIBLE PUBLISHERS, INC.
Iowa Falls, IA 50126 U.S.A.

To

Christian-Jewish organizations
that are interested
in winning Jews to Christ *today*

and in loving memory of

The author,
who went to be with the Lord
March 1, 2001.
By his wife, Peggy

Exploring Israel's History

Unless otherwise noted, all scripture quotations in this book are taken from the King James Version of the Holy Bible.

The author gratefully acknowledges permission to reproduce illustrations from the following sources:

Alva Museum Replicas, New York, New York (Fig. 15)
American Baptist Publications, Philadelphia, Pennsylvania (Fig. 33)
The British Museum, London, England (Figs. 6, 29, 30, and 32)
The Cairo Museum, Cairo, Egypt (Figs. 2, 3, and 23)
George Cameron, University of Michigan, Ann Arbor, Michigan (Fig. 31)
Delachaux & Neistle, Neuchatel, Switzerland (Fig. 18)
Fratelli Alinari, Rome, Italy (Fig. 39)
The Israel Museum, Jerusalem, Israel (Figs. 17 and 19)
David Livingston, Associates for Bible Research, Lititz, Pennsylvania (Fig. 34)
The Louvre Museum, Paris, France (Fig. 22)
The Metropolitan Museum of Art, New York, New York (Fig. 4)
The Oriental Institute of Chicago, Chicago, Illinois (Fig. 8)
Palestine Exploration Fund, London, England (Fig. 24)
Charles Pfeiffer (Figs. 7, 9, and 10)
James Pritchard, Berkeley, California (Fig. 16)

ISBN 0-529-11281-7

Published by
World Bible Publishers, Inc.
Iowa Falls, Iowa 50126 U.S.A.

Cover by Design Corps, Batavia, IL.

Printed in the United States of America

1 2 3 4 5 RRD 05 04 03 02 01

CONTENTS

APPENDIXES

ILLUSTRATIONS

FIGURES

MAPS

PREFACE

The Old Testament revolves around Abraham and his descendants—the Hebrews, Jews, Israelites. Abraham was called to be the father of a people, a nation, through whom the "Seed" of the woman, namely Messiah, would be born to defeat Satan and to be God's sacrifice for sin (Genesis 3:15; Galatians 4:4–5). These people were to obey God's commandments and be known as "a people called by His name" (Deuteronomy 28:9–10). They were promised a land in which to live, since they represented the true and living God among nations that were idolatrous and extremely wicked (Leviticus 18).

Among these people chosen by God was a small number who exercised faith in Him and His Word and who were called "the remnant" (of believers), but the majority of the Israelites disobeyed God throughout the Old and New Testament periods. We find in the Book of Judges, after their possession of this promised land, that their disobedience began to bring judgment upon them, even at times serving the people whom they had failed to drive out of the land as God had commanded. God outlined the blessings for obedience in Deuteronomy 28:1–14, and His judgments for disobedience in verses 15–68.

The apostle Paul provides the reason for us to learn through Scripture what befell these people because of their disobedience, mentioning the actions of some Israelites during their wilderness journey, actions that reveal characteristics of their behavior throughout their history. The word *some* does not refer to the believing remnant, but to those who disobeyed God and rebelled against Him. Paul wrote, "Now these things were our *examples,* to the intent we should not lust after evil things, as they lusted. . . . They are written for our admonition that we might profit by their wrongdoings and live a godly life in this present evil world" (I Corinthians 10:6,11). In other words, as we profit by their wrongdoings, we obey God's Word, and those who see and know us will know that we are a people called by His name. We will be *telling* others what great things God has done for us as we *show forth* the praises of Him who has called us out of darkness into His marvellous light (Mark 5:19; Luke 8:39; I Peter 2:9b).

It is imperative that every believer study Scripture, which has been given to us as God's inspired Word. In so doing, we are showing ourselves as being approved by Him, unashamed workmen before the ungodly world in which we live. This enables us to learn much about the "blessings of obedience" and the "judgments of disobedience."

This book begins with Israel's being chosen by God, the Israelites' bondage in Egypt followed by their exodus and wilderness journey to the Promised

Land under the leadership of Moses and Joshua. Once inside the land, the Israelites defeated one enemy after another in order to possess it, and they did possess the *whole* land (Joshua 11:23, 21:43–45). Obedience had brought them into the land that "flowed with milk and honey," and what a blessing it was to have their own homeland, a place that they could call their own after bondage in Egypt and forty years in the wilderness!

Although there was much complaining and disobedience prior to their entrance into Canaan, and disobedience in not driving out all the inhabitants whom God told them to, the Israelites' major rebelliousness began after Joshua and his elders died. In the Book of Judges, which recounts how the majority embraced Baal worship and chose a king so as to be like other nations, the stage was set for even more disobedience as they approached the division of the United Kingdom of Israel. From that point forward, their defiance took them to greater and greater depths.

Continued possession of the land was conditioned on obedience to God. The principle announced throughout God's dealings with His people in this matter was, "Obey Me and I will bless you; disobey Me and you will be taken out of the land" (Leviticus 26:27–35; Deuteronomy 4:1–2, 23–26). Israel failed to drive out certain nations from the land as God had commanded; she did not have full, effective control of all the land when she was taken into 70 years of Babylonian captivity; and upon her return she was under Gentile rule; but these facts do not mean that there had been any failure on God's part or of His divine promises.

At the beginning of the New Testament era, the Hebrews had become rebellious under Roman rule. Their religious leaders were blinded to the Scripture because of following the "traditions of their fathers," the oral law of the rabbis. Christians are familiar with the opposition that Jesus met during His earthly ministry, with His trial before Pilate, and with His death at Calvary, as well as with the opposition the apostles encountered as they witnessed in the establishment of the Church dispensation. Jewish disobedience and opposition finally brought about the fulfillment of Jesus' prophecy that Jerusalem and the Temple would be completely destroyed (Luke 19:43–44; 20:21–24).

This prophecy was fulfilled when a Roman army under Titus destroyed both the city and the Temple in A.D. 70. The Jews were driven out of their land and dispersed worldwide. Brutal anti-Semitic acts followed the Jews wherever they went; hundreds of thousands were destroyed. We are most familiar with the Holocaust before and during World War II under Hitler. So that Jews could return to their ancient homeland, the United Nations partitioned Palestine in 1947. In 1948, after a bitter war with the Arabs, Israel declared herself to be a nation—2,584 years after she was dissolved when Nebuchadnezzar destroyed Jerusalem in 586 B.C. Today there is still much unrest in the land, but there is also much prosperity as these people have fulfilled prophecy after prophecy in reclaiming the land.

My first visit to the Holy Land was in 1951. Along the Mediterranean coastline communities were flourishing, but there was a great deal of wasteland in the southern region. Over a period of 30 years that included eight more visits, it was amazing to see how cities, villages, farms, forests, and vineyards had blossomed forth. How true the Word of God has been as certain prophecies have been fulfilled since the Jews returned!

I am fully aware of future promises concerning Israel's having full possession of the land once more. God made a covenant with Abraham regarding His people and the land; the covenant included *everlasting possession* of the land from the river of Egypt to the great river Euphrates (Genesis 15:7–18, 17:8). Although this book mainly considers Israel's history *from day one to the present,* the ultimate vision for this book is to go beyond a study of the Jewish people to offer principles based on all scripture. The appendixes offer further insight and resources for reaching out to our Jewish friends given our common background growing out of the scriptures.

To avoid concerns about the authenticity of statements made, especially those that relate to Jewish actions recorded in the Old Testament, I use *their* Bible, the Tanakh, in three editions: *Tanakh: A New Translation of The Holy Scriptures According to the Traditional Hebrew Text* (1985), *The Holy Scriptures according to the Masoretic Text* (1937), and *The Holy Scriptures* (1936). Quotations from the Old Testament are taken from the last of these unless otherwise noted. Quotations from the New Testament are taken from the King James Version unless otherwise noted. I have italicized some words in Biblical quotations for emphasis. Following are abbreviations for the versions of the Bible used in this book:

H *The Holy Scriptures* (1936)
KJV King James Version
M *The Holy Scriptures according to the Masoretic Text* (1937)
NIV New International Version
T *Tanakh: A New Translation of The Holy Scriptures According to the Traditional Hebrew Text* (1985)

ACKNOWLEDGMENT

Many thanks to my wife, Peggy, in helping to research Israel's past in their Scriptures, the Tanakh, and their history since the days of father Abraham to the present; to Demi Tsiatsos and Thelma Ober for proofreading; and to Rev. Douglas May for his computer assistance.

I

ORIGINS

1

ORIGIN OF THE HEBREWS

For all things there must be a beginning. From the creation of Adam until God's choice of Abram to become the head of a great nation (Genesis 12:1–3), there were many nations: the Chaldean, Egyptian, Hittite, Canaanite, among others—chapters 12 through 15 of Genesis list at least 22. Races were known as "nations" or "peoples."

With the calling of Abram to become the head of a great nation, it is important to note that he is called "Abram the *Hebrew*" (meaning "exalted father"). This is the first use of the word "Hebrew" in the Bible. Abram's name was later changed to "Abraham," which means "father of a multitude of nations" (Genesis 17:4). When Jacob had his wrestling match with an angel, his name was changed to "Israel," which means "to strive with God" (Genesis 32:28). During the "exodus" wilderness journey from Egypt, Abraham's descendants were called "chosen" people, or as the Hebrew text puts it, "consecrated, chosen to be God's treasured people out of all the peoples that are upon the face of the earth" (Deuteronomy 7:6). The Hebrew Bible refers to these Hebrew/Israel people as "Jews" in Ezra 4:12 and Esther 3:6. Over a span of approximately 1,500 years, three names were given to this nation of people that issued from the loins of father Abraham—*Hebrew, Israel,* and *Jew.* The King James Version of the Old Testament constantly refers to other people as *Gentiles,* but the Hebrew Bible refers to them as "aliens" (Numbers 35:15), "strangers" (Deuteronomy 10:19), "nations" or "peoples" (Isaiah 49:22), and "foreigners" (I Kings 8:41). In the New Testament, people are usually referred to as *Jew, Greek,* or *Gentile.*

Besides *Hebrew, Israel,* and *Jew,* there is another term used in reference to Abraham's descendants: *Semitism,* along with its opposite, *anti-Semitism.* Simply defined, the latter term means hatred of the Jews—animosity toward those whom God chose to be His special people. Is there a *legitimate* reason why so many people hate the Jews? Is there any justification to so despise them that they are ostracized and even slaughtered? Certainly in God's sight, the answer is an emphatic *no,* especially in view of so many Old Testament prophecies that point to a Jewish Messiah sent by God because He loved every person of the human race regardless of national origin. Why, then, such hatred of only one race—the Jews? Why have they been singled out? Why have they paid such a tremendous price just for being Jews? Can we blame this hatred entirely on other races? Is the Jewish race the lowest form of humanity and for this they must suffer? Can anti-Semitism be justified?

We will deal with this subject in a later chapter, but for the moment, the answer, I believe, can be found in the Old Testament. We will consider Israel's calling by God, her position as God's nation on earth, the instructions that He gave to the Jews for His divine blessings to be theirs in return for obedience to His Word, and the consequences that would befall them if they failed to obey Him and *be* all that they were chosen to be. The Hebrew Scripture itself will provide the reason why so much opposition and so many problems have befallen this nation and people for centuries. In the meantime, pity the person who hates Jews simply because they are Jews!

11

THE BLESSINGS OF OBEDIENCE

2

ISRAEL, CHOSEN BY GOD

When we look at man's origin we note that after Adam's fall, God promised a "Seed" that would defeat the originator of sin, namely that old serpent, the devil (Genesis 3:14,15). Adam and Eve, expelled from the Garden of Eden, became fruitful and multiplied. Because the vast majority of people refused to retain a knowledge of God in their hearts and minds, by the time of Noah "the Lord saw great was their wickedness on earth, and how every plan devised by his mind was nothing but evil all the time" (6:5). As a result, nearly the entire human race was destroyed by a great flood; only Noah and his family were delivered.

The human race started all over again (Genesis 10:1) and, sad to say, most people left God out of their lives and desired to make a name for themselves by building a city and tower to reach to the top of heaven, lest they be scattered over the earth. The Lord interrupted their effort, confused their tongue (language), and scattered them over the face of the earth (11:1–9). In the resultant confusion, God needed one person to preserve the lineage through whom the "Seed" of the woman would come to be the Redeemer of mankind.

Abraham was chosen to be the head of that nation. He was told, "Go forth from your native land and from your father's house to the land that I will show you" (Genesis 12:1–3). This "promised land" was made known to Abraham once he arrived in the land shown him. It was "from the river of Egypt to the great river, the river Euphrates," which comprised ten nations (15:18–21). Later, God promised a son, or seed, to the aged Abraham to continue the promise he had given to him (15:1–6). Because Abraham's wife, Sarai, thought that she was too old to have a child, she persuaded her husband to have a child by his handmaid, Hagar (Genesis 16). Ishmael was born, and from his descendants through Esau and the Edomites have come the Arab nations of today.

We need to remember that Esau's descendants never forgave Jacob for getting Esau's birthright and Isaac's blessing (Genesis 25:27–34, 27:1–23). Their hatred was demonstrated when Moses wanted to pass through their land after the Israelites refused to enter the Promised Land at Kadesh-barnea (Numbers 20:14–21; Obadiah 10–14). We can see this hatred perpetuated in the Arab people of today, who trace their ancestry back through Ishmael to Abraham. This could be one cause of the hatred toward Jewish people.

Isaac, "the promised seed," was born after Ishmael. From Isaac came Jacob, father of the sons who later became the leaders (heads) of the twelve Tribes of Israel. One of Jacob's sons, Joseph, was hated by his brothers and was sold to merchantmen and taken to Egypt. Through no fault of his own, Joseph was imprisoned, but upon release he was elevated to a position second only to Pharaoh. Due to a famine throughout the known world, Jacob sent his sons to Egypt for food. In dispensing grain to foreigners, Joseph recognized his brothers. Revealing himself to them, he said, "God sent me before you to preserve you a posterity in the earth, and to save your lives by a great deliverance" (Genesis 45:5–11). According to this statement, it was not God's *permissive* will that placed Joseph in Egypt, but His *direct* will. "If Israel were to be the people through whom Messiah was to come, they would have to survive a seven year famine in which there would be no planting and harvest. God, who foresaw this famine in all the lands, engineered circumstances in such a way that His man was in a land of plenty to save His people from annihilation by starvation."[1] Jacob and his whole family moved to Egypt to be with Joseph, and there the Hebrews not only enjoyed a great measure of freedom but increased and multiplied.

Sometime after Joseph's death, there arose a king who knew him not. Aware of the Hebrews' numerical strength by this time and fearful that they might rebel and try to overthrow the government, Pharaoh placed them in bondage and set taskmasters over them. Realizing that Israel would increase further, all newborn males were to be killed (Exodus 1:6–22). Thus was the prophecy to Abraham fulfilled—the children of Israel sojourning in Egypt and, later, their bondage (Genesis 15:13,14; Exodus 12:40).

To bring Israel's years of bondage to a close so that she might be free to return to the homeland promised to Abraham and his seed, God executed ten plagues to force Pharaoh to his knees and allow Israel's exodus. The "Passover" was performed, and the Israelites left Egypt to begin their journey "home" (Exodus 10–12). It was at Mount Sinai that God revealed to them that, on the condition of their obedience to Him, He would make them a "kingdom of priests and an holy nation" (Exodus 19:6). The Ten Commandments (Decalogue) were given to Moses on Mount Sinai, along with instructions for the erection of the Tabernacle, the place in which God would dwell among His people (20:1–14, 25:8–9). The Books of Leviticus, Numbers, and Deuteronomy contain lists of certain feasts, codes, and sacrifices that Israel was to observe.

THE MAKING OF A NATION

Dr. George B. Fletcher has written,

> A race of people become a 'nation' when laws are made to govern, and we find in the wilderness that Israel is established as a nation. The nation's Ruler was to be Jehovah, its constitution was the Law given at

> Mount Sinai, its central national shrine was the Tabernacle, its bond of unity was the spiritual worship of the One True God, and its national hope was the 'prophet like unto Moses,' their Messiah (Deuteronomy 18:15,18 with Acts 3:22,23).
>
> It is important that we understand the meaning of the creation of this nation. It *was not* the election of a nation from among others in order that upon that nation God might lavish His love while He abandoned the others. The purpose was that of the creation of a testimony through this nation for the sake of others.[2]

Israel was chosen to be God's "holy, special, peculiar people unto Himself, above all people that are upon the face of the earth" (Deuteronomy 7:6–8). They were chosen to keep His oath that He had sworn unto their fathers—chosen not to be His *pet,* but His *pattern* in obedience to Him (7:6–11). So much emphasis has been and is placed upon Israel's being God's "chosen people," God's "holy nation," and rightly so, but Israel was *never* chosen or made holy in relation to *salvation.* They were not "saved" or "redeemed" just because of their calling. Nations round about, ignorant of God, were running rampant with sin. God was providing a "holy" nation in the world to set an example, "holy" referring to those who were consecrated, ceremonially and morally dedicated to Him. "Holy" carries with it the notion of being set apart or consecrated; examples are Moses being on "holy" ground (Exodus 3:5), the Temple building being "holy" (Hosea 2:20), Mount Sinai being "holy" (Psalm 68:17), and the city of Jerusalem being God's "holy" mountain (Daniel 9:16).

Nowhere does the Bible teach "national" salvation. Only on an *individual* basis is one saved, whether in Old Testament times or New Testament times. God's righteousness is imputed by an individual's faith, as was Abraham's (Genesis 15:6). The apostle Paul applies this concept both to Abraham and King David and to believers today (Romans 4; II Corinthians 5:21). We see the prophet Elijah as an individual standing for God, along with 7,000 others who had not bent their knees to Baal. Isaiah speaks of a "remnant" in contrast to the sinful Israelites (Isaiah 1:9–10). Christ told the hypocritical Jewish Pharisees of His day, "If ye were Abraham's children," you would do the works of your father Abraham (John 8:39). Even Nicodemus, a ruler of the Jews, a member of the Jewish race and the nation of Israel, was not saved just because of this heritage, nor was Saul of Tarsus with his national Jewish heritage (John 3:3–6; Philippians 3:3–6; I Timothy 1:15,16).

Let me repeat: Israel had been chosen to be "holy" in obedience to God's commandments, to be His *pattern* before wicked, sinful nations. Yes, chosen to be that nation or "seed" through whom Messiah would come, but proving that they were God's nation by obedience (Deuteronomy 28:9–10; Romans 9:6).

In relation to the nation of Israel's being "holy" unto God and before the other nations, Moses gave a vivid picture of the vulgarity and wickedness of the "religious" practices of the inhabitants of the Promised Land who worshipped the god Baal. Israel was warned "not to copy their practices, nor shall ye follow their laws" (Leviticus 18:2). Verses 6 through 30 of Leviticus 18 inform us that the Canaanites practiced open sex with family members and their neighbors, offered their sons and daughters as human sacrifices to their gods, and practiced homosexuality and bestiality. Such evil, ungodly behavior was an abomination to God, and His people were to obey *His* laws and have no part in the others' sin. Canaan's sin was so repulsive that God told the children of Israel, upon entrance into Canaan, to "utterly destroy them, make no covenant with them, do not intermarry, and destroy their idols" (Deuteronomy 7:1–5). They were also warned that if they did not drive out the inhabitants from the land, those whom they allowed to remain would be "as thorns in your eyes, as pricks in your sides, and they shall harass you in the land wherein ye dwell. And it shall come to pass, that as I thought to do unto them, *so will I do unto you*" (Numbers 33:50–56).

In Deuteronomy there is a review of the laws that God had given to His people and a setting forth of His purpose for them as a nation. They are told not only what they are to *do,* but also what they should *be* before heathen nations. As His "chosen treasure," His "holy people," God will keep His covenant faithfully to the thousandth generation of those who love Him and keep His commandments (Deuteronomy 6:7–9). Before Moses died, he sought to keep Israel informed of her heritage as God's chosen people and the blessings that could be hers if she obeyed His commandments once she entered the Promised Land.

In Deuteronomy 28:1–14, Israel is told what her blessings will be if she obeys the Lord. If obedient, she will be established as His holy people. It is one thing to say one is holy and quite another for one to reveal holiness. If the Jews reveal God's holiness, "all the peoples of the earth shall see that the name of the Lord is called upon thee [or that you are a people who are called by My name], and they shall be afraid of [fear or revere] thee" (verses 9,10). "The Lord will make thee the head [of nations] and not the tail. And thou shalt be on top and never at the bottom if only they *obey* and do not deviate to the right or left from any of His commandments to go after other gods and serve them" (verses 13,14).

From these verses, we must conclude that Israel's spiritual calling was to make known the true and living God among the sinful nations around them. When Solomon dedicated the Temple, he made it known that it was just as much for "strangers" or "*all* peoples of the earth to worship and call upon the Lord" (I Kings 8:41–43). When Isaiah gave the gracious invitation, "Ho, *everyone* that thirsteth, *come ye* for water, and he that hath no money, *come ye,* buy, and eat; Yea, *come,* buy wine and milk without money and without price" (Isaiah 55:1,5), this included Israel's witnessing and an invitation to a nation she knew not, one that would run to her, "aliens who would join themselves to Israel's God" (56:3,6). The calling of *all* God's people, whether His "holy nation" in the Old Testament or His "holy nation" in the New Testament, is a *tell-and-show* ministry to others of what great things God has done for them (Mark 5:19; Luke 8:39; I Peter 2:9).

Beginning with verse 15 of Deuteronomy 28 to the end of the chapter, it is almost unbelievable what will happen to and with the Jewish people if they disobey the Lord. Just as God had told Adam to obey and not eat of the fruit of His tree and live, or to eat and die, so Moses, in his last speech to Israel, said, "See, I have set before thee this day life and good, death and evil, in that I command thee this day to love the Lord thy God, to walk in His ways, and to keep His commandments and His statutes and His ordinances; then thou shalt live and multiply, and the Lord thy God shall bless thee in the land whither thou goest to possess it. But if thy heart turn away and thou wilt not hear, but shall be drawn away and worship other gods and serve them, I declare unto thee this day that ye shall surely perish. Ye shall not prolong your days upon the land whither thou passeth over the Jordan to go in to possess it. I call heaven and earth to witness against you this day that I have set before thee life and death, the blessing and the curse. Therefore choose life that thou mayest live, thou and thy seed, to love the Lord thy God, to hearken to His voice, and to cleave unto Him, for He is thy life and the length of thy days, that thou mayest dwell in the land which the Lord swore unto thy fathers, to Abraham, to Isaac, and to Jacob, to give to them" (Deuteronomy 30:15–20).

There is one other thought that must be mentioned from Deuteronomy 28: If Israel hearkens not unto the voice of the Lord, curses (judgment) shall come upon them and overtake them and these judgments shall be for a sign and wonder and "*upon thy seed forever*" (verses 45,46).

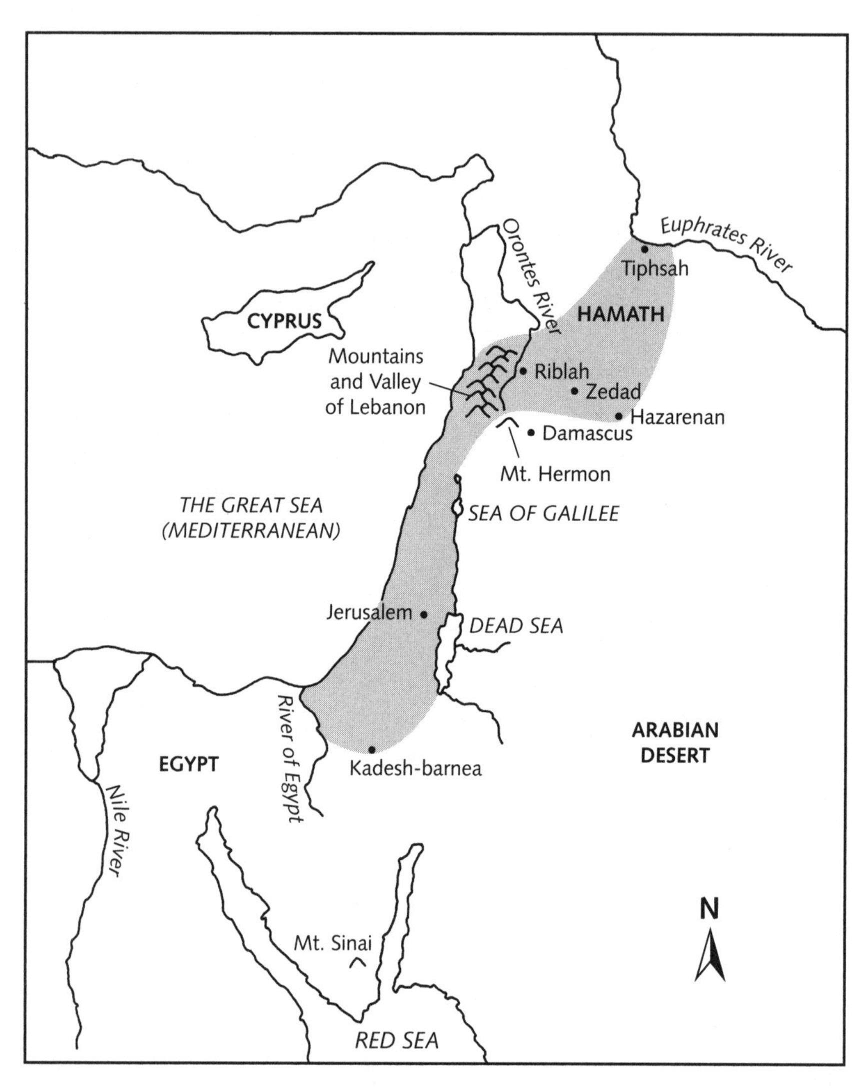

Map 1. Israel's Promised Land. From the river of Egypt to the Euphrates River (Genesis 17:8, 15:18; Deuteronomy 1:7, 8; Joshua 1:2, 4, 6). "From the wilderness to this Lebanon, even unto the great river Euphrates" (Joshua 1:4). Zedad and Hazarenan in Hamath (Numbers 34:8). Riblah in Hamath (II Kings 23:33; Jeremiah 39:5). Tiphsah in Hamath (I Kings 4:24).

3

GOD'S PROMISE OF CANAAN TO ISRAEL

As we approach the subject of Joshua's being used of God to possess the land that flows with milk and honey—the Promised Land—for His people, we must go back to an incident in the Garden of Eden. Due to Adam's sin falling upon the whole human race (Romans 5:12), God gave a promise that one day the "Seed of a woman" would defeat the cause of sin, Satan himself (Genesis 3:15).

Because the vast majority of Adam's descendants went the way of Cain, God preserved those who trusted in Him, such as Abel, Seth, Enoch, and Noah. Those who defied God were so wicked and evil because the imaginations of their hearts were evil *continually,* that God sent a flood to destroy them. He preserved only eight people, Noah and his family, to give the human race a new start, plus two of each animal (Genesis 8–10).

Sadly, the bulk of Noah's posterity became sinful; they ignored God and tried to reach heaven by their works in building the Tower of Babel. This angered God so that He came down and confused the tongues of the people. This was the formation of various nations, each speaking its own language (Genesis 11:1–9).

ABRAHAM, THE RECIPIENT

In order to make sure a lineage was preserved to finally produce the "Seed of the woman" who would redeem people of their sins, God called Abraham out of the pagan city Ur of the Chaldees. He was to go to a land unknown to him, but a land that God would show him that would be given to him and his descendants, making them a great nation. This land was called *Canaan,* the land that would be taken by Joshua to give the children of Israel for their inheritance (Genesis 12:1–3, 17:8). Abraham obeyed God and journeyed into the land of Canaan. Out from him came Isaac, the Seed of promise, and Jacob. Jacob's name was changed to "Israel" (32:24–28). From Jacob came the sons who made up the Twelve Tribes of Israel.

HOW ISRAEL GOT INTO EGYPT

In the course of His dealing with Abraham, the head and founder of the Jewish nation, God made a covenant with him according to which, before the Israelites would possess the land of Canaan and the nations there, they would be sojourners in a land not theirs and would be afflicted for 400 years, but would later come out of this land (Egypt) with great substance (Genesis 15:7–21).

In foreseeing a famine that would affect the whole world during the days of Jacob, God engineered circumstances in such a way that Joseph, Jacob's son, would be sold at Dothan to merchantmen who were going to Egypt. Upon their arrival in Egypt, Joseph was sold as a slave to Potipher, an officer of Pharaoh. His clean life caused Potipher to realize the Lord was with Joseph, whom he promoted to be the overseer in his house. Joseph was tempted by Mrs. Potipher, but refused to sin against God. When she falsely accused him, Potipher had him imprisoned. Later, when Pharaoh's wise men could not interpret his dream, he was told of Joseph's wisdom. Joseph said that the dream referred to seven years of plenty and seven years of famine. Released from prison, Pharaoh made Joseph what we would call today the Secretary of Agriculture, to oversee the good years and store grain for the seven lean years, a famine that would affect the whole world (Genesis 41:27).

Fig. 1. Ruins of Joseph's granaries.

When the famine came to pass and Canaan was affected, Jacob sent his sons to Egypt to buy grain. They were recognized by Joseph, and when his brothers found out who he was, they were remorseful. With a forgiving spirit, Joseph said unto them, "God sent me before you to preserve you a posterity in the earth and to save your lives by a great deliverance. So now it was not you that sent me here but God, and He has made me a father to Pharaoh, a lord (master) in all his house, and a ruler throughout all the land of Egypt" (Genesis 45:7,8). God *is* preserving His people.

Anxious for the whole family to be together, Joseph requested that his brothers return home and bring his father, Jacob, and the rest of his family down to Egypt. All the members of Jacob's family left Hebron and came down to be with Joseph and his family (Genesis 46:8–28). For a goodly number of years these families enjoyed freedom in a land not theirs.

ISRAEL IN EGYPTIAN BONDAGE

After Joseph and all of his generation had died, there arose a Pharaoh who knew not Joseph. The children of Israel had multiplied so great in number that this Pharaoh became fearful that these "foreigners" would rise up and rebel against Egyptian authority and seek to overthrow the government. They were then made slaves, put in bondage to make mud bricks for city buildings (Exodus 1:8–14). Taskmasters were placed over them to make sure that they worked from sunup to sundown and that none escaped.

Fig. 2. Likeness of an Egyptian taskmaster.

As the end of Israel's 400 years of slavery drew near, although she was hopelessly bound with no avenue of escape, God told Moses what He would do to Pharaoh. The Holocaust under Hitler was similar to Israel's bondage in Egypt. There was no deliverance for the Jews in the concentration camps until a force greater than Hitler arrived on the scene, namely the Allies, which set the remaining "branded" Jews free. It took a force greater than Pharaoh to defeat him, and that force was God Himself. How true the saying, "If God be for us, who can be against us?" (Romans 8:31). Note the "I Wills" in chapter 6 of Exodus[3]:

1. *I will* defeat Pharaoh, the *cause* of Israel's bondage: verse 1 with Hebrews 2:14; I John 3:8.
2. *I will* lift your burdens: verse 6a with Matthew 11:28.
3. *I will* set you free from bondage: verse 6b with John 8:32,36.
4. *I will* redeem you: verse 6c with Galatians 3:13; I Peter 1:18,19.
5. *I will* make you My people: 7a with I Peter 2:9,10.
6. *I will* be your God to deliver you: verse 7b with Galatians 1:4.
7. *I will* bring you into a land and *I will* give it to you for your own inheritance: verse 8 with Colossians 1:12–14.

Redemption or deliverance could not come for the children of Israel until *first* the very *cause* of their bondage was defeated. The Passover (redemption) was not instituted until after the judgments of the plagues were levelled against Pharaoh and Egypt (Exodus 7:1–12:23). God did not provide "coats of skin" for Adam and Eve until he pronounced judgment upon that old serpent, the devil, the *cause* of their sin (Genesis 3:14,15). Redemption or salvation could not come to "all who have sinned and come short of God's glory" until the *cause* of sin was dealt with. Jesus *first* judged the prince of this world and spoiled principalities and powers before a victorious redemption or salvation could become operative (John 12:31; Colossians 2:14,15; I John 3:8). How effective would our salvation be if our foe were not defeated? We could never "resist the devil, and he will flee from [us]" (James 4:7). We would have no armor to overcome his fiery darts of temptation (Ephesians 6:10–17; I Corinthians 10:13), and we could not be "more than conquerers through [Christ] that loved us" (Romans 8:37). He came forth from the grave with the keys of hell and of death to prove that He had treated the *cause* of sin (Revelation 1:18). Now we can say, "Thanks be unto God for His unspeakable gift" and "thanks be to God, which giveth us the victory through our Lord Jesus Christ" (II Corinthians 9:15 and I Corinthians 15:57).

MOSES VERSUS PHARAOH—THE TEN PLAGUES

Moses spent 40 years in royalty, having been found by Pharaoh's daughter in the bulrushes where his mother hid him so that he wouldn't be slain by Pharaoh. In a confrontation with an Egyptian who was persecuting a Jewish slave, Moses murdered the Egyptian and fled to the backside of the desert. He spent 40 years tending flocks for his father-in-law. One day Moses was standing by a bush that began to burn but was not consumed. Curious, Moses stepped forward to get a good look, and God spoke to him, telling him that he was on holy ground. God told Moses to go back to Egypt and tell Pharaoh to "let My people go." Moses began to make excuses, but God prevailed, and Moses and Aaron appeared before Pharaoh to bring to pass the *I wills* of God. Pharaoh defiantly refused their request to let Israel go.

How, then, did God begin the process of His *I wills* to free His people? Judgment has always been God's method upon those who rebel against Him, so He sent ten plagues upon the Egyptians for Pharaoh's defiance. None fell upon the Israelites. The first nine plagues were as follows:

1. The Nile River was turned into blood.
2. Frogs covered the land.
3, 4. Gnats and flies swarmed all over the people.
5. Their livestock were stricken.
6. Boils afflicted both man and beast.
7. Hail, lightning on the ground, and thunder killed herbs and felled trees.
8. Locusts, so many that they darkened the sky as they flew overhead, flew into and filled the houses.
9. Darkness covered the land (but there was light for the Israelites).

During the plague of the swarm of flies, Moses requested permission of Pharaoh for the people and their animals to go into the wilderness for three days to make sacrifices unto the Lord. Pharaoh agreed to grant permission if Moses would lift the plague of the flies. Moses did so, but Pharaoh reneged on his promise to let Israel go (Exodus 8:24–29). After the ninth plague, Moses again requested permission to take the people, children, and animals into the wilderness to make sacrifices unto God. Pharaoh said that they could on the condition that only the people and children would leave, but that the animals would remain behind. Thus the animals would not be with the people to make sacrifices, and with no cattle, there would be no milk for the smaller children. Moses refused, whereupon Pharaoh drove Moses out of the palace, saying he didn't want to see his face again (10:24–29).

The Plague of the Death of the Firstborn. The tenth plague involved the death of the firstborn, one that would surely drive Pharaoh to his knees. The Israelites were instructed to slay a lamb and sprinkle its blood on the side and top doorposts, so that when the death angel came and saw the blood, he would pass over that house. Since none of the Egyptian homes had blood on the doorposts, all their firstborn sons were killed, including Pharaoh's firstborn.

This plague instituted the Feast of the Passover, a feast that Israel celebrated in appreciation of God's blood sacrifice that "passed over" them. We see its fulfillment in chapter 12 of Exodus, where death came to families whose homes had no blood on the doorposts: "It came to pass that at midnight the Lord struck down all the firstborn of Egypt from Pharaoh down to the common man. Pharaoh and all his officials got up during the night. There was loud wailing in Egypt for there was not a house without someone dead" (Exodus 12:1–30). Pharaoh had no alternative but to let God's people go.

ISRAEL PREPARES FOR THE EXODUS

When God finished the second and third *I Wills* with the death of Egypt's firstborn sons, Pharaoh gave up, realizing that he could no longer fight the God of Israel. Having awakened that night, he discovered that all of the Egyptians had lost loved ones. Pharaoh called for Moses and Aaron and said, "Rise up and get out of Egypt, leave my people and go and worship the Lord according to your heart's desire as you have requested. Take your flocks and herds, and go, and bless me also" (Exodus 12:31,32). As the people prepared to leave, they gathered what belongings they could, taking what extra clothing they had and wrapping it around the dough (food) they had. Surprisingly, the Israelites found great favor with the people of Egypt, who gave them silver, gold, clothing, and precious jewels (12:31–36). God had prophesied that in the country where they would serve as slaves, they would receive great substance (Genesis 15:14). The Israelites were now ready to follow Moses out of the land they had despised for so many years, thinking that they would be in their permanent homeland in just a few years.

4

CHARACTERISTIC ATTITUDES OF THE ISRAELITES

Before continuing our historical journey with the children of Israel as they enter and settle in the Promised Land, let us review some of the human traits of those chosen to be God's holy, peculiar, treasured people. One feature of the Bible is that it "tells it like it is": it pulls no punches when it comes to revealing facts, whether good or bad, especially in bringing out the meaning of events as they happened. From Abraham to the death of Moses, there is no attempt to sit in judgment of another's faults, to condemn anyone for wrongs or sins committed. It is important to see how one generation after another follows in the footsteps of their ancestors, whether they obey God's commandments or not. This is true of the whole human race, no matter who our ancestors were. None is perfect, "for all have sinned, and come short of the glory of God" (Romans 3:23). More is expected from those who are "chosen to be holy," and as a result, we look to them for examples. Since the Old Testament is a record of these people, here are a few examples:

Abraham enters the picture as a citizen of Ur of the Chaldees and living in an idolatrous home (Genesis 11:31; Joshua 24:2). None will deny that he was a man of great faith, yet at times his wavering faith created trouble. His faith in God led him to leave his home in Ur, but he disobeyed God's command to leave his kindred and his father's household; instead, he took his nephew, Lot, an act that had adverse consequences (Genesis 12:1, also chapters 13 and 19).

Abraham's faith took him to Canaan, where God confirmed His promise that the land would be his and his descendants', but lack of faith due to a famine caused Abraham to leave the place of God's choosing and go to Egypt. Because of Sarai's beauty and for fear that the Egyptians would kill him for her if they knew she was his wife, he persuaded her to tell them that she was his sister. This was a "half-truth" because Sarai was his "half-sister" (Genesis 20:10). But a "half-truth" is a "whole lie" where deception is involved, and when the Pharaoh found out that she was Abraham's wife, orders were given for them to leave the country. Abraham repeated the same lie to King Abimalech, which would have caused the king to have sinned greatly had he taken Sarai to be his wife (20:1–10).

When God told Abraham that he would have an heir to inherit the promises given to him, Abraham believed Him (Genesis 15:1–6). However, considering his and Sarai's ages as well as her barrenness, he probably, as a "henpecked" husband, said "yes, dear" when she told him to have a child by his housemaid, Hagar. This offspring, Ishmael, was not *the* heir, the "Seed of promise," but the "seed of the flesh" (Genesis 16). Ishmael became the father of many nations when he sired twelve sons (Genesis 17:20, 25:12–16). Other nations sprang from Esau's marriage to one of Ishmael's daughters, one of which was the Edomite people (Genesis 28:8,9, 36:1–9; Obadiah). Many Arabs of today are descendants of these nations, claiming "father Abraham" through Ishmael.

Isaac, the "Seed of promise," proved the wisdom of "like father, like son" when he told the men of Gerar that Rebekah was his sister. His sin found him out when he was seen caressing his wife (Genesis 26:6–10).

Moving a few centuries forward, we find a multitude of Abraham's seed living in Egyptian bondage. Suffering under the lash of taskmasters, Israel cried out to God for relief. When Moses tried to encourage them by revealing what God would do to Pharaoh to free them, a streak of stubbornness surfaced as "they hearkened not unto Moses for impatience of spirit and for cruel bondage" (Exodus 6:1–9). It appears that there was such bitterness for having been in Egyptian bondage that throughout their exodus and wilderness experience the Israelites set themselves to mischief (32:22):

1. They complained at the Red Sea: Exodus 14:11,12.
2. They murmured and became obstinate due to lack of food and meat: Genesis 16:1,2; Numbers 11:4–6, 18–33.
3. They complained due to lack of water: Exodus 15:22–24; Numbers 20: 2–11.
4. They were dissatisfied with both food and water: Numbers 21:5,6.
5. They rebelled, taking active steps to return to Egypt, but Moses prayed in their behalf and God overruled: Numbers 14:1–4, 11–20. Had God not answered this prayer,[4]
   - Who would have led them back to Egypt?
   - Who would have fed them?
   - Who would have supplied them with drinking water?
   - Who would have clothed them?
   - Who would have sheltered them from the noonday heat and the chilling nights of the desert?
   - Who would have parted the waters of the Red Sea to get back into Egypt?
   - Who would have been their spokesman if they desired to leave Egypt again?
6. They were demanding and arrogant: Exodus 16:8.

7. They became impatient due to Moses' delay on Sinai and resorted to idolatry: Exodus 32:1–8. Idolatry was not something new for these people; Joshua later mentioned that they had practiced this in Egypt: Joshua 24:15.
8. They lost the privilege of being a "kingdom of priests" when they worshipped the "golden calf," and the Levites were appointed priests: Exodus 32:15–26 with Numbers 3:1–13.
9. They rebelled at Kadesh-barnea when ten spies gave a discouraging report of the Promised Land: Numbers 14 and 15. They failed to pass the test to "walk by faith" and instead, *unbelief* ensued and they "walked by sight."
10. They became violent and almost stoned Moses: Exodus 17:3,4.
11. They were stiff necked (cruel): Exodus 32:9.
12. They manifested self-pity: Numbers 11:5,6; 14:1,2.
13. They showed disrespect for authority: Numbers 16:1–25.
14. They were called "rebels": Numbers 20:10.
15. They became discouraged and spoke against God: Numbers 21:4.
16. They accused God of hating them: Deuteronomy 1:27.
17. They committed harlotry with Moabite women and worshipped their idols: Numbers 25:1–3.
18. They provoked the Lord throughout their entire journey: Deuteronomy 9:7.

It is also interesting to note that there were times when Israel's leaders did not set a good example:

1. Moses disobeyed God by striking the rock for water after God had told him to speak to it: Numbers 20:7–13; Deuteronomy 32:51,52.
2. Aaron disobediently assisted in Israel's idolatry at Sinai; he also rebelled against God at the waters of Meribah with Moses: Exodus 32:1–8; Numbers 20:24.
3. The Levites (priests) were rebellious and stiff necked: Deuteronomy 31: 25–27.
4. Miriam, speaking against Moses, contracted leprosy: Numbers 12; Deuteronomy 24:9.

It would be wrong to single out the faults of a people and leave the good qualities unmentioned, but as we pursue Israel's arrival and settlement in the Promised Land, we will see that her history, according to *her* Scriptures, reveals the predominance of the characteristics mentioned above. Of course, we will note good qualities as we see them in her leaders and prophets and in the remnant.

5
THE EXODUS

THE DATE OF THE EXODUS

There has been much controversy as to the date of Israel's exodus from Egypt. Some liberal scholars give a late date (twelfth or thirteenth century B.C.). Conservatives give an earlier date, around 1450–40 B.C. I prefer to stick with what the Bible has to say. By taking into account the time that Solomon began building the Temple, we can reach an approximate date for Israel's leaving Egypt. It has been calculated that Solomon's reign began in 971 B.C. Work began on the Temple four years later, in 967 B.C., 480 years after the Exodus, according to I Kings 6:1. By adding 480 to 967 we arrive at the approximate date of the beginning of the Exodus—1447 B.C. Forty years later, Israel arrived at the Jordan River, and several days later Joshua led the Israelites into the Promised Land—about 1407 B.C.

THE PHARAOH OF THE EXODUS

Who, then, was the Pharaoh at this time? Amenhotep II began his reign as Pharaoh around 1450–1445 B.C., which would make him the Pharaoh of the Exodus. Some scholars accept Rameses II, who began his reign in 1225 B.C., as the Pharaoh of the Exodus. Since Moses' date of the birth is generally accepted to have been in the 1500s B.C., it would be impossible for Rameses II to be the Pharaoh of the Exodus.

Fig. 3. Amenhotep II, Pharaoh of the Exodus.

THE NUMBER OF ISRAELITES IN THE EXODUS

Can we arrive at an approximate number of Israelites fleeing Egypt? Adam Clarke lists 3,262,000. Others have estimated one to three million people. A Jewish writer has said that the figure of 600,000 men over the age of 20 is an error in copying and that

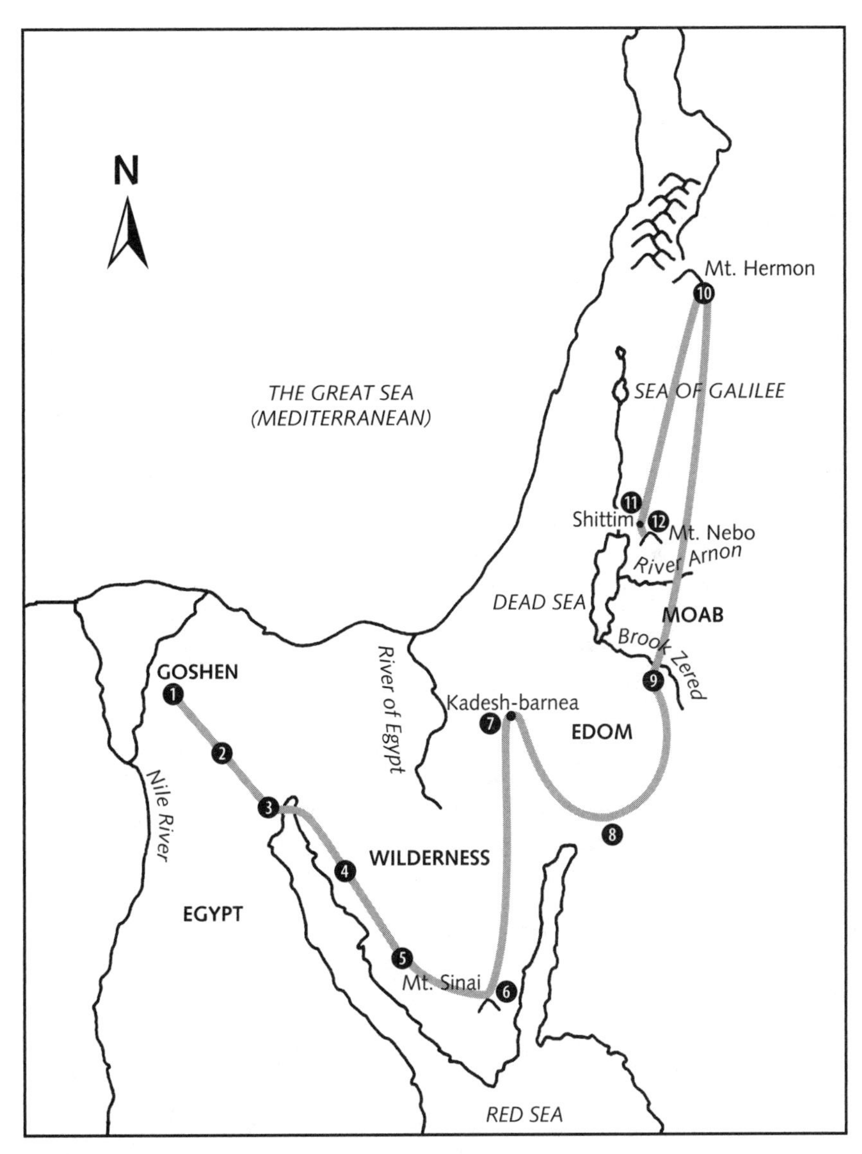

Map 2. Israel's Exodus.

KEY

1 Land of bondage
2 Cloud by day, pillar of fire by night
3 Crossing the Red Sea
4 Manna
5 Water at Horeb
6 The Ten Commandments
7 Spies sent into land
8 Go around Edom's land
9 The brazen serpent
10 Advance through Moab, conquest of land up to Mount Hermon
11 Encampment at Shittim
12 Moses' view of Promised Land and death

the figure should be only 6,000. Only God knows the exact number of people and animals involved in the Exodus. It would be impossible for us to know the number of animals, but we can arrive at an approximate number of men, women, and children, including the mixed multitude. Scripture does not say who the "mixed multitude" people were, but we can assume that they were Egyptians probably at odds with Pharaoh.

Men over the age of 20 (Exodus 12:37; Numbers 1:30)	600,000
Approximate number of women	400,000
Approximate number of children	890,000
Approximate mixed multitude (Exodus 12:38)	10,000
TOTAL	1,900,000

THE JOURNEY BEGINS— GOD'S PROVISIONS

When we think of all the protection that God gave these 1,900,000 people from enemy nations, as well as all the provisions that He gave them in a barren land on their pilgrimage journey, it staggers the imagination. Space does not allow detailing all of them, but several illustrations will show that "If God be for us, who can be against us?" (Romans 8:31; Philippians 4:19).

1. **The Cloud by Day and the Pillar of Fire by Night.** The Israelites started out by venturing into an unknown territory. They had no road maps and really didn't know which way to go. But God gave them the Cloud by Day to lead them and the Pillar of Fire by Night to give them light (Exodus 13:21). When the Cloud moved they were to go forward. When it stopped, they stopped (40:36,37). There are times when God would have us on the move; there are also times when we should be still and wait upon Him (Psalm 4:4, 46:9a). The *steps* of a good man are ordered of the Lord (Psalm 37:23). So are His *stops* (Psalm 27:14). "Order my steps in Your Word and let not any iniquity have dominion over me" (Psalm 119:133). For us to walk in the light as He is in the light without sin becoming victorious over us, there is only one thing to do: "follow his steps" (I Peter 2:21).

Not only was the Cloud by Day for direction, but in the wilderness (desert) it is terrifically hot from the blazing sun, so the Cloud protected the Israelites from a blistering sunburn or sunstroke. Although it is hot in the desert during the daytime, sometimes reaching 120–125° Fahrenheit, during the night it gets extremely cold, so the Pillar of Fire helped to keep them warm.

2. **Crossing the Red Sea.** With the Cloud and Pillar to direct them, God led the Israelites toward the Red Sea. After Pharaoh let them go, he had second thoughts and sent his charioteers in hot pursuit to catch up with them and bring them back to Egypt. When the people heard the sound of chariots as Pharaoh's army drew near, they were in great fear and cried unto the Lord. Moses encouraged them to stand still and see the salvation of the Lord (Exodus 14:1–13).

Fig. 4. Ancient Egyptian chariot.

Behind them was Pharaoh's army, *before* them was the sea, and *around* them, left and right, was the shoreline. There was no avenue of escape, and the people complained bitterly that Moses had brought them out into the wilderness to die. The "pillar of the cloud," which had gone before them, moved to their rear and settled between Israel and the Egyptians (Exodus 14:19). When Moses *looked up* and lifted up his rod, God revealed His salvation (deliverance) in parting the waters, and Israel walked over dry-shod. The Lord was

- For them: Romans 8:31.
- With them: Genesis 28:15; Isaiah 41:10–13.
- Before them: Genesis 13:21.
- Behind them: 14:19; Isaiah 30:21.
- Above them: Joshua 2:11; Psalm 18:16; 144:7.
- Underneath them: Deuteronomy 33:27.
- Around them: Psalm 125:2.
- Over them: Song of Solomon 2:4.

3. **Manna (Food).** As Israel followed the cloud and the pillar, the food they had brought with them ran out (Exodus 12:34a). Complaining to Moses in their hunger, God began to rain down manna (bread) from heaven for their daily meals (Exodus 16:1–15). Manna was furnished for almost 40 years except on the Sabbath, since twice as much was gathered on the sixth day (16:21–22). The manna ceased right after Israel crossed the river Jordan and entered the Promised Land (Joshua 5:10–12).

Can you imagine all the Israelites eating and sleeping together for 40 years?

Can you imagine each of them gathering an omer (six dry pints) of manna *daily* during this period (Exodus 16:16)? They did it for at least 14,400 days (using a lunar year of 30 days per month). If the Israelites numbered 1.9 million people, they would have about 119,000 bushels a day to collect. This is truly a miracle of God's provision for his people.

Manna is a type of Christ, the Bread who came down from heaven (John 6:32–35). Paul refers to it as spiritual meat or food (I Corinthians 10:3). Manna is[5]

- Of divine origin: Exodus 16:15; John 1:1, 2.
- Undeserved: verse 12 with Romans 5:6–8.
- Essential: verse 15 with John 6:35, 15:5.
- Suitable: verses 16–18 with John 6:51.
- Adequate: verse 18 with Philippians 4:19.
- Satisfying: verse 35 with John 6:35; Psalm 34:8.
- The free gift of God: verse 15 with Romans 6:23b.

4. **Water.** This item is very scarce in desert regions. Although oases are widely scattered, at least two are mentioned in Israel's journey: one at Elim and the other near the river Arnon (Exodus 15:27; Numbers 21:14–16). God performed many a miracle in giving water, such as the time Moses struck a rock at Horeb to quench Israel's thirst. We can be sure that the 1,900,000 people drank more than usual in the hot climate of the desert, but it is difficult for anyone to determine the amount of water God furnished daily for 40 years. Suffice it to say God *did,* and the amount was supplied.

Water is a type of the Lord Jesus Christ, who is the "Water of life," providing eternal life with the promise of never thirsting again (John 4:10,14). He is our "Rock" in our journey in a weary land (Isaiah 32:2).

A little Sunday School girl was being chided by an unbeliever for saying God had to supply so much manna and water for Israel. When asked to explain how much, she said she would have to wait until she got to heaven, and then she would ask Moses. The unbeliever said, "What if Moses isn't there?" She replied, "Then *you* ask him!"

The Rock at Horeb (Exodus 17:1–7 with I Corinthians 10:4) was

- Chosen by God: verse 6 with Matthew 3:16,17.
- In the wilderness—Christ is a Rock in a weary land: Isaiah 32:2.
- Smitten: verse 6 with Isaiah 53:4. God instructed Moses to *speak* to the Rock at Meribah when Israel needed water (Numbers 20:8). Instead, Moses, in a fit of anger with the people, struck the rock twice. In disobeying God, he forfeited the privilege of entering the Promised Land. The rock at Horeb, once smitten (a type of the crucifixion of Christ), did not need to be smitten again. His offering was *once and for all* (Hebrews 9:25–28, 10:10). The water gushing out of the twice-smitten rock, in spite of Moses' disobedience, reveals the grace of God to a needy people (Numbers 20:10–12).

- A merciful provision: verse 6 with Psalms 68:19, 78:15–20 and John 4:10,14.
- Free: verse 6 with Isaiah 55:1.

The "Rock" (Christ) followed them, providing a continual supply, full of unseen blessings: I Corinthians 10:4 with Psalm 68:19.

The Scripture is silent in the matter of supplying food and water for the Israelites' animals. Moses said that flocks, herds, and very much cattle were taken on the journey (Exodus 12:38). Sheep and oxen were used as sacrifices in the Tabernacle worship. Much of this is related in the Book of Leviticus.

When the Israelites were in the land of the Midianites east of the Dead Sea and Jordan River, a battle was fought and Israel won. The men and adulterous women were not spared, but all the female virgins were to be spared. Among the spoils of victory were 675,000 sheep, 72,000 oxen, 61,000 donkeys, and 32,000 virgin women (Numbers 31:1–3, 31–35). It had required plenty of faith for the Israelites to take a large number of animals when they left Egypt, considering that these would have to be fed all those years in the wilderness, but to combine these with what they took from the Midianites presents a problem that Congress couldn't figure out.

5. **Defeating Enemies.** After crossing the Red Sea and heading south toward Mount Sinai, Israel encountered the army of the Amalekites (Exodus 17:8–14). A battle ensued, and Moses and his assistants ascended a hill to observe the fighting; Joshua had been selected to lead the Israelite army. As long as Moses' hands were raised, Israel was winning. When Moses became tired and lowered his hands, the Amalekites would overrun them. But when Aaron and Hur held up Moses' hands, Israel defeated their enemy. Moses built an altar on the spot to commemorate God's victory and named it *Jehovah-nissi*—"Our Banner." Moses' trust was in "the Lord, a man of battle" (Exodus 15:3).

Throughout Israel's journey, God went before them to defeat the nations determined to destroy them, protecting His people to fulfill His promise to Abraham concerning the Promised Land. He not only had defeated the Amalekites, but gave Israel victory over the Canaanites at Mount Hor (Numbers 21:1–4). As they approached the land of the Moabites (Deuteronomy 2:19), the Israelites were victorious over the Amorites (Numbers 21:31), the Midianites (Numbers 31:1–8), Og, king of Bashan (Deuteronomy 21:32–35), and northward to Mt. Hermon (Deuteronomy 3:8).

MOUNT SINAI AND THE GIVING OF THE COMMANDMENTS

After crossing the Red Sea and defeating the Amalekites in battle, the Israelites continued on to Mount Sinai. After setting up camp in the valley, Moses told the people that if they obeyed God and kept His covenant, they would be a peculiar treasure above all people and would be a kingdom of priests and a holy nation. They promised God they would obey (Exodus 19:1–8).

After God spoke to Moses on Mount Sinai, Moses came down and was

Fig. 5. Mount Sinai.

given the Ten Commandments *orally* (Exodus 19:20–20:17). God also gave Moses instructions regarding sacrifices and Tabernacle worship (21:1–24:11). Once again, Moses was called by God to ascend the mountain, and this time he was given the Ten Commandments on tablets of stone (24:12). But before he received the Commandments the second time, Moses was given instructions for the materials of the Tabernacle, its implements, garments for the priesthood, sacrifices, and discipline regarding worship (25:1–34:28).

It is often said that Mount Sinai is a *type of the Law,* and rightly so, since it was there that the Ten Commandments were twice given to Moses. Note, however, that it is also a *type of grace,* since instructions were given for the priesthood and for Tabernacle sacrifices for sin, all of which is a *type of Christ.* We can sum it up in two verses: "The Law is the schoolmaster which leads to Christ" and "The Law was given by Moses, but grace and truth came by Jesus Christ (John 1:17; Ephesians 2:8,9).

Remember the promise that the children of Israel made to Moses about obeying God when they were told that God would make them a peculiar and holy people? (Exodus 19:18). Their promise didn't last long. While Moses was on top of Mount Sinai receiving the Ten Commandments written by the finger of God, the Israelites, irritated because Moses had been gone for so long, persuaded Aaron to make them a molten calf (like the god Apis) from the jewelry that they had received from the Egyptians. They then worshipped the calf, eating, drinking, dancing naked, and making merry. When Moses started down the mountain and met Joshua, he was told that the loud noise he heard was coming from the people. Descending farther, Moses saw what the people were doing and, in a fit of anger, he cast down the stones containing the Ten Commandments, breaking them. Once he had quieted the people, Moses asked who was on the Lord's side, and the Levites responded affirmatively. Instead of the people becoming a "kingdom of priests," as they were told they could be if they obeyed the Lord, in their disobedience they forfeited this privilege, and the Levites became God's priesthood. The Book of Leviticus explains many of their duties.

Fig. 6. The golden calf.

As a result of Israel's gross sins, God punished about 3,000 men by putting them to death, and because they were not forgiven, God struck the people with a plague (affliction) for their sins of immorality and idolatry (Exodus 32:15–35). The Jews have a saying, "No affliction has ever happened to Israel to which there was not some particle of the dust of the golden calf."[6] Interestingly, about 3,000 men died after Moses received the Law and about 3,000 souls were saved when Peter preached the Gospel on the Day of Pentecost (Acts 2:41).

As a judge in Greensboro, North Carolina, was administering the oath of citizenship to 50 persons, he advised them to obey the Ten Commandments. If they would, he said, they need not worry about keeping over 35 million laws that have been enacted by their new country! After giving Moses the Ten Commandments orally, and with the second set on stone now broken, God instructed Moses to return to the top of Mount Sinai for a third set of the Commandments on stones that Moses had cut (Exodus 34:1–28). Vance Havner has said that the reason God put these Commandments on stone was because you cannot *twist* or *bend* stone. You either keep the Commandments, or you *break* them! It is said that Moses was the greatest sinner mentioned in the Bible—he broke all Ten Commandments at one time!

KADESH-BARNEA AND SPYING THE LAND

After the mess at Mount Sinai had been cleaned up and the people had been reproved, they marched northward to Kadesh-barnea. It was here that God had set the southern boundary of the Promised Land. Straight ahead was the land that God had promised to Abraham. For Israel to know what lay ahead for them in the land, God instructed Moses to send twelve spies, one from each Tribe, to comb the whole land up to the Euphrates River to determine whether the current inhabitants were weak or strong, few or many, as well as agricultural and other possibilities.

Joshua the Ephraimite was one of the spies, as was Caleb. They searched out the land from the river of Egypt to the entrance of Hamath on the Euphrates River. Their journey, during the ripe grape season, took 40 days. Bringing back some of the delicious fruit, they reported to Moses.

Why bring back some fruit? As Joshua and Caleb were the only two who gave a favorable account of the whole land, they were the ones most likely to have gathered fruit. The "cluster of grapes" is interesting. In ancient Biblical lands grapes were very large. This cluster was so large, along with the other fruit they gathered, it was carried on a pole between two men. It was gathered a short time before their arrival back at camp to assure its freshness. They wanted to convince the people the land was fertile, that it "flowed with milk and honey" (Numbers 13:23–27).

The spies also reported that the inhabitants of the land were strong, there were giants, and the cities were enclosed with huge walls. When Caleb suggested that they should enter the land then to possess it, the *belief* of Joshua and Caleb contrasted with the *unbelief* among the ten other spies and the people. Ten spies had a *walk of sight,* while Joshua and Caleb had taken the *walk of faith.* Notice the conversations that took place in Numbers 13 and 14:

1. *The Ten:* We are not able to go up: 13:31.
   Joshua and Caleb: We are well able: 13:30.
2. *The Ten:* They are stronger than we: 13:31.
   Joshua and Caleb: Their protection has been removed: 14:9.
3. *The Ten:* They gave an evil report of the land: 13:32.
   Joshua and Caleb: It is an exceeding good land: 14:9.
4. *The Ten:* It is a land that devours its inhabitants: 13:32.
   Joshua and Caleb: They shall be our prey: 14:9.
5. *The Ten:* We are grasshoppers in their sight: 13:33.
   Joshua and Caleb: The Lord is with us; fear them not: 14:9.

Accepting the report of the ten unbelieving spies, the people refused to enter the Promised Land at this point. Their anger was so aroused against these believing two that they threatened to stone Joshua and Caleb (Numbers 14: 7–10). Although the minority lost the decision to enter the land then, it proves that the majority is not always right. Israel was now to learn a bitter lesson the hard way. It always turns out this way.

God's anger was so aroused that He pronounced two judgments upon them:

1. For each of the 40 days the men spent in spying out the land, Israel must spend a year wandering in the wilderness—40 years. It didn't take God 40 years to get Israel out of Egypt; it took Him 40 years to get Egypt out of Israel.
2. The people's refusal to heed Joshua and Caleb's advice brought about a death sentence for men over 20 years of age, whose lack of faith caused them to murmur against God, who promised to take them into a land of powerful, hostile enemies. All the men died in the wilderness journey except Joshua and Caleb, who were exempt from this penalty due to their faith in God's ability to deliver (Numbers 14:27–30).

WANDERING IN THE WILDERNESS

Wandering in a barren wasteland for so many years seems like an awful punishment, but not when we consider all God had done for the Israelites in getting them out of Egypt, supplying their physical as well as spiritual needs, and giving them victory over their enemies. Since they refused to enter the land that God had promised, they would soon learn that man reaps what he sows. God does not tolerate disobedience no matter what one does when it comes to defying His commandments.

While still at Kadesh-barnea, Moses asked permission to go through the land of the Edomites. Descendants of Esau, the Edomites were still bitter toward the descendants of Jacob, blaming him for stealing Esau's birthright, even though Esau had sold it to him for a meal to satisfy his hunger (Exodus 25:27–34). Later, when Isaac blessed Jacob, who deceived his father (by obeying his mother) to get the blessing of birthright, Esau hated Jacob and threatened to kill him because he thought that he was the one who was supposed to get the blessing (Genesis 27:1–41). The prophet Obadiah has much to say about the animosity of Esau's descendants toward Jacob.

Since the Edomites did not allow the Israelites to pass through their land, they left Kadesh-barnea and headed south toward the Gulf of Aqaba of the Red Sea, thus circling around the Edomites' land. Here they did battle with the Canaanites and defeated them (Numbers 20:14–21:4). This part of her wilderness journey, lasting 38 years, was nothing more than going around in circles, sort of like the "blind leading the blind." This is what happens when we get out of the will of God. There is no advancement, just going from one place to another. Out of His will, walking by *sight* and not *faith,* we become critical, bitter, vindictive, unruly, and downright mean sometimes. This happened to Israel.

After the Israelites made their way around the land of the Edomites, there was much discouragement on the part of the people—again they complained about lack of food or water, telling God how much they hated the light bread (manna). This was an awful indictment against God, who had been feeding them all along. As a result, fiery serpents were sent and many died from their bites. Crying loudly unto the Lord, they confessed to Moses that they were wrong for complaining and asked Moses for help.

The Brazen Serpent (Numbers 21:5–9).[7] Moses asked God what to do and was instructed to make a fiery (brazen) serpent, put it on a pole, and tell all who were bitten by the snakes to look at the fiery serpent and they would live. It was a matter of personal choice; all who exercised faith and looked were cured—they lived.

This brazen serpent is the only shadow or type of the Cross pointed out by our Lord (John 3:14–18). In the midst of vast hoards of human sinners, sin bitten and dying, there rises a lonely Cross. It was our Lord who said that just as the uplifted serpent was the only means of deliverance for the snake-bitten Israelites, so the uplifted Son of Man is the only means of deliverance now. From this experience we learn, from chapter 21 of Numbers:

1. The *need* of salvation: verse 6 with Romans 3:23, 6:23a.
2. The *method* of salvation: verse 8 with John 19:17,18. Salvation is of the Lord. By a serpent the Israelites had been bitten, and by a symbol in the form of a serpent they must be healed. Through man's disobedience came sin and death, and by One in the form of man came justification by His blood that we might be saved from wrath through Him (Romans 5:9).
3. The *condition* of salvation: verse 8 with John 3:14,15; 12:32.
   - They were not told to look to their wounds to be saved.
   - They were not told to look to Moses to be saved.
   - They were not told to shake off the serpent to be saved.
   - They were not told to keep the law to be saved.
   - They were not told to help one another to be saved.
   - They were not told to go through a ritual to be saved.
   - They were told to look to the fiery serpent to be saved.

   (See Isaiah 45:22.)
4. The *extent* of salvation—it was for *everyone* who was bitten to look: verse 8 with John 3:16.
5. The *effects* of salvation—instantaneous life: verse 9 with John 5:24; II Corinthians 5:17.

The distance from Kadesh-barnea to the southern end of the land of the Edomites at the Red Sea and then up to the Brook Zered just below the southern tip of the Dead Sea is about 200 miles. Israel's wanderings, or going around in circles, during this part of her journey lasted 38 years, as mentioned. It took this amount of time for all the men over 20 years old to die (except Joshua and Caleb), as a penalty for unbelief at Kadesh-barnea in not going into the Promised Land that was to be theirs (Deuteronomy 2:13,14).

GOD'S PUNISHMENT FOR UNBELIEF IN THE WILDERNESS

There is a common saying, "I've got some good news for you and some bad news. Which do you want first?" I'll give the bad news first. Israel, being fickle and a people set to mischief (Exodus 32:22), exercised unbelief at Kadesh-barnea in refusing to enter the Promised Land and constantly revealed their dissatisfaction with the Lord and their leader, Moses. As a result, God said that all males aged 20 years and upward who left Egypt would die in the wilderness (Numbers 14:20–38 with Hebrews 3:15–19).

It was about a year and a half after leaving Egypt, during the building of the Tabernacle, that males 20 years and older were counted. About 600,000 left Egypt (Exodus 12:37); at the time of the counting there were 603,550 (Numbers 1:46). This means that 3,550 19-year-old fellows had reached the age of 20, so we know for sure that 600,000 did leave Egypt in the Exodus. Excluding Caleb and Joshua, we have 599,998 of these males who died in the wilderness. Children were spared, but adults were included in this "death penalty." There were deaths due to plagues or "sin in the camp." Because of the golden calf incident, 3,000 had to be buried. Only God knows how many had to be buried after complaining and being bitten by "fiery serpents" (Numbers 21:6). It was fortunate for Israel that God was the "undertaker" for Korah and his henchmen when they rebelled against God (16:35,49). We also have to consider the 24,000 graves that had to be dug when Israel's men died after committing harlotry with Moabite women and serving their pagan gods (25:1–9).

Would we be safe in saying that no fewer than 1,250,000 Israelites died in the wilderness? Maybe more! Counting 30 days to the lunar month, we would have 360 days per year times 40 years, or at least 14,400 days on which these people died, resulting in at least 85 funerals daily. Undertakers must have worked overtime. Tombstones would probably have had the epitaph, "I expected to die someday, but not in a place like this!" How true the Word of God: "Be sure *your* sin will find *you* out" (Numbers 32:23 with Romans 6:23a).

Leaving the area of Zered, the Israelites headed north up to Moab and crossed over the river Arnon. They were forbidden to take the land of the Ammonites because these people were descendants of Lot (Deuteronomy 2:19). Advancing, they defeated King Sihon of the Amorites at Heshbon (Numbers 21:21–31) and Og, king of Bashan (21:33–35), and then went up to conquer the land as far north as Mount Hermon (Deuteronomy 3:8).

Having finished the Northern Conquest, the Israelites came back and encamped at Shittim on the Jordan River across from Jericho (Numbers 25:1; 33:51), in the land of the Midianites. As they settled there, the Midianite king, Balak, sought out Balaam, the prophet, and asked him to curse Israel because they outnumbered the Midianites and he was fearful of a war that would destroy his kingdom. Balaam, a compromiser who was willing to take a bribe, thought that he could assist Balak. When a sacrifice was offered unto God, which pleased the Lord, Balaam's eyes were opened to his wrong, and he left Balak, returning to the camp of the Israelites (22:1–24:5).

It was here at Shittim that Israel, after all that God had done for them in bringing them through the wilderness and supplying their every need, hit the skids spiritually. Many men began to commit adultery with the heathen Moabite women and embraced and worshipped their gods. God then pronounced a plague upon his people, and 24,000 men died as a result (Numbers 25:1–9). God ordered Moses to utterly defeat the ungodly Midianites, which Israel did (25:17). As previously mentioned, Israel was to keep the animals and all the Midianite women who were virgins. There were 675,000 sheep, 72,000 cattle, 61,000 donkeys, and 32,000 women (Numbers 31:32–35). Again God was gracious unto them.

As Moses was distributing the spoils of victory, the Tribes of Reuben and Gad and the half-Tribe of Manasseh requested that they be given the land from the river Arnon northward. They had much cattle and desired this land because of its fertility. Moses granted their request under the condition that the men of war of these Tribes would cross over the Jordan River with the other Tribes to conquer and possess the whole of the Promised Land. The men promised to stay until the whole land was conquered and then return to their families. They chose not to receive their inheritance in the land God promised them (Deuteronomy 3:12–20). See Map 5 on page 67.

CONCLUSION

As Israel's 40-year wilderness journey came to a conclusion, the question arises, How many Israelites were left? Taking into account all the men over 20 years of age who died (and there were almost 600,000, excepting Joshua, Caleb, and women and children), those who died at Mount Sinai, those who died in battle, the 24,000 at Shittim, and so on, the number of funerals is impossible to determine. Only those men under 20 years of age were left, plus all who were born during the journey. When Moses took a census at Shittim the number of males over 20 was 601,730, only 1,730 more than had left Egypt at that age (Numbers 26:4,51). It has been estimated that 1,900,000 survived. Only God knows.

We have already mentioned how rebellious many of the people were, as indicated by the number who died. A brief review will help us to see that too often *self* is the "besetting sin," a person's biggest enemy. Tragically, the Israelites took their feelings out on God and Moses by "setting themselves on mischief" (Exodus 32:22b); note their record in their journey. They

1. Complained at the Red Sea: Exodus 14:10–12.
2. Became violent and were ready to stone Moses: Exodus 17:3,4.
3. Became stiff necked (cruel): Exodus 32:9.
4. Manifested self-pity: Numbers 11:5, 6; 14:1,2.
5. Exhibited disrespect for authority: Numbers 16: 1–25.
6. Were classified as rebels: Numbers 20:10.
7. Became discouraged and spoke against God: Numbers 21:4.
8. Accused God of hating them: Deuteronomy 1:17.
9. Committed adultery with Moabite women and worshipped their idols: Numbers 25:1–25.
10. Murmured and became obstinate due to lack of food and meat: Numbers 11:4–6, 18–33.
11. Became rebellious and took active steps to return to Egypt (but Moses prayed in their behalf and God overruled): Numbers 4:1–4, 11–20. Had God not answered this prayer,
    - Who would have led them back to Egypt?
    - Who would have fed them?
    - Who would have supplied them with drinking water?
    - Who would have clothed them?
    - Who would have sheltered them from the noonday sun and the chilling nights of the desert?
12. Provoked the Lord throughout their wilderness journey: Deuteronomy 9:7. See Acts 13:18.

In spite of all the opposition that Moses endured from his brothers and sisters, his love for them was demonstrated in his prayer to the Lord in their behalf. God was so disgusted with His people that He was ready to destroy them, but Moses prayed for God not to do it. His prayer was heard and answered, and God let them live (Deuteronomy 9:23–26).

Many critics of the Bible have branded God as a hateful, unloving, judgmental God for the way He punished ungodly, heathen nations. No matter what awful sins Israel committed, He was committed to His covenant promises in their behalf. Now, as we approach their entrance into the Promised Land, He is still with His people, going before them and fighting their battles, so that the promises that were made to Abraham would be fulfilled (Genesis 17:8).

In view of all that the Lord did for Israel throughout her wilderness journey, it is impossible to comprehend the infinite, boundless greatness of our omnipotent, omniscient, and omnipresent God. No wonder the psalmist, standing on the horizon of the universe and considering the heavens, the work of God's fingers, the moon and the stars, said, "What is man that thou art mindful of him?" (Psalm 8:3). God is big enough to control this vast domain, big enough to make every provision for any man's need (II Peter 1:3), and big enough to have stooped to become a Man and be the Saviour to all who receive the Lord Jesus Christ (John 1:12,13, 3:16, 5:24).

How big is God?
How big His creative act?
One's words fail to express.
But our faith accepts as fact
He's big enough to master His universe,
Yet small enough to live within *my* heart!

6

ISRAEL'S EXODUS IS OVER

I am quite sure that all Israelites who survived the wilderness journey were glad within their hearts that such a trek was over. If they had only gone into the Promised Land at Kadesh-barnea, the misery and suffering that befell them would not have occurred. They were now settled down in Shittim at the Jordan River, opposite Jericho, the first city they must conquer. They were aware that only God had brought them this far, supplying guidance, food, water, and victory over all enemies. Believe it or not, their clothes did not become old upon them and their shoes did not wear out (Deuteronomy 29:5). My wife once told me, "No wonder so many women died in the Exodus. If I had to wear the same old dress for 40 years, it would kill me too!" And think of this: When God supplies the shoe leather, we can keep on keeping on. God orders our steps (Psalm 37:23).

MOSES' FINAL WORDS

The days of Moses were numbered. Although he was 120 years old, his vision was 20-20 and his strength had not lessened. Gathering all the people together, he was given God's final message to deliver to those who had followed him for so many years.

He began his farewell speech by assuring the people that God will go before them and that they must be strong and of good courage. He also spoke of God's mercies toward them if they obeyed His commandments, but emphasized that if they disobeyed, apostasy would follow and God's judgment would befall them. A person would do well to look up Deuteronomy 31:1 through 33:29 and meditate upon this section, letting God speak to him personally about His "do's and don'ts."

Israel's behavior among the people of Canaan was to be consistent with every command of God. If the Israelites were to exhibit godly living, they must obediently submit to God's divine order of life in order to be recognized by Him. Such consistency would prove that their God was the true God and not a false god like the others' gods. The impression that Israel was to get of God through His laws left no room for them to think that He would in any way live after the ways of heathen gods, nor induce Israel to follow the ways of these false gods. Israel was given God's laws for the express purpose of guiding them on the straight and narrow path, fleeing the ungodly actions of pagans and showing reverence for their God.

The heart's desire of Moses was that Israel would see that she was not chosen to be God's *pet,* but to be His *pattern* in the midst of a world gone mad with sin. He had told them previously that they were to *prove* their calling as His holy people by keeping His commandments so that the people they confronted daily would know that they were a people called by His name. This was Israel's *spiritual* calling—the same calling that believers in this age have. She was to be the head of nations, not the tail (Deuteronomy 28:9,10,13). She was to let her light shine (Matthew 5:16).

MOSES' DEATH AND BURIAL

After Moses' "sermon," he asked God's blessing upon His people and "went up to the top of Mount Nebo to view the land." He had forfeited his right to lead Israel into it when He was commanded to *speak* to the Rock at Meribah but, in anger against the people, disobediently chose to strike it twice (Numbers 20:8). See Water from Rock in the index.

On Mount Nebo God permitted Moses to see the land. He gazed upon much of it, seeing the palm trees of Jericho and on to the Mediterranean Sea—the Promised Land in which he longed to dwell. Suddenly, he became absent from the body and present with the Lord. Scripture tells us *he went up to die.* One translation tells us that he "died by the kiss of God. God kissed Moses good night and put him to sleep. What a lovely way to go."[8] He was buried in an unknown tomb in the valley of Moab (Deuteronomy 34:1–7).

If God had given Moses a public funeral, I am sure that the following words would have been engraved on the tombstone:

> And there arose not a prophet since in Israel like unto Moses, whom the Lord knew face to face. In all the signs and wonders which the Lord sent him to do in the land of Egypt to Pharaoh, and to all the servants, and to all his land, and in that mighty hand, and in all the great terror which Moses showed in the sight of all Israel.
>
> (Deuteronomy 34:10–12)

It is strange how some people act when a person close to them dies. Israel had been a *thorn* in Moses' side all during the Exodus, but at his death they mourned for him for 30 days (Deuteronomy 34:8). This is typical of many funeral attendees—at odds with the deceased but shedding "crocodile tears" for them. When we truly love one another in the Lord as we should, our conscience is clear when they leave this world. For the believer, there is no room for hypocrisy.

THE PROMISED LAND

Before we turn the leadership over to God's choice, Joshua, we need to consider what property Israel was to possess and who and what the people were like whom she was to destroy.

The Borders of the Promised Land. The first mention of the land was to Abraham, that it was to go from the river of Egypt to the Euphrates River (Genesis 15:18); it must be noted that "the river of Egypt" was *not* the Nile. Abraham was told that his seed would be a stranger (sojourner) *in a land not theirs.* During their bondage the Israelites were in a section of Egypt called Goshen, which was east of the Nile River and the Nile Delta (Exodus 8:22). Since this land was Egyptian territory and not part of the Promised Land, the river of Egypt was located northeast of Goshen. The land from this river to the Euphrates River was all of Canaan (Genesis 17:8). It had been spied out by the 12 tribesmen when they left Kadesh-barnea for Hamath on the Euphrates River (Numbers 13:3, 21, 25–26). The borders of the land are listed in chapter 34 of Numbers:

- Southern border (verses 3–5): the wilderness of Zin to the far end of the Salt (Dead) Sea, to Kadesh-barnea to the river of Egypt.
- Western border (verse 6): the Great (Mediterranean) Sea coastline.
- Northern border (verses 7–9): the entrance of Hamath at the Euphrates River. (The entrance will be discussed later in the section on Israel's final conquest.)
- Eastern border (verses 10–12): From the city of Riblah to the Chinnereth Sea (Sea of Galilee) and down the Jordan River to the Dead Sea.

As we consider the takeover of the land after Israel crossed the Jordan River, we must keep in mind that the borders that Moses gave were on the western side of the Jordan (Deuteronomy 11:31). The Tribes of Reuben and Gad and half of Manasseh chose land on the eastern side of the Jordan. Permission for this land was given by Moses, not by God, and it was in no way part of the original Promised Land (Numbers 32:1–22; Joshua 13:8, 15, 24, 29, 32).

The Nations that Israel Must Conquer. When God told Abraham that Canaan was to be the land for all his descendants, several nations were mentioned, four of which were not listed among those to be destroyed: the Kenites, Kenizzites, Kadmonites, and Rephaims (Genesis 15:18–21). The others mentioned are on God's list to be defeated. Moses was also informed that some people and cities were to be spared (Deuteronomy 20:10–15).

The land in which these people lived was called Canaan, which derived its name from the descendants of Noah's grandson, Canaan (Genesis 10:6, 15). Due to an act of immorality, he came under God's curse of judgment (9:20–23). The list of the seven nations that God told Moses to utterly destroy were "greater and mightier than Israel" (Deuteronomy 7:1). They were as follows[9]:

1. The Hittites. These were the descendants of Heth, Canaan's son (Genesis 10:15). An archaeological team discovered the ruins of a Hittite city in Boghazkoy, Turkey in 1906; it is believed to be the capital of this nation. Hittites lived in groups from that city at least to Hebron, below Bethlehem, where Abraham bought a cave to bury Sarah (49:32). *Hittite*

means "fear," fear because they were brutal, a nation to dread. They were the *terrorists* of their day.

2. The Girgashites. Little is known of these people, who were scattered throughout the land of Canaan. They have been referred to as nomads or pilgrims, "those who return from a pilgrimage."
3. The Amorites. Known as the "talkers," the "sayers," these people lived in the mountains and were scattered throughout the land. They were also known for their iniquity, even in the days of Abraham (Genesis 15:16).
4. The Canaanites. Canaan had 11 sons, whose descendants were all living throughout the land (Genesis 10:15–19). *Canaan* means "humiliation," and these people were merchants, *traffickers* in shady business deals.
5. The Perizzites. These were not descendants of Canaan. A restless people, they lived in open country. The Canaanites and Perizzites were living in the land when Abraham and Lot had a parting of the ways and when God gave Abraham a view of the land that his descendants would one day possess (Genesis 13:7–15).
6. The Hivites. They were also known as the "Gibeonites" because many of them lived in the city of Gibeon (Joshua 9:3–7). Their name means "deceitful," "craftiness," "one who lives wickedly."
7. The Jebusites. These were a warlike people. Their city was Jebus, renamed Jerusalem, and their name means "pride," "loathe," and "polluted."

It should be pointed out that in Old Testament days the word *nation* does not always mean a number of cities that constitute a nation as we conceive of one. Although a nation may have a capital city like the Hittites', an individual city could constitute a nation with its own king. Note Joshua 10:23: "They brought forth those five kings unto [Joshua] out of the cave, the king of Jerusalem, the king of Hebron, the king of Jarmuth, the king of Lachish, and the king of Eglon."

The Ungodliness of These Nations. After Moses gave Israel a list of the seven nations that she was to cast out, he said, "When the Lord your God shall deliver them before you, you shall smite [kill] them and utterly destroy them. Make no covenant with them, nor show any mercy unto them. Neither shall you marry any of them; your daughters you shall not give unto their sons, nor their daughters are to be given unto your sons. For they will turn away your sons from following Me that they may serve other gods, so will the anger of the Lord burn against you and destroy you suddenly. But thus shall you deal with them; you shall destroy their altars, break down their idols [groves] and burn their carved images" (Deuteronomy 7:2–5).

This portion of Scripture is very perplexing, since we are taught that God is a "God of love." Why, then, would He be so merciless in telling Israel to go into a land and slaughter the inhabitants of seven nations, show them no mercy, make no covenant with them, and utterly destroy them? Why be so cruel, especially to women and children? Why destroy all their idols and altars and not let your children marry their children? To completely annihilate these people sounds like premeditated murder. Modernists and liberals call God a "dirty bully" for telling Israel to exterminate these people. So what is the answer?

First, we must find out what God knows that Israel didn't know. The answer, I believe, is found in chapter 18 of Leviticus, where a graphic picture is given of the lifestyle—the sins and abominations—of these seven nations.

When Abraham first entered the land of Canaan, sin was running rampant, but not to the extent that it is being labelled in this chapter of Leviticus. Genesis 15:16 refers to sins or iniquities not having reached full measure, implying that people were very sinful but that wickedness would increase in their lives. In Moses' day, their "cup of iniquity" was overflowing. The Israelites were told that, once they entered the land, they must not do after the sins of Egypt, which they had already done in worshipping the golden calf. They were also warned not to do *after the doings* of people in Canaan, nor walk in their ordinances (verses 2,3). This warning was given before Israel entered the land. Nothing was known about the repulsive sins of these people and how low in sin these people had stooped. What, then, were these people doing?

God does not tell His people to do something without telling them why they should, nor does He tell them not to do something without telling them why they should not. In this chapter of Leviticus, He spells out what the Canaanites were doing. In verses 4 and 5, He tells the Israelites that if they keep His ordinances, they shall live. In verses 6 through 20, He begins to detail the sins of these nations. Adultery was the *norm* of the land. It was nothing for sex to be performed by mothers with their sons, fathers with their daughters, uncles with their nieces, nephews with their aunts, and neighbors with their neighbors. The people offered their own sons and daughters as human sacrifices to their gods. Sodomy, or homosexuality, was common, and sex was also performed with beasts. All these things were being done, and such abominations had defiled the land.

What an awful picture of sin God paints of the Canaanites in Leviticus! What He told Israel to do was not hatred or murder on His part. It was moral surgery for these nations to be blotted out. Their sins and the consequences were a menace to the whole human race. They were deliberately, not accidentally, immoral. The Canaanites were not victims of circumstances; they were not primitive in the strict sense of the word. They hated knowledge of truth and devised their own ways. They loved sin and delighted in their acts of vulgarity. Through Israel, God's wrath would be revealed from heaven against their ungodliness and unrighteousness. He would give them up to vile affections and uncleanness and to a reprobate mind. Even though they had pleasure in what they did, they were worthy of death (Romans 1:18–32). Their wickedness had put them outside the pale of humanity, and their right to occupy Canaan had been forfeited by their contempt of right. Both the love of God and His righteousness demanded this particular condemnation. It was to be through His people that Messiah, the Redeemer, was to come, and His chosen ones would not be safe if these people lived.

Archaeological Confirmation of Canaanite Wickedness. To counter the critics who say that God was wrong in instructing Israel to "wipe out" the inhabitants of these seven Canaanite nations, a discovery by an archaeologist has brought to light even deeper evidence of their sins than Moses mentioned in chapter 18 of Leviticus. Their religion was Baalism (Baal worship).[10]

In the late 1920s, a French archaeologist excavated the ancient Canaanite city of Ugarit, known today as Ras Shamra, in northern Syria. He discovered the Royal Library, located between the temples of Dagon and Baal. A set of clay tablets was found that unfolded the mythological and historical background of Baal worship, the main religion of the Canaanites. El was the father god, and Atharit was the mother goddess. She was the "sex" goddess, having given birth to 70 gods and goddesses. El had made his son, Baal, the chief god, the god of nature (rain and harvest), heavenly bodies (sun, moon, and stars), fire, war, and sex. His sister, Anat, was his mistress, and he became the international god of all the nations.

Atharit's name in Hebrew is *Asherah,* translated "grove" in our English Bible. In the plural it is *Asherim,* and groves are mentioned in II Kings 13:6 and 17:10. We normally think of a grove as a number of trees in a given area. In the case of Baal worship, however, a tree was cut down to a stump about six feet high, on which woodcarvers carved an image of a nude man. About 20 feet away, the same thing was done with the carving of a nude woman. It was these carved tree stumps that were called "groves." Between these groves an altar was built. As priests visualized Baal and his sister, Anat, committing sex acts, priests and prostitute priestesses would commit open sex at the altar, thus venting the lustful desires of the people, who would then imitate the religious leaders. This is one reason that God warned Israel not to "plant a grove of any trees near an altar of the Lord your God, neither shall you set up any images which the Lord hates" (Deuteronomy 16:21,22).

Baal, as the god of nature, led his subjects into astrology and the worship of heavenly bodies. They observed times, used enchantments, dealt with familiar spirits and wizards, and practiced witchcraft, which is sorcery. Tied in with these activities were necromancy, soothsaying, dreamers, divination, black magic, augury (fortune-telling), (false) prophesying, and incantations. God warned Israel about this in Deuteronomy 17:2–5 and 18:9–14.

Child sacrifice was common in Baal worship. It was performed to appease Baal should there be a drought or a defeat in war (even though he was the god of war), or for trivial matters relating to an unwanted answer by a medium. The child could be cut up, with the body parts put on an altar and burned;

Fig. 7. The god Baal.

Fig. 8. Baal, god of sex.

Fig. 9. The god El, father of Baal.

Fig. 10. Bestiality.

Fig. 11. Site of altar for child sacrifice.

Fig. 12. Altar to the sun, moon, and stars.

Fig. 13. Remains of child sacrifice in building foundation.

laid in a wall or temple foundation and crushed to death; or placed in a large jar, which was then sealed so that the child would die of asphyxiation. See Joshua 6:26 with I Kings 16:34.

Demon worship was also associated with Baalism, in which its adherents embraced the worship of Satan, the devil. Baal was often designated as *Zebul,* meaning "prince." *Baal-zebub,* god of the Ekronites, is a derivation of the name *Baal-zebul.* In demon worship, "Princely Baal" was the name for Satan. During Christ's day, the Pharisees referred to the devil as "Beelzebub the prince of the devils" (Matthew 12:22–27). The serpent is a symbol of the devil, and "snake priestesses" were prostitutes who danced at ceremonies. Israel was reminded that the Canaanites sacrificed to devils or demons, and that their rock was not *"our Rock"* (Deuteronomy 32:17,31).

Fig. 14. Stone snake used in demon worship.

CONCLUSION

The information that God gave Israel as related in chapter 18 of Leviticus and the evidence unearthed at Ugarit and other related sites in Palestine give us insight into the worship of Baal in Old Testament days. They indicate that the Canaanites were fully dedicated to their gods and would do *anything* to appease them. It may be difficult for us to comprehend what has been presented thus far, but an unfolding of God's commandments will help us to have a better understanding of why He demands obedience and loyalty from those who name His name. New light will be shed on many passages of Scripture, confirming and illuminating many portions that heretofore may have been obscure, confusing, or even doubtful. Certainly, Romans 1:18–32 has taken on new meaning now that we have greater knowledge of the ancient Canaanites as they practiced their ungodly demonic religion.

We can see now why God told Israel to destroy the Canaanites, for if they didn't, it wouldn't be long before these people would bring Israel down to their level of sin. Instead, Israel was to lift these nations up to the level God demanded of them. Moses warned Israel that destroying them was a necessity, else they would be taught to do after their abominations. God said that if they "do not dispose the inhabitants of the land, those whom you allow to remain shall be stings in your eyes and thorns in your sides, and they shall harass you in the land in which you live, so I will do to you what I planned to do to them" (Numbers 33:55,56).

As recounted in chapter 28 of Deuteronomy, blessings were promised when obedience to God's commands was exercised so that Israel might have heaven's best in the land—every need supplied, both physical and spiritual. Moses outlined those blessings in the first 14 verses. Beginning with verse 15 and through the end of the chapter, various judgments were outlined that would befall the Israelites if they were not obedient. The judgments God would put upon His people for their disobedience "shall come upon them, . . . and they shall be upon them for a sign and for a wonder, and upon their seed [not for several generations] *but forever* (verses 45,46).

7

JOSHUA, ISRAEL'S NEW LEADER

PREPARING TO ENTER THE LAND

As we approach the Book of Joshua, which tells us about the conquest of the Promised Land, a review of the Books of Moses from Exodus through Deuteronomy can teach us much about the character of this man. To get the job done, God needed a man qualified to continue where Moses left off.

Joshua was born about 1500 B.C., while Israel was in Egyptian bondage. He was the son of Nun, of the lineage of Ephraim, Joseph, and Jacob (Numbers 13:8). We know him as *Joshua,* but he was called other names, such as *Oshea* (Numbers 13:8) and *Hoshea* (Deuteronomy 32:44), meaning "deliverer," and *Jehoshua,* meaning "Jehovah-saves" or "Saviour" (Numbers 13:16). When Stephen referred to Joshua in his witness to the Jews in Acts, his name, Joshua, was translated into Greek as *Jesus* (Acts 7:45).

Soon after Israel's exodus in about 1450–1446 B.C., Israel crossed the Red Sea and was confronted by an enemy, Amalek. Moses appointed Joshua commander of Israel's army, and soon the Amalekites were defeated (Exodus 17: 8–14). When Israel arrived at Sinai, Joshua, Moses' minister (servant), accompanied him partway up the mountain as Moses proceeded to receive the Ten Commandments (24:13). It was Joshua who informed Moses of the celebration of the Israelites worshipping the golden calf that Aaron had made (32:14). Being as close to Moses as he was, Joshua became a little jealous when two men in the camp began to prophesy, but Moses had to remind him that others could be used by the Lord (Numbers 11:26–29). Christ had to similarly remind John when he complained about one who was casting out demons and was not of them. Jesus said, "He that is not against us is for us" (Luke 9: 49–50).

As the Book of Joshua opens, God was speaking to Joshua as he took over the leadership of His people, who were sometimes very rebellious. Joshua was to lead them over the Jordan River to face brutal nations, but he had the promise that as God was with Moses, so would He be with him.

Conditions for Success.[11] God outlined for Joshua certain conditions for success (Joshua 1):

1. Arise and go to fulfill God's purpose (verse 2). Israel had to get *out* of the wilderness before God could bring them *into* the land of their inheritance (Deuteronomy 6:23). The child of God must get *out* of the "wilderness" of this old world before he/she can go *in* where the fields are white unto harvest (Mark 16:15; John 4:35,36).
2. Exercise faith in the promises of God (verse 3). "Faith without works is dead" (James 2:26). Whatever is not of faith is sin (Romans 14:23b).
3. Be assured of the presence of God (verses 5 and 9b). God the Father will not forsake us (Hebrews 13:5b), Jesus the Son is always with us (Matthew 28:20; Colossians 1:27), and the Holy Spirit abides with us forever (John 14:16). The believer is the possessor of the Triune God.

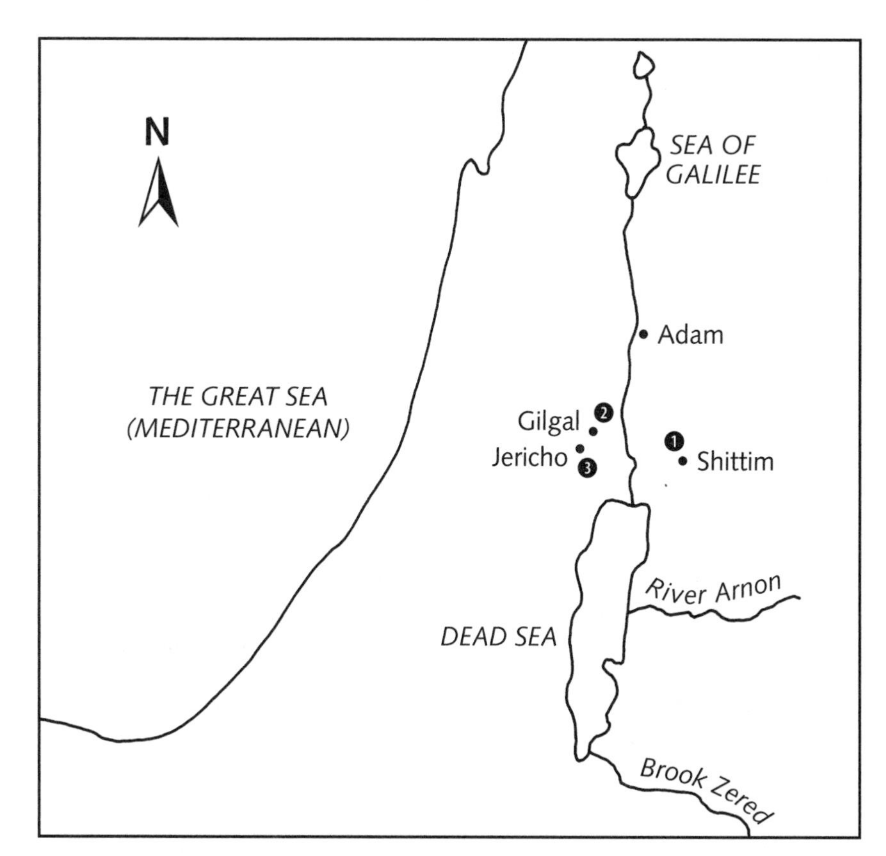

Map 3. Israel enters the Promised Land.

KEY

1 Preparation to cross the Jordan River
2 Crossing the Jordan and encampment at Gilgal
3 Spiritual preparation, spying out Jericho, and preparation for battle

4. Observe—do (faithfulness to God's leading) (verse 7). This assures us that He will lead us in a right path for His name's sake (Psalm 23:3). The steps of a good man are ordered of the Lord (Psalm 37:23).
5. Meditate upon the Word of God and practice—apply it (verse 8). This alone assures us of God's approval (Psalm 1:2; II Timothy 2:15).
6. Be strong and courageous; be not afraid, neither be dismayed (verse 9). We must rise above our circumstances as we labor together with Him, knowing that "if God be for us, who can be against us?" (Romans 8:31) and "we are labourers together with God" (I Corinthians 3:9a).
7. Yield to God's will (verse 16). This involves setting ourselves apart unto Him, walking in His footsteps, setting our affection on things above, and in everything giving thanks (I Thessalonians 4:3; I Peter 2:21; Colossians 3:1–3; I Thessalonians 5:18).

What an encouragement this must have been to this man of God! He had been assured by God that success in conquering the land depended upon his faithfulness to Him and His Word (verses 7 and 8).

Military Preparations. Joshua needed assurance from the 40,000 men of war of the Tribes of Reuben and Gad and half the Tribe of Manasseh that they would keep their promise to cross the river Jordan to help conquer the whole land (Deuteronomy 3:18–20). They assured Joshua that they would (1:12–18, 4:12,13).

No doubt, Joshua reviewed in his mind those to whom God had made the promise of the land:

First to Abraham: Genesis 15:7, 18, 17:8.
Then to Isaac: Genesis 24:7, 26:4.
To Jacob: Genesis 28:13, 35:9–12.
To Moses: Exodus 6:8, 12:25; Deuteronomy 4:21–22. God also promised Moses that Israel would inhabit and possess the land: Leviticus 20:24; Numbers 35:34.

With these promises running through Joshua's mind, God laid out the land to him—from the wilderness of Kadesh-barnea, Lebanon, to the river Euphrates, including all the land of the Hittites unto the Mediterranean Sea. Every place that the Israelites' feet would tread upon would be theirs. Joshua was convinced that victory would be theirs, that no man would be able to stand before him all the days of his life (Joshua 1:3–5).

Spying On Jericho. Evidently, it was during the period of Israel's mourning for Moses that Joshua sent two men to secretly spy out the city of Jericho (Joshua 2). He had learned in the wilderness as commander against the Amalekites that he must get the lay of the land of this first city to be conquered. The spies headed for the house of Rahab the harlot.[12]

To the Western mind the word *harlot* refers to prostitution and immorality. The question is often raised, Did the trusted spies of Joshua ignore their responsibility and seek to satisfy their own lust and passion in the home of such a person? (2:1–11). Scriptural evidence would hardly lend support. It is quite possible that Rahab was a widow who had turned her house on the wall into a lodge, and she was the desk clerk. Travellers would frequent such a place rather than spend the night deep inside the city. To hold such a position as meeting the public (men in particular), Rahab would have to remove her veil. This would put her in a likely position of shame, since only a woman of ill repute would dare permit a man to see her face. It was probably for this reason that she was classified as a harlot. The fact that the spies *lodged* there would indicate that her house was for tourists.

Why go to her house? Could it have been the providence of God? It hardly seems likely that they had gone there for an immoral purpose. Whatever the reason behind their strategy, it became public knowledge that they were in the city. Even the king of Jericho knew of their presence there and came to inquire of Rahab. When asked about the spies, Rahab lied about their presence. Had she been a harlot, it would appear that she would have been glad to cooperate with the king. It would have been bad for business to fall out with those in authority.

We cannot condone her sin of lying, but it hardly seems possible that a harlot would converse in the things of the Lord and confess Him to men who had sought to buy her services. She knew about the dividing of the Red Sea and Israel's victory on the east side of the Jordan River. She was willing to identify herself and her family with God's people rather than with the Jerichoites. This certainly would not have been in keeping with the character of a harlot. Being an innkeeper, she would have important information from conversations with travelling guests, as well as connections with prominent city officials that would be vital to the spies. Probably for this reason, the spies headed for such a place and there met Rahab the harlot.

Because of her confession of faith in Israel's God and her hiding them from the king, the spies granted her request that she and her family would be spared when Israel invaded the land and defeated Jericho. She was given instructions to hang a "scarlet thread" out the window to identify her house when the invasion took place. Not knowing the day when the invasion would occur, she immediately hung the thread out her window. What a lesson for us when Christ comes to take us to be with Himself. We must watch daily for His coming, for we know not the day nor the hour, and we want to be ready and not ashamed before Him at His coming (I John 2:28).

CROSSING THE JORDAN RIVER AND ENTERING THE LAND

Upon their return, the spies reported to Joshua, giving him confidence that victory would be theirs. Three days were necessary for the people to prepare for the crossing, and the officers went through the camp to give instructions. They were to reconsecrate (sanctify) themselves unto the Lord and be prepared to follow the priests bearing the ark at a certain distance. When the priests arrived at the edge of the river, the waters would part for all to pass over on dry ground to enter "their land" (Joshua 1:11). Many had already had such an experience crossing the Red Sea.

How was the miracle of parting the waters of the Jordan River performed? The dividing of the Red Sea was an act of nature—a strong wind that God sent (Exodus 14:21). Was the parting of the Jordan a direct miracle, or did God use an act of nature? It could have been either. Our sovereign God can do anything—"nothing is too hard for Him" (Jeremiah 32:17). The Canaanite god was Baal, who was supposed to be the god of nature. What a wonderful opportunity for God to show these people that He, not Baal, was the *God of Nature!*

This is exactly what God did. Scripture tells us that the waters of the Jordan were stopped in the vicinity of Adam and Zaretan (Joshua 3:16). Adam is about 16 miles north of the area that lies between Jericho and Shittim, and it is three or four miles from Shittim to the Dead Sea, which would be drained as it flowed southward, making the total dry stretch from Adam to the Dead Sea about 20 miles long. Verse 13 tells us that the water is "upon" or "in one heap." Since it was the harvest season, the river was overflowing and much wider than normal, probably 200 feet wide at this point (3:13–16).

Assuming that there were 1,900,000 people ready to march across and that each person would take up the area of a square yard, 1,760 people would stretch one mile walking abreast, and 10,560 would stretch six miles. Since a person can easily walk 300 feet in about three minutes, twenty rows six miles wide could cross in one hour, equalling 211,200. Thus it would take the 1,900,000 people about nine hours to cross—more of course if animals were included. Joshua 4:10 says that the people hastened to cross over.

The possibility has been suggested that God used an earthquake to cause a landslide at Adam, thereby stopping the flow of the river. God could use any method He chose to stop the flow, but, regardless, it was a miracle. It is true that Scripture does give some evidence of an earthquake at the time of Israel's entrance into Canaan. In Psalm 114:1–5 we read, "When Israel went out of Egypt . . . Israel had dominion. The sea saw it, and fled, Jordan was driven back. . . . What ailed you, o you sea, that you fled? and you, Jordan, being driven back." The Psalmist could be referring to an earthquake at the time of Israel's crossing.

At the site of Adam there are high banks. A landslide here could easily block or dam up the water. According to records at the Rockefeller Museum in Jerusalem, such an earthquake occurred toward the end of the 19th century that dammed up the Jordan for 16 hours. In 1927, in a similar occurrence, a section of the cliff 150 feet high fell and blocked the water for almost 22 hours.

We need to keep in mind that God often used acts of nature to miraculously accomplish His purpose:

1. Hailstones in Egypt afflicting man, beasts, and crops: Exodus 9:22–25.
2. Darkness for the Egyptians and light for the children of Israel: Exodus 10:21–26.
3. Hailstones to slay Israel's enemies: Joshua 10:11.
4. Prolonging daytime: Joshua 10:12–14.
5. Flood to destroy Sisera's army: Judges 5:20b–21a.
6. Rain to damage Israel's crops: I Samuel 12:13–18.
7. Rain withheld in Ahab's day, causing first famine, then a downpour: I Kings 17 and 18.
8. A storm to bring Jonah to his senses: Jonah 1:4.

Whatever method God used to get Israel across the Jordan on dry ground, it was a miracle that only He could perform. We must ever keep in mind that He brought them *out* of bondage to bring them *in* for their inheritance (Deuteronomy 6:23).

After all of the Israelites had crossed the Jordan, Joshua instructed a member of each Tribe to take a stone from the riverbed and make a memorial where they were to lodge for the night. It was to be a "sign" among the people. When their children would ask its meaning, they would be told that the waters of the Jordan were cut off when the priests stood on its banks with the Ark of the Covenant of the Lord so that all Israel could march forth into their Promised Land (Joshua 4:9,10). Another set of stones was gathered and placed in the river to mark where priests who carried the Ark stood. When Joshua called them out of the river, the water began to flow again over the banks as before (4:16–18). God's "miracle avenue" through Jordan's riverbed was to let all people of the earth know that the hand of Almighty God is powerful and that they might fear Him and Him alone. Such an act melted the hearts of the Amorites and Canaanites who were living nearby (4:19–5:1).

ISRAEL'S SPIRITUAL PREPARATION

Circumcision (Joshua 5:2–9). During their 40-year wandering, no Israelite males had been circumcised. This rite did not originate with the Jews; ancient Semites, Arabians, Egyptians, Canaanites, and Philistines practiced this as a religious act. With the Jews it was instituted by God as a sign of the covenant between Him and Abraham: "My covenant shall be in your flesh for an everlasting covenant" (Genesis 17:13).

According to the terms of the covenant symbolized by circumcision, the Lord undertook to be the God of Abraham and his descendants and they were to belong to Him, worshipping and obeying Him. The rite effected admission to the fellowship of the covenant people and secured for the individual, as a member of the nation, his share in the promises that God made to the nation as a whole. Circumcision reminded them of the duties that they were to perform for the promises to become effective.

The prophets often reminded them that the outward rite, to have any significance, must be accompanied by "circumcision of the heart" (Leviticus 26:41; Deuteronomy; Ezekiel 44:7). Jeremiah said that his countrymen were no better than the idolaters, for they were "uncircumcised in the heart" (Jeremiah 9:25–26). Paul used the word *concision* for this outward circumcision not accompanied by a spiritual change (Philippians 3:2). Acts 15 brings out that salvation is "by faith" and not by the works of circumcision. Paul also points out that circumcision is of the heart and that all who say they are of Israel are not of Israel (Romans 2:9, 9:6).

The Passover. The Passover was instituted prior to Israel's exodus from Egypt. It involved the sacrifice that spared the firstborn from death when blood was sprinkled on a house's doorposts. Judgment was put into action upon the firstborn when no blood was applied to the doorposts on the Egyptian houses (Exodus 12:1–26). Israel observed the Passover at Mount Sinai (Numbers 9:1–5), but not again until they crossed the Jordan River. After their encampment at Gilgal, they observed it for the first time in their new homeland (Joshua 5:8–10).

With the Israelites' taking care of their *spiritual needs* as their first act of worship, the Passover is a symbol or type of Christ shedding His blood as God's Lamb at Calvary. As our Passover, when we by faith believe and apply His blood for His forgiveness of our sins, He passes over us and we do not come into condemnation but are passed from death unto life (John 5:24 with I Corinthians 5:7b). We noticed in the sprinkling of the blood on the doorposts that no blood was sprinkled on the threshold. Judgment comes to those who trample underfoot the Lord Jesus Christ and count His blood of the covenant, whereby we are cleansed and set apart, an unholy thing (Hebrews 10:29).

Encampment at Gilgal (Joshua 5:9). The name of the Israelites' first encampment is interesting. *Gilgal* means "a place of rolling." Their past bondage and wilderness (barren) experience were behind them, and they were on new territory. The reproach of Egypt was rolled away. The manna had ceased, and they were now eating the fruit of the land (5:9–12). What a beautiful picture of one's sins being blotted out, removed from him as far as the east is from the west, becoming a new creation in Christ Jesus (I Corinthians 5:17). Walter D. Kallenbach has written a chorus about Gilgal's meaning:

> Rolled away, rolled away, rolled away,
> Ev'ry burden of my heart rolled away.
> Rolled away, rolled away, rolled away,
> Ev'ry burden of my heart rolled away.
> Ev'ry sin had to go, 'neath the crimson flow, Hallelujah,
> Rolled away, rolled away, rolled away,
> Ev'ry burden of my heart rolled away.[13]

How wonderful God was to "roll away" Israel's past and give them a fresh start in bringing them into a land of his choosing. We can never outdo God! For us Gilgal means a place[14]

- Of deliverance from the broad road leading to destruction: Matthew 7:13b with Psalm 40:2,3.
- Where the past is blotted out: Psalm 103:12; I John 1:7.
- Of freedom: Joshua 5:9 with John 8:32,36.
- Of rest: Matthew 11:28,29.
- Of joy, symbolic of our tasting the fruits of salvation: Joshua 5:11,12 with Psalm 34:8.
- Of blessing: Ephesians 1:3.
- Of challenge: Philippians 3:13,14.

I wonder how I would have felt if I had been one of the Israelites. After a gruesome trek for so long a time through "no man's land," with any love in my heart at all for the Lord, I would have had to shout, "Home at last!" My mind would have focussed on God's bigness—big enough to make all the provisions He made over a period of 40 years for 1,900,000 people and their animals. How big is God? He's even bigger than all He did for Israel, but thanks be unto Him, He's small enough to live in my heart!

Captain of the Lord's Host. With all the blessings and encouragements that God had given to Israel and Joshua after crossing over the Jordan, Joshua does one more thing to prepare for the next step—attacking Jericho. He went to get a good look at the walled city, probably to survey or get the lay of the land (Joshua 5:13). The weapons that Israel had at that time to defend themselves were no match for a powerful army on Jericho's city walls. Suddenly Joshua was granted a most unusual experience, that of seeing a man with a drawn sword in his hand. Knowing that God was with him, he asked if the man was a soldier of the Jericho army. Maybe Joshua thought that he was coming to spy on the Israelite army at Gilgal. Joshua got his answer: "The man said, 'no, but as *Captain of the host of the Lord,* I am now come.' And Joshua fell on his face to the earth and did worship, saying unto him, 'What does my lord say unto his servant?' And the Captain of the Lord's host said unto Joshua, 'Loose your shoe from off your foot, for the place where you are standing is holy.' And Joshua did so" (5:13,14). Moses had a similar experience when he stood on holy ground (Exodus 3:2–5).

This is what we call a *Theophany* or *Christophany:* an appearance before someone of God or Christ prior to His virgin birth. There are other examples of this: God's appearance to Moses at the burning bush and at Mount Sinai; God's appearance to Samuel, who said, "Speak, Lord, for your servant hears"; and the appearance of the fourth person in the fiery furnace to Nebuchadnezzar.

Joshua is being encouraged as well as instructed. This Captain was as much as saying, "Fear not, I am from heaven to save you and My people from defeat. Israel is the Lord's host and the Lord is Israel's Captain. You are my captain under Me and you must obey My orders" (Joshua 5:13,14). No wonder Joshua fell on his face and worshipped Him. In a sense the battle was over before it started, for God said, "I have given you the king and this city" (6:2). "Captain" Joshua had a lot to look forward to as the people prepared to go to Jericho.

8

CONQUERING THE WHOLE PROMISED LAND

THE CENTRAL CONQUEST

The Battle of Jericho (Joshua 6:1–24). With Jericho's king aware of Israel's multitude, he and his army were prepared to meet an invasion by them. All the city gates were securely closed. But Joshua, with the assurance that God was going to give them victory, shared his faith with the people, and they, without the necessary weapons for warfare, followed God's instructions and just marched around the city every day for six days. After about the third day, the soldiers on the city wall must have relaxed, thinking that victory would be easy. As the priests carried the Ark of the Covenant on the seventh day, the people marched around the city seven times. Probably by this time the soldiers of Jericho had laid down their weapons and fallen asleep, figuring that no one would enter the city after wearing themselves out walking around the city repeatedly. They didn't know that God was in charge and that His ways were not man's ways. During their last march around the city, the priests blew their trumpets, the people shouted, and the walls came "a tumblin' down." Israel gained access to the city, and victory was "in the bag," as the little Sunday School boy would say!

As the priests blew their trumpets and the people shouted, the wall began to crumble, *falling down flat* (Joshua 6:20). Cities were typically built on hills, and when a wall was bombarded in battle, one would expect the stones to start rolling down the hill, crushing the invading people. But God performed another miracle—the wall fell down flat, meaning that it fell down right on its foundation, so that the Israelites were able to climb over the open space and invade the city. Only enough of the wall fell down to make room for an entrance, and the rest of the wall, left standing, hemmed in the Jerichoites so that there was no possible way for any of them to escape. The majority of the soldiers were on the wall at the main entrance, and as the wall fell down flat, they met their fate.

The city was utterly destroyed, including all the people and animals, and then reduced to ashes by fire. A British archaeologist in the late 1920s excavated this Old Testament site, and his discoveries confirmed that the walls did indeed "fall down flat"; they had not rolled down the hillside, as would have been expected.

Overcoming Jericho, or the Victory of Faith

1. The *act* of faith—compassing the city: Joshua 6:3 with Hebrews 11:30.
2. The *use* or means of faith—blowing the trumpets: verse 4 with our *tell-and-show* witness: verse 4 with Mark 5:19; Luke 8:39.
3. The *substance* of faith—carrying the Ark: verse 6 with Romans 13:14.
4. The *anticipation* or hope of faith—shouting of the people: verse 20a with Hebrews 11:6. The people shouted as the priests blew the trumpets. We cannot leave *all* the work to the ministers. They do the work of the *minister,* and we are to do the work of the ministry—working together (Ephesians 4:11–16).
5. The *victory* of faith: verse 20 with I John 1:5. The weapons of Israel's warfare were not strong, but the weapon of faith was mighty to the pulling down of Jericho's strongholds (II Corinthians 10:3,4).

When the spies left Rahab's house, it was with the promise that she and her family would be rescued if she hung a scarlet thread out of her window, which she did immediately (Joshua 2:15–21). The two spies saw it and rescued the whole household (6:22–25). This scarlet thread is a type of Christ, symbolizing His blood (Hebrews 9:19–22). As the hymn writer put it, "When I see the blood I will pass over you." See Exodus 12:13. Let us review Rahab's testimony:

1. She believed in the God of Israel: 2:9–11.
2. She accepted God's message: 2:12–18.
3. She obeyed God's Word: 2:21.
4. She and her family were saved from wrath: 5:22–25.
5. She entered the "Faith Hall of Fame": Hebrews 11:31.

The victory of Joshua and the people, under God, was so outstanding that Joshua's fame was proclaimed throughout the countryside (Joshua 6:27). What God did in conquering and destroying Jericho was but His announcement to the seven nations in Canaan that He was out to do the same to them that He did to Jericho (Deuteronomy 7:1–5).

Jericho Is Judged. From the very beginning, Jericho was on God's "hit list." It was an *accursed* city (Joshua 6:17). All was to be destroyed but the silver, the gold, and the vessels of brass (bronze) and iron. These metals were to be consecrated and go into God's treasury (6:21, 24). Anyone taking any portion of this treasury would make themselves accursed, and judgment would fall upon the whole camp of Israel and trouble it (6:18). The whole city was destroyed because of its sinfulness, and God put a curse on any man who would rebuild it. If one did, he would offer two of his sons as human sacrifices to his god, probably Baal (6:26). Ironically, a man by the name of Heil, about 500 years later, rebuilt Jericho and did offer two of his own sons in the gate and wall foundations (I Kings 16:34). See Fig. 13 on page 45.

Achan's Sin in the Camp and Defeat at Ai. The children of Israel were warned, under threat of severe punishment, not to take the precious metal after Jericho was conquered (Joshua 6:18–19). One man, Achan, secretly stole some, and the anger of the Lord was against the whole camp (7:11). Sometimes just one person can hinder the flow of the Holy Spirit's blessing upon a congregation. In the Northwest, lumberjacks fell trees, trim them, and get them down to the river to float them to the sawmill. Occasionally, the logs jam, causing a blockage, and a lumberjack will jump from one to the other until he finds the cause. Usually it is just one log turned the wrong way that stopped the flow. What a tragedy when just one person brings God's judgment upon the whole!

Achan's sin was unknown to Joshua and the people, who were basking in the victory over Jericho. The city of Ai was next to be attacked and defeated. Instead of consulting the Lord as to what strategy to follow, Joshua sent some men to spy out the area. The report convinced him that a large army was not necessary, so he sent a small battalion. Defeat was imminent for the Israelites, and depression struck the people. Instead of admitting he had done wrong in not consulting the Lord for instructions, Joshua immediately had a "pity party." He tore his clothes, fell on his face, and started blaming the Lord for bringing them over the Jordan. He even told the Lord that they would have been better off if they had not crossed the Jordan. His first concern was about himself as leader and about Israel's name being cut off from the world; only later did he mention God's name, saying that if the inhabitants of Canaan heard about the defeat, they would surround the Israelites and cut off their name from the earth. He even put God's name last, asking what they would do with His great name (Joshua 7:2–9).

How typical of many individuals when things begin to go wrong. The natural "out" is to blame someone else, like Adam did when Eve said, "Take a bite" (Genesis 3:12). Joshua's prayer was a selfish prayer, acting in the energy of the flesh. By no means can we excuse him for his actions as God's captain, but let us not forget that he, like us, was not perfect. In Joshua's case, it really was not the time to pray but to act in finding the problem and trying to resolve it. There is a time to pray, and there is a time to act.

God told Joshua to get up from the ground, that the sin that brought Israel to defeat at Ai was going to be brought to light. He was instructed to bring all the Tribes before him, and by the process of elimination God would point His finger to the one Tribe that included the family of the guilty party. The family was singled out, and Achan was taken. Moses had warned the people that if they sinned, "be sure your sin will find you out" (Numbers 32:23). Achan's sin had found him out (Joshua 7:20–28).

The first thing to do when sin is committed, is not to try to hide it, as Achan did, but to confess it. As Joshua faced Achan, he said, "My son, give, I pray you, glory to the Lord God of Israel and make confession to Him [first] and then tell me what you have done. Hide it not from me" (Joshua 7:19). Achan answered and said, "I have sinned against the Lord." He had no alternative but to face up to the situation.

Adam's one act of disobedience was a *full-grown sin.* So was Achan's. The temptation came to him by the only method the devil uses—*see, desire, and take.* He invented this method in heaven (Isaiah 14:12–17): he *saw* the glory of God and the honor He received, he *desired* within himself to be above God, and he sought to *take* God's place.

Eve did likewise: she *saw* the fruit was good to be *desired* and she *took* a bite (Genesis 3:6). It has been said, "It wasn't the *apple* up in the tree that brought about sin, it was the *pair* on the ground." Lot *saw* the fertile plains of Jordan, *desired* them, *took* them, and ended up as a compromiser in Sodom (13:10–11). David *saw* Bathsheba, *desired* her, and *took* her (II Samuel 11:2–4).

Satan used the same method with Christ's temptation to *look at* the kingdoms of the world, to *desire* food, and to *take* His life in His own hands by casting Himself down from the pinnacle of the Temple (Matthew 4:11). Achan followed suit when he confessed by saying, "When I *saw* among the spoils a beautiful, expensive Babylonian garment, about twenty pounds of silver and about five pounds of gold, I *coveted* them, I *took* them and hid them in my tent" (Joshua 7:20,21).

Though Achan's sin was *individual,* its result was *collective.* The effect of his secret sin was so powerful that it not only caused defeat at Ai, but involved his whole family as well, bringing shame and humiliation to all. Why his family? They must have been aware of Achan's possession of the stolen items when he entered the tent and hid them. Some member of the family should have told Joshua about his guilt after Ai's defeat, but silence reigned, making them guilty by association. We often sing "Calvary Covers It All," but Calvary does not cover the consequences—we reap what we sow. As a result, Achan's whole family suffered the penalty of death in the valley of Achor (Joshua 7:22–26).

In Achan's confession, one thing stands out. Joshua said to him, "Give glory to the Lord and make confession" (Joshua 7:19). When a believer sins, it breaks the heart of God, but He is glorified when sin is *confessed* and *forsaken.* Achan's confession proves this. How do we glorify God when we confess our sin? First, we acknowledge that He, and He alone, can forgive sin, and second, we plead the only source of forgiveness, the blood of Jesus Christ. This is what glorifies Him. When we *confess* our sin and *forsake* it, He shows mercy and is faithful and just to forgive us and cleanse us. He is not faithful to us, but faithful unto Himself and to the shed blood of His Son. For *this* reason He forgives us (Proverbs 28:13; Ephesians 1:7; I John 1:9).

Restored Fellowship and Victory at Ai. With the sin of defeat dealt with, instead of trying to figure out for himself how to defeat Ai, Joshua now lis-

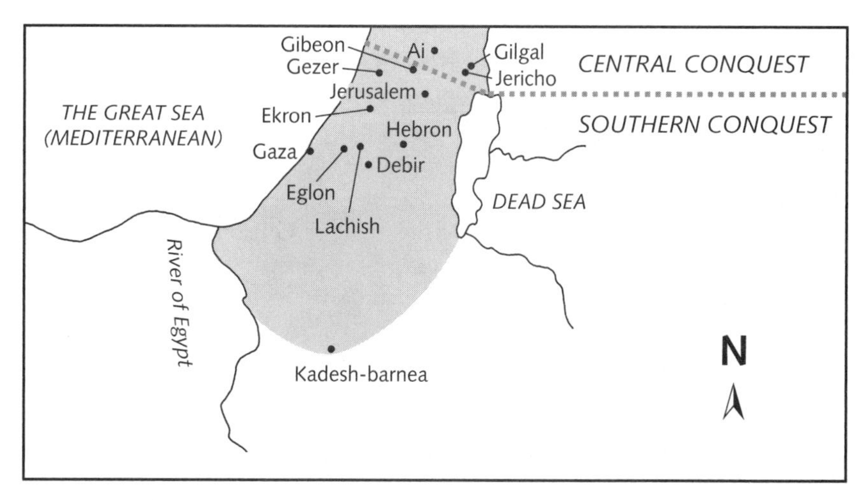

Map 4. Israel conquers central and southern Canaan.

tened to God's instructions. He needed to be reminded again that God's ways are best, that His ways are not man's. The plan was very simple: 30,000 soldiers were to go at night and lie in wait between Bethel and Ai (Joshua 8:1–9). Why at this location? When Abraham arrived in Canaan from Ur, he built an altar east of Bethel, between Bethel and Ai. *Bethel* means "house of God." When Abraham left Egypt after the famine, he returned to the same place, Bethel, where he had built an altar (Genesis 13:1–4). Joshua's soldiers were thus stationed on *sacred ground,* awaiting God's call to advance. God always knows where to place His own (Psalm 37:23).

The next morning Joshua, the people, elders, and men of war encamped in the valley between Jericho and Ai (Joshua 8:10–11). Five thousand men were secretly placed between the 30,000 soldiers and Ai. That night Joshua and the people moved from the valley toward Ai. When the king of Ai saw them, he and his men went out to battle them. Joshua and the people pretended to be fleeing, and when the king started to pursue, the city was left wide open to attack by the 30,000 soldiers, who entered the city, destroyed the people, and set the city on fire. When the king and his men saw the flames, they turned to go back to the city, but Joshua and his army overtook them. At last there was victory over the once victorious Aiites (8:14–29).

Conclusion. In the battle of Jericho we saw how God gave victory because of Israel's faith and obedience. In her defeat at Ai, Israel learned lessons because of her disobedience and Joshua's not seeking God's leadership. When confession was made and God's orders were followed, their obedience paid great dividends in their victory. The best thing anyone can do when they attain victory is to give thanks unto the Lord. Joshua did by offering a sacrifice, reading the Scriptures, and blessing the people (Joshua 8:30–35).

THE SOUTHERN CONQUEST

As word spread of Israel's victories at Jericho and Ai, kings of the southern nations of Canaan gathered themselves together to fight against the people of God with one accord (Joshua 9:1–3).

The Deceitful Gibeonites and the Battle of Gibeon. Among the Hivites was a group called the Gibeonites, who lived in Gibeon, just seven miles southwest of Ai. Fearing that they would be captured, they devised a deception to save their lives. They feigned to be ambassadors from a far-off country. Dressed in old clothes and shoes and carrying old moldy bread and patched-up wine skins, they made their way to see Joshua. Telling Joshua that they had come from a distant country, they asked Israel's captain to make a league with them. Having heard of Israel's fame, they desired to dwell among the Israelites. Joshua was fooled and, without taking counsel with God, made peace with the Gibeonites and made a league or covenant to let them live (Joshua 9:4–15). It appears that Joshua still hadn't learned the need for divine guidance for every step he was to take. Moses had said *not* to make *any* covenant with the inhabitants of the land (Deuteronomy 7:2). Blinded by pity for the lying Gibeonites, Joshua made a second error in letting them live, done lest wrath should come upon Israel because of the oath made (Joshua 9:20). Here he is thinking of self.

Joshua did punish the Gibeonites, however, making them laborers—woodcutters and water carriers for the community. That may sound like a small sentence, but when we consider that it was the job of women in the Near East to carry jugs of water from the wells or reservoirs, this was a humiliating task for men (Joshua 9:20–27). Gibeon had huge cisterns to catch rainwater for use in dry seasons. It had become known as a "city of great waters" (Jeremiah 41:11–12). Fig. 15 shows one of the many large cisterns that have been discovered; this one is 37 feet in diameter, 87 feet deep, with 40 steps and a tunnel to reach the water table.

After Joshua had made the league or covenant with the Gibeonites, he left and went back to Gilgal. When the king of Jerusalem, Adoni-zedek, heard what the Israelites had done to Jericho and Ai and that the Gibeonites had made peace with Israel, he sent unto the kings of Hebron, Jarmuth, Lachish, and Eglon, requesting their help in warring against Gibeon, a city that was strategically important to these nations. When the Gibeonites heard of this plot, they sent to Gilgal for Joshua and his army to come to their rescue. Joshua responded, slew many and put to flight those who escaped. God used a miracle of nature by sending down huge hailstones to kill more of the enemy than were killed by the sword. Again, Baal, the supposed god of nature, was unable to cope with the true God of Nature. Baal also failed when darkness was falling at the end of the day and some of his subjects were still fleeing. Knowing that they would soon be out of sight, Joshua looked to God to pro-

Fig. 15. Cistern at Gibeon.

long time, saying, "Sun, stand still in the midst of heaven and it hastened not to go down about a whole day." This miracle gave Israel's army sufficient time to catch all the enemy and destroy them (Joshua 10:1–14).

Joshua's Long Day. Critics of the Bible have taken this statement of Joshua's—"Sun, stand still"—to be scientifically incorrect. For them, it is but another mistake in the Bible. It is a scientific fact that the sun does not revolve around the earth. In the original Biblical language, Joshua was telling the sun not to "stand still," but to "be silent." Time slowed down and "the sun hastened not to go down."

> Did Joshua have this scientific data of his day? Did he think the sun moved from East to West and that for time to be lengthened the sun must stand still? By modern standards he was a primitive man, in a primitive culture, with primitive misconceptions. He probably knew very little about the planet upon which he lived, its chemical compounds or shape. He knew even less about the solar system. As far as Joshua was concerned, almost everyone believed the earth was flat, the sun rose in the East and hours later sank into the West. Did Joshua know that the earth upon which he stood really was a sphere about 8,000 miles in diameter? He had no idea there were close to 200 mil-

lion square miles of earth's surface, 71 percent of which was water. He was unaware the earth was spinning on its axis in a cycle every 24 hours (23 hours, 56 minutes, and 4.09 seconds to be exact). And he didn't even know that the earth was traveling through space about eighteen and a half miles per second. Did he know that the sun he was commanding to stand still was 93,000,000 miles away, and that at its core it was over 30,000,000 degrees Fahrenheit, or that it was over 1000 times bigger than the earth? Did he know that the earth made a complete orbit around the sun yearly?

No, he didn't. But he knew his God! He knew that God had promised to go before His people and fight their battles to give them victory (10:8). And in this battle he saw victory in his grasp, but time was running out. If he didn't conquer the enemy before darkness set in, they would regroup and attack Israel the next day. Knowing his God, his God's power, and his God's promise, he called on Him for help and in the presence of all the children of Israel he commanded the sun to cease working.

Joshua had no idea that his command slowed down 6.6 sextillion tons of spinning gravel and water to give Israel victory over her enemies. But did Joshua know something that would have met with the approval of today's scientific establishment? To repeat, his command in the Hebrew tongue was not "Sun, stand still," but "Sun, stop working." It was then that the work of the sun lessened and had its effect upon the earth. It was then that the earth began to slow down and the day lengthened. The "God of Nature" had done it again!

There is indisputable evidence from the modern science of ethnology (a study of the races of mankind) that such an event occurred as Joshua records. In ancient Chinese writings there is a legend of a long day. The Incas of Peru and the Aztecs of Mexico have a similar record. There is a Babylonian and a Persian legend of a day that was miraculously extended. Herodotus, an ancient historian (484–425 B.C.), recounts that while in Egypt priests showed him temple records where he read of a day that was almost twice the natural length of any day ever recorded.

A British astronomer, Sir Edwin Ball, found that twenty four hours had been lost out of solar time. Where did it go and what was the cause of this strange lapse, and how did it happen? Such would puzzle any scientist. Professor C. A. Totten of Yale challenged the famous astronomer to read the Bible to see if it would account for the missing day. When Sir Ball came to the portion of the long day in Joshua, he rechecked his figures and found that at the time of Joshua there were only twenty-three hours and twenty minutes lost. His skepticism justified, he told Dr. Totten that the Bible was in error because it had made a mistake of forty minutes.

Showing the skeptic that the Bible record does not say *twenty-four hours,* but rather *about the space of a whole day,* he suggested the astronomer continue reading through the Bible. Coming to the Book of Isaiah, he noticed in Hezekiah's prayer that God extended this sick man's life fifteen years. To confirm this promise, the sundial was turned back ten degrees (II Kings 20:1–11; Isaiah 38:1–21). Ten degrees on a sundial is forty minutes on a clock. The missing time had been found. The unbelieving astronomer saw for himself that the Bible accounted for the missing time, and said, "Lord, I believe."[15]

Conclusion. Due to the miracle-working power of God in Israel's behalf, they have now conquered the southern section of Canaan, having pursued their enemies during "extended daylight" and captured the five kings who were determined to destroy Israel. The kings were placed in a sealed cave until their armies were destroyed, and then the five kings were released. They were slaughtered and hanged on separate trees until sundown. Their bodies were then taken down and put back in the cave, which was sealed. After all the soldiers and the kings were utterly destroyed, there was a "mopping up" campaign of smaller nations in southern Canaan to complete the capture of this section of the Promised Land (Joshua 10:15–43).

The victorious army of Israel returned to Gilgal, the place where their "past was rolled away." To Israel, this was *sacred ground,* the place where they erected a stone memorial to commemorate deliverance from their Exodus and God's bringing them into His land. As we live for the Lord and participate in His victories in our lives, we always need to take a trip back to Calvary, the place where Christ took us *out* of darkness and brought us *in* to His marvellous light of salvation (I Peter 2:9b). We must never forget that we were once purged from our old sins (II Peter 1:9).

THE NORTHERN CONQUEST

As we look back over the previous battles, Israel had done a fine job taking possession of the central and southern portions of their inheritance, the Promised Land. When Jabin, king of Hazor, heard about all of Israel's victories, and especially of the Gibeonites' making peace with Israel, he got together with four other northern kings at the waters of Merom to decide how best to attack Joshua and his army. They declared war on God's people (Joshua 11:1–5).

Josephus, the noted Jewish historian of the first century A.D., wrote that these confederate forces totaled 300,000 foot soldiers, 10,000 cavalry, and 20,000 war chariots. The Scripture says, "They went out, they and all their hosts with them, much people, even as the sand of the sea that is upon the seashore in multitude with horses and chariots very many" (Joshua 11:4). It was Jabin, king of Hazor, who took the lead in the proposed invasion, "for Hazor beforetime was the head of all these kingdoms" (11:10).

Once again, God spoke to Joshua, saying, "Do not be afraid because of them, for tomorrow about this time I will deliver them up all slain before Israel." Taking God at His Word, Joshua led the people to the waters of Merom, and the Lord fulfilled His promise by delivering the enemy into the hands of Israel. The people of these nations, the Amorites, Hittites, Perizzites, and Hivites who dwelled in various northern cities, had no chance for victory since they trusted in Baal, the god of war. Not only did the Israelites utterly defeat them, thus gaining possession of the whole land, but to make sure that no one could use the horses and chariots against them, the chariots were burned and the horses were "hocked" (a nerve in the leg was cut, causing the animal to limp) or "hamstrung" (Joshua 11:1–15).

Knowing that it would be necessary to capture or put under control the people in the upper part of Canaan, why didn't Joshua use the chariots and horses as weapons of war, to empower his people as they marched through the whole land up to the river Euphrates? Joshua's trust was in God, not the natural implements of war. He remembered all that Moses had told him: "When you go into battle against your enemies and see horses and chariots and a people greater in number than you, be not afraid of them" (Deuteronomy 20:1). The psalmist also said, "Some put their trust in chariots and horses but we will remember the name of the Lord our God" (Psalm 20:7), and "A horse is a vain thing for safety, Neither shall any be delivered by his great strength" (Psalm 33:17). A horse may be prepared against the day of battle, but Joshua knew full well that his safety was in God (Proverbs 21:31). Isaiah pronounced a woe upon those who rely upon horses and trust in chariots because "they . . . look not to the holy one of Israel, neither seek the Lord" (Isaiah 31:1).

What a lesson for us in our spiritual warfare with the enemy of our souls, namely Satan! Nahum reminds us that in our battles against the prince of the power of the air, the "Lord is our stronghold in the day of trouble" (Nahum 1:7). Paul reminds us that "though we walk in the flesh, we do not war after the flesh: (For the weapons of our warfare are not carnal, but mighty through God to the pulling down of strong holds." Our battles start in the mind, and we are to cast down "imaginations, and every high thing that exalteth itself against the knowledge of God" bring "into captivity every thought to the obedience of Christ," and "have in a readiness to revenge all disobedience" like Joshua did (II Corinthians 10:3–6). We can thank God that we have His whole armor, that we can stand up to Satan and resist him, thus becoming more than conquerors through Christ who loves us (Ephesians 6:10–18; James 4:7; Romans 8:37).

CONCLUSION

The most important spiritual blessing in preparing Israel for conquest of the land was the appearance unto Joshua of the "Captain of the Host of the Lord" (Joshua 5:13–15). At first, Joshua did not know who this Person was, but when he realized it was an appearance of the God of Israel, he fell on his face

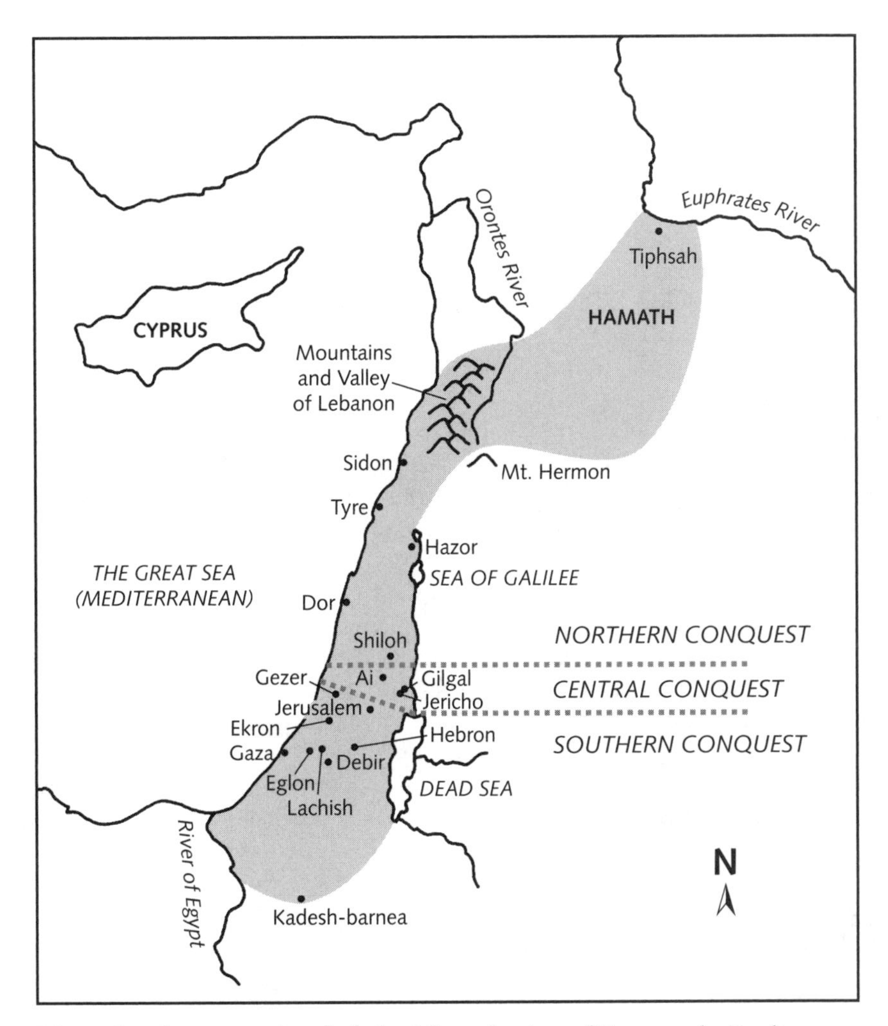

Map 5. Israel conquers the whole land from the river of Egypt to the Euphrates River. "So Joshua took the whole land, according to all that the Lord said unto Moses; and Joshua gave it for an inheritance unto Israel according to their divisions by their tribes. And the land rested from war" (Joshua 11:23). "And the Lord gave unto Israel all the land which he sware to give unto their fathers; and they possessed it, and dwelt therein. And the Lord gave them rest round about, according to all that he sware unto their fathers: and there stood not a man of all their enemies before them; the Lord delivered all their enemies into their hand. There failed not aught of any good thing which the Lord had spoken unto the house of Israel; all came to pass" (Joshua 21:43–45).

to the earth and worshipped Him. Even though the land of Canaan was defiled, the spot on which Joshua fell was made holy. It was here that he was assured by the Lord that every place the sole of the Israelites' feet would tread, they would conquer. This experience was the highlight of all the spiritual help that Joshua and the people needed to advance.

Looking back over Israel's history from her encampment at Gilgal and her first battle and victory at Jericho, she covered much territory as she marched against the nations from the south to the north of Canaan. She encountered all seven nations that Moses mentioned for her to destroy: the Hittites, Girgashites, Amorites, Canaanites, Perizzites, Hivites, and Jebusites (Deuteronomy 7:1). There were others mentioned in the land, but God told Moses that they could be spared, provided they made peace and paid tribute. If not, Israel was at liberty to make war against them and permit the women and children to survive (20:10–15).

Joshua recounts all the land that he took from the south up to the valley of Lebanon (Joshua 11:16–22). Then in chapter 12, there is the record of what Moses conquered on the eastern side of the Jordan and a list of all the kings whom Joshua defeated on the western side of the Jordan—the land that was promised to Abraham.

After the Israelites had gone through the land and defeated the prescribed nations, some remained who should have been *finalized.* We will discuss the effect of these survivors in a later chapter. But having defeated those whom God had listed, "Joshua took the *whole* land, according to all that the Lord said to Moses, and Joshua gave it for an inheritance unto Israel according to their divisions by their Tribes. *And the land rested from war*" (Joshua 11:23). One may review the following verses, which support God's promise of the land to Moses: Exodus 6:9; Deuteronomy 4:21,22; Leviticus 20:24; and Numbers 35:34.

Having defeated the kings of the north and rested from war, Israel's army still needed to continue northward to possess all the land to the entrance of Hamath on the river Euphrates. But the immediate need was for Joshua to give the Tribes their inheritance—their portion of the land.

9

DIVIDING THE LAND TO THE TWELVE TRIBES

The Lord's promise to Abraham of a land that flows with milk and honey as an inheritance for his people has now been fulfilled. God had said, "*Little by little* I will drive them out from before you until you are increased and inherit the land" (Exodus 23:30). Once the northern section of Canaan had been captured, Joshua returned to Gilgal for a much-needed rest. It has been suggested that it took approximately seven years to conquer the land. Caleb, Joshua's right-hand man, was 85 years old at this time. He was 40 years old when he was sent out as a spy from Kadesh-barnea, and having wandered for 38 years more in the wilderness, he was 78 at the end of the Exodus. Thus, seven years had passed since Israel crossed the Jordan River and started her mission to conquer the enemies of the Promised Land. It could be argued that Israel fought for at least five years. Either way, it was a lengthy struggle.

At the war's end we find Joshua making mention of the Tribes of Reuben, Gad and half of Manasseh being given their inheritance by Moses (Joshua 13:8–33). Since these Tribes remained on the east side of the Jordan River, only nine and a half Tribes received their inheritance west of the river, in the land that was promised to the Israelites (Deuteronomy 2:29, 3:20). Chapters 14 through 19 of Joshua recount how the nine and a half Tribes were given their inheritance.

THE TRIBES OF JACOB'S SONS

Judah (Joshua 15:6–15:63). The borders of this tribe were to extend from the southern tip of the Dead Sea westward, including Kadesh-barnea and the river of Egypt to the Mediterranean Sea. Northward, it included Jericho, Jerusalem, and westward to the coast. Joshua also listed Judah's family members. Located in Judah's territory was the city of Hebron, one of the Cities of Refuge. We will list these cities later, after all the Tribes have received their portion of the land and Joshua has received the city in which he will dwell, as well as the cities of the Levites.

Judah had a record that left a stain on his memory (Genesis 39). To his credit, he saved Joseph's life by persuading his brothers to sell him at Dothan

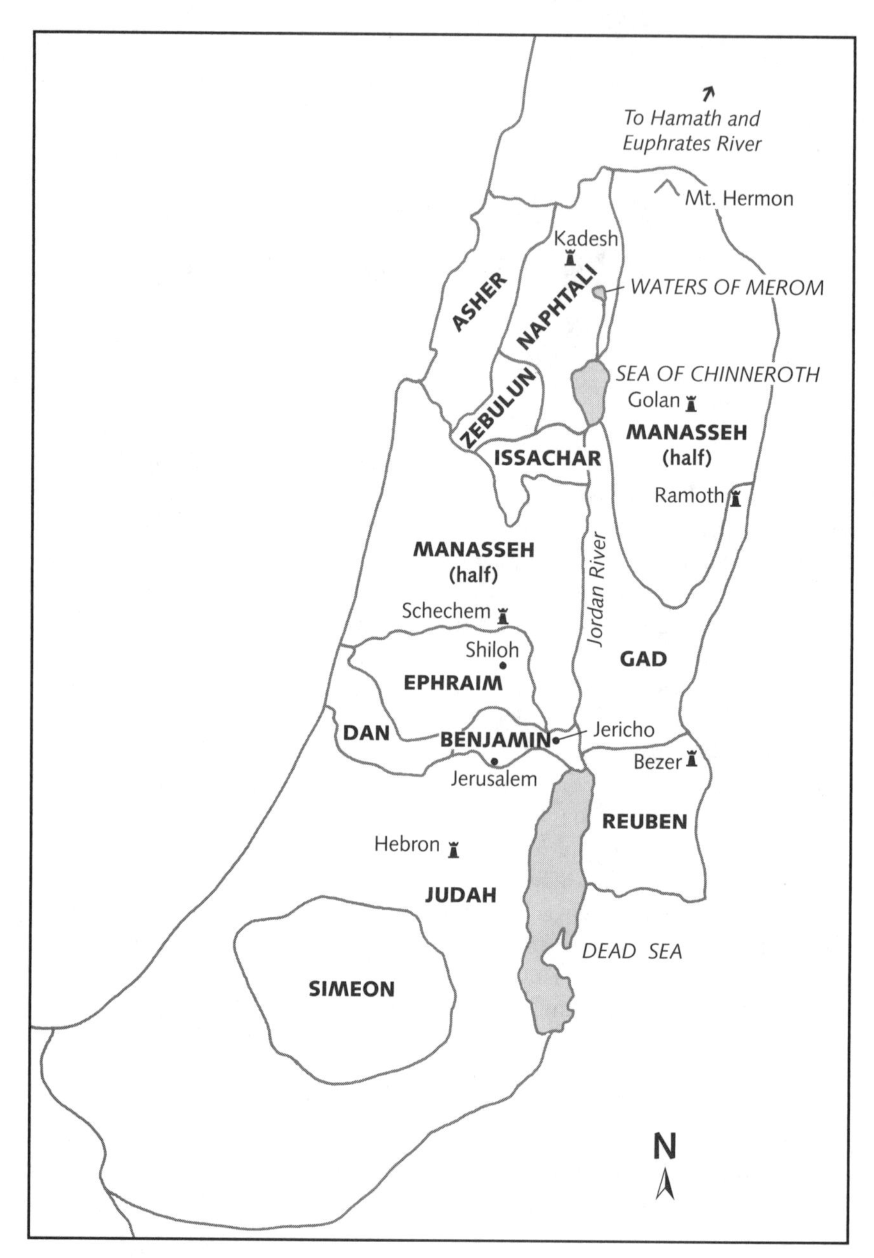

Map 6. Division of the land among the Twelve Tribes. *West of the Jordan River:* Asher (Joshua 19:24–31), Naphtali (19:32–39), Zebulun (19:10–16), Issachar (19:17–23), Manasseh (half) (chapters 16 and 17), Ephraim (chapters 16 and 17), Dan (19:40–49), Benjamin (18:11–28), Judah (chapter 15, 18:5, 19:9), and Simeon (19:1–8). *East of the Jordan River:* Manasseh (half) (18:7), Gad (18:7), and Reuben (18:7). ♜ denotes a City of Refuge (Deuteronomy 35:6 with Joshua 20).

to merchantmen who were going to Egypt (Genesis 7:26–28). It is interesting to note that the first Tribe Joshua mentioned to receive its inheritance was the one through whom Messiah was to come. As mentioned in Chapter 1, Abraham was chosen to start a race through whom the "Seed of the woman" would come. As we read Christ's genealogy (Matthew 1:1–6), we note that David came through Judah and that Christ would receive the "throne of his father David" (Luke 1:32). The virgin Mary was Christ's chosen mother, and she was also from the Tribe of Judah. Before Jacob died, he praised and blessed Judah, saying that his brothers would praise him, that he would be as strong as a lion, and that the sceptre would not depart from him till Shiloh come (Genesis 49:8–10). Some have suggested the sceptre remark is a prophecy relating to the coming of Messiah. Christ's kingship is also represented in the sceptre (Psalm 45:6). In the Book of Revelation (7:5), the Tribe of Judah is listed with the 144,000 Jews.

Caleb's Inheritance. Another descendant of Judah was Caleb, the spy who saw a mountain while passing through Hebron and desired it as his inheritance when Israel took the land. He was promised this mountain because he "wholly followed the Lord" (Deuteronomy 1:36). When the land was conquered, Joshua granted him his request (Joshua 14:6–14). Why was this man labelled with such a title as the one who "wholly followed the Lord"?

- He was honest: Joshua 14:7. He spoke as it was in his heart.
- He was charitable: verse 8b. Even though he disagreed with the spies whose report brought about the wilderness journey, he called them "my brethren." See Spies in the index.
- He was yielded: verse 8b. "I wholly followed the Lord." This expression is used four other times of him (verses 9 and 14; Numbers 32:12; Deuteronomy 1:36).
- He trusted God's Word: verse 9. His faith at Kadesh-barnea was now turned into sight when he saw the mountain again and took it.

What a testimony this man had for the Lord! He praised God for

- His faithfulness: verse 10 with Philippians 1:6; I Peter 1:5; Jude 24.
- His goodness: verse 11 with Psalm 31:19.
- His power: verse 12 with I Corinthians 15:57.

It is not surprising that in claiming his inheritance, Caleb received Joshua's blessing and God's inheritance (Joshua 14:13). God always has great dividends for those who "wholly follow Him" (Psalm 23:6). God is always "able to do exceeding abundantly above all that we ask or think, according to the power that worketh in us" (Ephesians 3:20; see also 1:19).

Ephraim (Joshua 16:1–10). Technically, Joseph was Jacob's son and was to be recognized as the head of a Tribe, but Jacob blessed the two sons of Joseph, Manasseh and Ephraim, and adopted them as his own sons. Although Joseph objected, Jacob's two grandsons were given the chosen blessing, signified by the right hand (Genesis 48:1–22). When Jacob blessed his own sons, he did not mention his grandsons, but he did give a special blessing to Joseph (49: 22–26). Ephraim's territory is bounded on the east by the Jordan River, on the south by Benjamin, on the north by Manasseh, and on the west by Dan.

On a scale of one to ten, it is difficult to know where to place this Tribe; you be the judge. *Ephraim* means "double fruit," implying a good crop. He is described as "strength" (Psalm 60:7). Although this Tribe was of the Northern Kingdom of Israel under Jeroboam's idolatry, it did join Manasseh in making a covenant to seek the Lord during King Asa's reign in the Southern Kingdom of Judah (II Chronicles 15:9–15). Also, Ephraimites went to Jerusalem and attended the Passover under King Hezekiah's reign; so did Manasseh (30:18).

The Ephraimites defected in battle, refused to walk in God's Law, and forgot God's Works (Psalm 78:9–11). By their not walking with the Lord, they turned to idolatry and mixed with the wrong people (Hosea 4:17, 7:8). They failed to drive out God's enemies from their land (Judges 1:29). God had said if any of His people failed to drive out their enemies, the latter would become "pricks in their eyes and thorns in their sides" and would become one of them (Numbers 33:55,56). Since the Tabernacle was pitched in their land at Shiloh, one would think that the Ephraimites would have set a good example to all who came to worship the Lord there (Joshua 18:1). As we think of the meaning of his name, "double fruit," the Ephraimites certainly were known by their fruit, and so are we (Matthew 7:20).

Manasseh. This Tribe's territory was situated from the west bank of the Jordan River to the Mediterranean Sea between the lands of Dan and Ephraim on the south and Asher, Zebulun, and Issachar on the north. One of the Cities of Refuge, Shechem, was located in this territory.

This Tribe was a much more faithful servant of the Lord than that of Manasseh's younger brother Ephraim. They joined David when he was a fugitive from King Saul (I Chronicles 12:19–22) and furnished David with 18,000 soldiers when he was made king at Hebron (I Chronicles 12:31). After Manasseh was settled in the idolatrous Northern Kingdom of Israel, the Tribe went over to the Southern Kingdom while Asa was king and made a covenant with the Lord (II Chronicles 15:9–15). Its people also went to Jerusalem and observed the Passover when Hezekiah was king (II Chronicles 30:10–22). However, there were those of this Tribe who built altars and worshipped idols (II Chronicles 34:9), although they later contributed to an offering for the cleansing and opening of the Temple when Josiah was king (II Chronicles 34:9). This Tribe is mentioned with the 144,000 Jews in Revelation 7:6.

Although Ephraim and Manasseh had their inheritance in the land with the other Tribes, their father, Joseph, did not. He is listed as one of the Tribes among the 144,000 Jews in Revelation 7:8. His father, Jacob, listed him as faithful. He suffered much at the hands of his brothers, and after arriving in Egypt, his fruit spread wherever he went (Genesis 49:22). What a difference between his fruit and that of Ephraim, his son!

There seemed to be a lull before the other seven Tribes received their inheritance. Joshua told them to divide the upper part of the land into seven portions, and he would cast lots for them in Shiloh for them to receive their inheritance (Joshua 18:2–10). The Levites were to receive cities, but no land.

Benjamin (Joshua 18:11–28). Benjamin's lot fell between the Jordan River and the northern part of the Dead Sea, with Dan to the west and Judah to the south. The meaning of his name is interesting. Joseph was the firstborn son of Jacob and Rachel. Upon his birth, Rachel said, "The Lord shall add to me another son" (Genesis 30:24). When the other son was born, she called his name *Ben-o-ni,* meaning "son of my sorrow" (35:18). Rachel was Jacob's favorite wife, and the two sons by her were his favorites. After Jacob was lied to about Joseph's death, he changed the name of Ben-o-ni to Benjamin, meaning "son of my right hand," and Benjamin became Jacob's favorite. There was much rejoicing and weeping on Joseph's part when he saw his "baby brother" once again in Egypt (43:16, 29–34).

There is a sad story involving this Tribe. As a result of their failure to drive out the Jebusites, they dwelt among them and embraced their sinful way of life and worshipped their gods (Judges 1:20). A number of them from Mount Ephraim raped and killed a concubine of a travelling Levite who had sought shelter there. This led to a civil war between them and other Tribes, a war that almost wiped out the Benjaminites (19:1–21:25). Jacob had said that this Tribe would be as a devouring wolf (Genesis 49:27). Finally, there was repentance, and this Tribe was not wiped out. They are mentioned among the 144,000 Jews in Revelation 7:8.

There were several well-known Benjaminites:

- Ehud, a judge who delivered Israel from Moab: Judges 3:12–15.
- Mordecai, who was instrumental in getting Esther to be queen, who in time saved the Jews from Haman's death sentence: Esther 2:5.
- Saul, Israel's first king: I Samuel 9:21.
- The prophet Jeremiah: 1:1.
- Saul of Tarsus (Paul): Philippians 3:5.

Simeon (Joshua 19:1–9). The inheritance of this Tribe was within the territory of Judah, yet some were scattered. Eventually most of them disappeared. Jacob said Simeon was self-willed and as ravenous and destructive as a wolf (Genesis 49:5–7). They too are listed with the 144,000 Jews in Revelation 7:7.

Zebulun (Joshua 19:10–16). Very little is said about this Tribe. Its territory was bordered by Asher, Naphtali, Issachar, and Manasseh. It was in this land that Jesus fulfilled the prophecy of Isaiah that people who were in darkness would see a great light (Isaiah 9:1,2 with Matthew 4:12–16). His Tribe is mentioned with the 144,000 Jews in Revelation 7:8.

Issachar (Joshua 19:17–23). With the Jordan River as its eastern border, this Tribe was bound by the land of Naphtali, Zebulun, and Manasseh. Its people were as strong as a burden-bearing donkey that bore the burdens of others as they served the Lord (Genesis 49:14). What a lesson for us to "bear one another's burdens"! By so doing we fulfill the law of Christ (Galatians 6:2). This Tribe also took part in helping Deborah and Barak defeat Sisera in order to free the Israelites from the Canaanites (Judges 5:15). The Tribe of Issachar is mentioned among the 144,000 Jews in Revelation 7:7.

When David was anointed king of Israel at Hebron, men of this Tribe were on hand with others. It is said of them that "they were men who had understanding of the times" (II Chronicles 12:32), a knowledge that prepared them to face any situation or circumstance with readiness. It was in their land that Jesus fulfilled the prophecy of Isaiah to reach the lost in the region of Galilee (Isaiah 9:1,2 with Matthew 4:11–16).

This should challenge us to take heed of the "signs of the times." The need for Issachar was to be helpful, and ours is to consider the times of the last days as "the coming of the Lord draweth nigh" (James 5:8; see also Matthew 16:3). Paul reminds us of the happenings of perilous times that will come in the last days (II Timothy 3:1–5). When we think of all the looseness of sin in our country today, we need to "abide in [Christ], that, when he shall appear, we may . . . not be ashamed before him at his coming" (I John 2:28).

Asher (Joshua 19:24–41). Very little is said about this Tribe. When Jacob's wife, Leah, gave birth to Asher and named him, she said, "Happy am I," and "happy" is the meaning of his name (Genesis 31:13). Jacob said of him that his bread shall be fat and that he would yield "royal dainties" (49:20). This seems to imply great fertility for his land along the Mediterranean coast. It also implies that these would be a nurturing people. Moses said of this Tribe, "Let Asher be blessed with children, let him be acceptable to his brethren, and let him dip his foot in oil" (Deuteronomy 33:24). The figure "his foot in oil" implies that he would enjoy the fruit of his labors. Asher is listed with the 144,000 Jews in Revelation 7:6.

We are told that whatever a man sows, that shall he reap. If we sow to our sinful nature, we will reap destruction, but if we sow to the Spirit, we will reap an abundance of fruit if we sow the "Seed of the Word." Let us not lose heart in doing good, for we shall reap in time if we walk daily in the footsteps of the "oil" of our fruits and not become weary in our well-doing (Galatians 6:7–9; I Corinthians 15:58).

Naphtali (Joshua 19:32–39). The territory of this Tribe stretched from the tip of the Sea of Galilee northward between Asher and the river Jordan. Naphtali's father, Jacob, likened him to a running deer, giving beautiful or goodly words as a counsellor (Genesis 49:21). The land of Naphtali was also where Jesus preached to Gentiles according to Isaiah's prophecy (Isaiah 9:1,2 with Matthew 4:12–16). Kadesh, one of the Cities of Refuge, was located in Naphtali's land. They are listed with the 144,000 Jews in Revelation 7:6.

Dan (Joshua 19:40–48). The people of this Tribe are branded as a "serpent by the road, a viper by the path, that bites the horse's heels so that his rider is thrown backward" (Genesis 49:17 Tanakh). Their territory was located on the Mediterranean Sea, bordered by Manasseh, Ephraim, Benjamin, and Judah. Some members of the Tribe were not satisfied with the allotment given them by Joshua, so a group set out to look over a part of the land suitable to them. They settled north of Asher and Naphtali, west of Mount Hermon, in the area of the city Laish, which they destroyed by fire after killing its inhabitants. There they built a new city, calling it Dan (Joshua 19:47).

In the Book of Judges it reveals that Dan, less than forty years after Joshua's death, became known as the first Tribe to openly build altars and worship graven images (Judges 18:1–31). With the division of the United Kingdom, king Jeroboam of the Northern Kingdom of Israel set up two golden calves to be worshipped, one at Bethel and one in Dan (I Kings 12:25–30). Dan's role of idolatry in the Northern Kingdom could possibly be one reason why this Tribe is omitted from the list of Tribes in Revelation Seven.[16]

In the Book of Judges, it is said twice that "every man did that which was right in his own eyes" (Judges 17:6, 21:25). Once we take our eyes off the Lord, we are in trouble. Scripture says that it is possible for one to "see, but not see" and that it is possible to see and not perceive (Matthew 13:13; Mark 4:12). The child of God is to look "unto Jesus the author and finisher of our faith" (Hebrews 12:2). When we do this, we "seek those things which are above, where Christ sitteth on the right hand of God . . . not on things on the earth," where Satan is having a field day (Colossians 3:1,2). A songwriter has given us a timely thought in the chorus of "Turn Your Eyes Upon Jesus":[17]

> Turn your eyes upon Jesus,
> Look full in His wonderful face;
> And the things of this earth
> will grow strangely dim,
> In the light of His glory and grace.

It is too bad that Dan didn't look to the God of Israel and follow the commands that He had given to Israel as a whole.

Levi (Joshua 21:1–42). The Levites, the priests of Israel, were not given a specific territory in the Promised Land. Since their ministry called for their being present throughout the nation to minister to the spiritual needs of the people, God appointed 48 separate cities throughout the lands of the Tribes to be their dwelling places (Numbers 35:7). The Book of Leviticus outlines their duties, including special duties in the Tabernacle at Shiloh. Because they did not have a specific portion of land, it became the responsibility of the people to supply their daily physical needs. Scripture teaches that the "labourer is worthy of his hire" (Luke 10:7). This Tribe is listed with the 144,000 Jews in Revelation 7:7.

Joshua's portion (Joshua 19:49–51). It was now the children of Israel's turn to do something for Joshua, and they gave him a city in Mount Ephraim, Tim-nath-serah, which he and the priest Eleazar had built. It was near Shiloh, where the Tabernacle rested.

This concluded the dividing to the Tribes of the land promised to Abraham and all his descendants (Genesis 15:18, 17:8).

THE CITIES OF REFUGE

After Joshua received his portion of the land and before he gave the Levites their cities, he appointed six Cities of Refuge[18]—three on the west side of the Jordan River for the nine and a half Tribes and three on the east side for the two and a half Tribes there (Joshua 20). These were cities that belonged to the Levites and were to be a haven for anyone who accidentally killed someone (Numbers 35:6). This gave protection from a revenge-minded member of the deceased family. The killer must flee to the closest City of Refuge, residing there until the priest of that city died. Upon his death, the "manslayer" was at liberty to return to his own home without fear of retribution. If the act of murder was not accidental, capital punishment was to be carried out (Genesis 9:6).

The six Cities of Refuge have New Testament significance:

1. They were to be a shelter appointed for a refuge from judgment. So is our Refuge from judgment appointed: John 1:29; Romans 5:6–8.
2. They were situated so that they were easily accessible in all parts of the land. Christ is within easy reach of any sinner: Luke 19:10; Revelation 3:20.
3. The way to these cities was prepared—each city was marked out. The Holy Spirit has been sent to testify of Christ, using the preaching of the Word, tracts, hymns, and the witness of faithful Christians to point us to do the right thing for security: John 16:7–9; Romans 10:3–17.
4. The manslayer must be inside the city gate to be safe. One cannot be *almost* saved. "Almost cannot avail, almost is but to fail." We must be *in* Christ: II Corinthians 5:17.
5. Refuge was provided for only *one* kind of offender. So is our salvation in Christ—it is for the sinner *only:* Luke 18:9–14.
6. The manslayer had to believe and appropriate this provision for himself to escape punishment. So must we: John 1:12, 5:24.

The names of the cities are also significant, in that each relates directly to the Person of Christ, our *Refuge.* The Cities of Refuge west of the Jordan River were the following:

1. In Asher, *Kadesh,* meaning "holy": Joshua 20:7 with Mark 1:24.
2. In Manasseh, *Shechem,* meaning "a shoulder": Joshua 20:7 with Isaiah 9:6; Luke 15:4,5.

3. In Judah, *Hebron,* meaning "fellowship": Joshua 20:7 with I John 1:7; I Corinthians 1:9.

The Cities of Refuge east of the Jordan River were the following:

4. In Reuben, *Bezer,* meaning "fortification": Joshua 20:8 with Psalms 18:2 and 91:2; John 16:33.
5. In Gad, *Ramoth,* meaning "high" or "exalted": Joshua 20:8 with Philippians 2:9.
6. In Manasseh, *Golan,* meaning "joy" or "exultation": Joshua 20:8 with John 15:11.

It is good to know that God makes every provision necessary for His child (Philippians 4:19). He is my salvation, my glory, the rock of my strength and my refuge, and unto Him will I pour out my heart because He is nigh unto me (Psalm 145:18). Because my confidence is in Him, He daily loads me with His benefits and I will speak of the glorious honor of His majesty and of His wondrous works (Psalms 69:18 and 145:5).

10

ISRAEL POSSESSES THE WHOLE LAND

The northern part of Canaan was the final section of the Promised Land to be conquered. God's original promise to Abraham, handed down to Moses and Joshua, was the land from the river of Egypt in the wilderness through Lebanon unto the river Euphrates (Genesis 15:18; Joshua 1:4). Yet when Joshua and Eleazar divided the land among the Tribes, they only settled in portions as far north as opposite Mount Hermon, about 225 to 250 miles south of Hamath on the Euphrates. With this conquest, Joshua declared that they had taken the *whole* land that God had promised them and that the land was resting from war (Joshua 11:23).

Some scholars say that Israel possessed only the land that became the inheritance of the Tribes and that at a future date Israel will possess all of it up to the great river Euphrates. They say when the land rested from war, what she dwelt in was all that she possessed *at that time.* This viewpoint raises several questions.

Having conquered the central, southern, and northern land in Canaan, did Joshua and Israel actually possess *all* the land God had promised from the river of Egypt to the Euphrates River? (Genesis 15:18). It must be kept in mind that one can possess land without living on it.

After Joshua made the statement that Israel had taken the whole land and that the land rested from war, he reviewed what had been accomplished in their battles. He listed not only the conquests by Moses east of the Jordan River, but also the kings whom he himself had defeated in Canaan (Joshua 12). Before he began to divide the land, he said, "*There remaineth yet very much land to be taken over.*" He then listed several border areas that reached up to the entering in of Hamath (Joshua 13:1–5); this section was included in the territory the spies looked over (Numbers 13:21). Joshua had previously said in defeating the northern kings that there were many strong cities that still stood (Joshua 11:12,13).

A second question must be asked. Did Joshua contradict himself when he said that Israel took the *whole* land (Joshua 11:23), meaning all that God had promised, and then said that "there remaineth yet very much land to be taken over"? (13:1). Joshua stated that with the defeat and destruction of the northern kings, people, and key cities, the *whole* land was taken (chapter 11).

What Israel now needed to do was to spread out and take the remaining cities in the north and along the seacoast, cities that still stood in their strength. An analogous situation happened in World War II. Hitler and his German forces conquered Paris, the capital of France. As a result, France as a whole fell, but Hitler's armies had to fan out through the whole country and take control of all the cities. This is what Israel must now do to take full possession all the way to the Euphrates River in Hamath. God had promised Israel that "every place the sole of your foot shall tread upon, that have I given unto you, as I said to Moses, from the wilderness and this Lebanon unto the great river, the Euphrates, all the land of the Hittites, and unto the great sea toward the going down of the sun, shall be your coast" (Joshua 1:3,4).

The Scriptures are silent in the matter of Israel's "mopping up" in the territory northward to the Euphrates, but note Joshua's summation of their doing just this after the land was divided for Israel's main dwelling place: "The Lord gave to Israel the whole country which He had sworn to their fathers that He would assign to them; they took possession of it and settled in it. The Lord gave them rest on all sides, just as He had promised to their fathers on oath. Not one man of all their enemies withstood them; the Lord delivered all their enemies into their hands. Not one of the good things which the Lord had promised to the House of Israel was lacking. Everything was fulfilled" (Joshua 21:41–43 T [21:43–45 KJV]).

If the Bible thus quoted does not mean that Israel received *all* that God promised concerning possession of *all* the land, then someone is not telling the truth, and I don't believe it is God, for He cannot lie (Titus 1:2). To say that God gave Israel only what the Tribes inherited is a "half truth"—and that is a "whole lie." So who is telling the truth, certain Bible teachers or God? Both cannot be right, so I cast my lot with God!

THE ENTRANCE INTO HAMATH

Just what is the meaning of the "entrance into Hamath"? Hamath was bordered by two rivers, the Orontes on the southwest and the Euphrates on the northeast. People who were travelling north entered Hamath at Riblah on the river Orontes (II Kings 23:33; Jeremiah 39:5). People who were travelling westward and planned to go south into Palestine would enter Hamath at the city of Tiphsah on the Euphrates River (I Kings 4:24).

According to the *Encyclopædia Britannica,* some areas along the Euphrates could be forded by traders or armies coming over from the Fertile Crescent to head south into Syria, Palestine, and Egypt, passing through the city called Tiphsah. This, then, was the "entrance to Hamath" of which God's promise spoke. See Map 1 on page 12.

If the only land that Israel possessed was what Joshua gave them as their inheritance to live in, how were some of the dissatisfied members of the Tribe of Dan able to move north of Naphtali's territory and establish residence in a city they called Dan? (Joshua 19:47). When Moses gave the Tribes of Reuben, Gad, and Manasseh territory on the eastern side of the Jordan River, he made them promise that their men of war would cross over the river and help the rest of Israel conquer the land. They agreed not to return home until the land was fully possessed (Numbers 32:1–32; Joshua 1:10–18). When the land was fully possessed, Joshua gave these Tribesmen permission to go back to their families. It is hardly likely Joshua would have done this if all the land were not possessed (21:43–45 with 22:9).

When they arrived at the Jordan River on the return home, these Tribesmen built a huge altar on the west bank, Canaan's side. The children of Israel heard of it and gathered together to war against them, thinking that the Tribesmen had turned their backs on the Lord and that the altar was to an idol. When they found out it was an altar to be a witness between God and all Twelve Tribes on both sides of the Jordan so that future generations might know there was peace between them, they were blessed and went home (Joshua 22:10–34).

After their return, the Tribe of Reuben, because they had great numbers of cattle, moved northward and inhabited an area by the river Euphrates for grazing land (I Chronicles 5:3–9). It would not be possible for them to invade another's land and live there if it were not possessed by Israel. Tragically, Israel later lost part of the northern territory, but King David "recovered his border to the Euphrates river" (II Samuel 8:3). "Recover" means that this territory was Israel's possession—it belonged to God's people, and David took it back.

After the Philistines had taken the Ark of God, the men of the city of Kirjath-jearim returned it to Israel. David wanted to take it to Jerusalem, so he requested all the brethren (Israelites) from Shihor (or "Sihor," the river of Egypt) unto the entering of Hameth (or Hamath) to join him. Why request Israelites to come from the river of Egypt and the entrance of Hamath to Jerusalem if none were living in these areas? (Joshua 13:3; I Chronicles 13:1–5). David's dominion was established from the whole of Israel's possession—the river of Egypt to the entrance of Hamath on the Euphrates River. He encouraged Israel to help Solomon build the Temple by reminding them that the Lord had given them rest, that He had given the inheritance of the land into his hand, and that the land was *subdued* before the Lord (I Chronicles 22:17,18). What else could David be referring to than Israel's conquest of the whole land under Joshua?

King Solomon reigned from the river Euphrates unto the border of Egypt (I Kings 4:21; II Chronicles 9:26). When he kept the Seven Day Feast and all Israel was with him, it was done "from the entering in of Hamath unto the river of Egypt" (II Chronicles 7:8). How could Solomon reign over the whole land and observe feasts throughout the whole land if Israel did not possess it? Upon completion of the Temple, Solomon offered a dedicatory prayer in which he thanked God with a loud voice, saying, "Oh praise the Lord who has

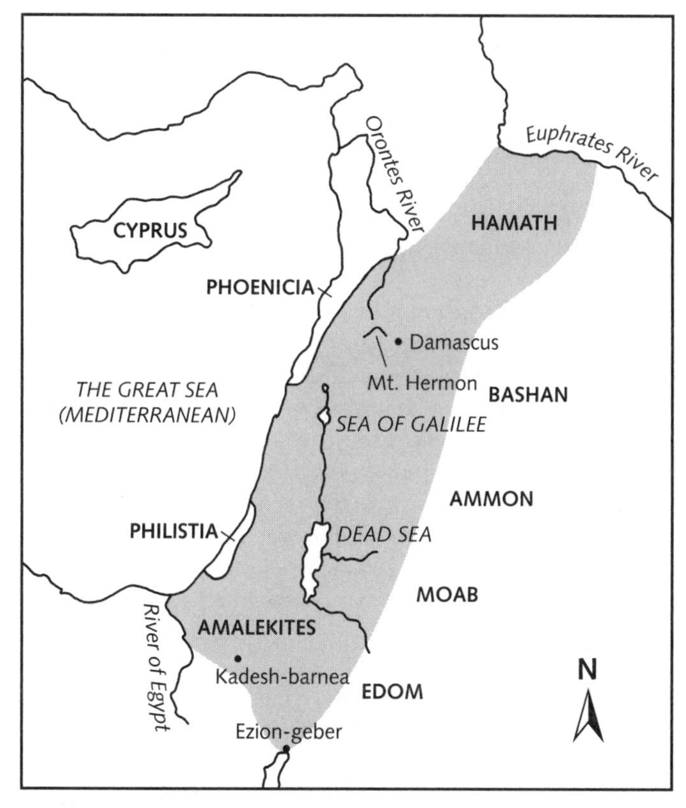

Map 7. The empires of David and Solomon. *David:* II Samuel 8:3. *Solomon:* I Kings 4:21; II Chronicles 9:26, 7:8; I Kings 9:26.

granted a haven for His people Israel, just as He promised; not a single word has failed of all the gracious promises He made through His servant Moses. May the Lord our God be with us as He was with our fathers" (I Kings 8:56,57). There is no doubt Solomon was referring to the promise that God gave Moses in Leviticus 20:24, Deuteronomy 4:21,22, and Joshua 1:2–4: that He would give them *all* the land.

The prophet Jeremiah, in reminding Israel of God's goodness, spoke of how they came out of Egypt, were given the land that He swore unto their fathers, and went in and possessed it (Jeremiah 32:21–23).

Amos prophesied against the Northern Kingdom of Israel concerning their Assyrian downfall, mentioning that these brutal people would afflict their prisoners (impaling, blinding, and decapitating them) "from the entering in of Hamath to the river [of Egypt] of the wilderness" (Amos 6:14).

Nebuchadnezzar besieged Jerusalem three times. The third time, he stopped at Riblah in Hamath, a part of Israel's possession, and sent his soldiers down to Jerusalem to finally conquer it. When King Zedekiah of Israel's Kingdom of Judah was captured, he was brought before the king of Babylon at Riblah, saw his two sons killed and then was blinded (II Kings 25:6,7).

After the exiles returned from Babylonian captivity and had the Word of God read to them, they were reminded of the covenant that God had made with Abraham in giving him the land, how their fathers went in, subdued the nations, and possessed the land, and how God richly rewarded them once they had settled there (Nehemiah 9:7,8; 24,25). Once again, the word *subdued* is used, and here again we see that Nehemiah took notice that Joshua had conquered the seven nations spoken of by Moses, that they were brought to subjection, bondage, and humiliating defeat by a miracle-working God. Possibly the Holy Spirit had reminded Nehemiah of the time when the Tabernacle was first pitched at Shiloh, how the land was *subdued* before them (Joshua 18:1).

A third question is, Why did Joshua, in dividing the land to the Tribes, not scatter them from the river Euphrates to the river of Egypt. It is quite possible that for unity's sake it would be better for God's people to be closer to the Tabernacle for worship purposes. Even if the northern sector were not as densely populated, worshipping God in person and trusting Him together would be strengthening to all the Tribes on both sides of the Jordan River.

Fig. 16. Impaling prisoners.

Fig. 17. Blinding prisoners.

Fig. 18. Decapitating prisoners.

CONCLUSION

If Abraham and Moses, by faith, along with Joshua, members of the Tribes of Reuben, Gad, and half of Manasseh, kings David and Solomon, Nehemiah, the Levites, and the prophets Jeremiah and Amos all believed that Israel possessed land beyond the stated boundaries of the Tribes, all the way up to the river Euphrates, why do some people, even many who claim to believe the Bible, still argue that Israel didn't conquer it all but will at a future date? We need to quit listening to these people and become like the Bereans, who daily sought the Scriptures to see if what they were being taught was actually Biblical (Acts 17:10–11).

11

JOSHUA'S FAREWELL

Possibly seven years had passed since Israel conquered "much more land" and the Tribes had received their inheritance (Joshua 13:1–5). Old age had caught up with Israel's leader, Joshua (13:1). He called together all Israel to give them some final words of advice and encouragement. The Bible does not state where this meeting took place, whether in Joshua's hometown or Shiloh. He not only wanted all the families to be present, but made sure the leaders of the people were present to hear what he had to say. There were (1) the *elders,* or what we would call today the "senate," (2) the *heads* of the Tribes (or families), (3) the *judges,* who interpreted the law for the people, and (4) the *officers,* who enforced the decisions that were made. Joshua wanted to make sure that what he had to say was understood by all and would be carried out by those in charge after he died.

JOSHUA'S FIRST MESSAGE

Joshua began his speech by reminding the people of what God had done for them in defeating the nations in the land that they would possess (Joshua 23:35). They were advised to be very courageous and obey the Word of God, to *observe* and *do* it by walking the straight and narrow road. His desire was for them to be successful, as he had been told by God (1:7,8). They were not to fear anyone, for God was with them, and one man, with God, could chase a thousand. To do this, they must be in love with God and not themselves, which meant loving the Lord with all their heart, soul, mind, body, and strength (Joshua 23:6–11 with Mark 12:30).

A strict warning was given to anyone who decided to fraternize with any of the people left in the land who should have been driven out. Joshua told them of Moses' warning that if they joined in with their enemies, the latter would become snares and traps, whips in their sides, and pricks in their eyes until they (Israel) would perish off the land that God had given to them. Just as the Lord had seen that good things befell His people, that no promise He had made unto them failed, He would bring evil things upon them, even destroying them from the good of the land that He had given to them if they disobeyed God. He even gave a stiff warning about idolatry still being practiced in the land and cautioned them not to embrace the worship of false gods (Joshua 23:12–16).

JOSHUA'S SECOND MESSAGE

Joshua called for a second "business meeting" to be held with all the people—families and leaders—at Shechem, one of the Cities of Refuge.

1. For this gathering, the people came not necessarily just to *hear about* God as in times past, but to *present themselves unto Him* (verse 1). To be successful with God, we must "present [our] bodies a living sacrifice, holy, acceptable unto [Him]" (Romans 12:1).

2. Joshua opened his discourse with the formula of the prophets, "Thus saith the Lord" (Joshua 24:2). He knew that his speech would be with enticing words and man's wisdom if he spoke on his own, so he reminded all Israel that it was God speaking through him.

3. Joshua began this speech by reviewing the history of God's dealing with Abraham and the promise that He made to him and his seed about the land of Canaan being given to them as their "Promised Land," a land that "flows with milk and honey." He reminisced about Jacob and his family going down into Egypt and bringing the children of Israel out of Egyptian bondage; crossing the Red Sea and dwelling in the wilderness for a long season; gaining victory over several enemies; crossing the Jordan River and conquering the land, starting with Jericho and defeating the Amorites, Perizzites, Canaanites, Hittites, Gergashites, Hivites, and Jebusites; and the whole land being given to them by God (verses 1–13). He praised the Lord for fulfilling His Word with one victory after another in giving them a land of cities, vineyards, and olive yards for which they did not labor.

4. Joshua then turned to a spiritual need for self and the people to practice; this point in his sermon had to do with idolatry. We notice that his first mention of idolatry had to do with Abraham's father and family (Joshua 24:2). It was on the basis of this practice of idolatry on the other side of the flood and those days of Abraham's time that he said to all his people, "Now therefore fear the Lord and serve Him in sincerity and in truth and put away the gods which your fathers served on the other side of the flood and in Egypt, and serve the Lord" (Joshua 24:14).

This verse is an acknowledgment that many of the Israelites were still serving idols. What a pity in view of God's undertaking in their behalf! It appears that Joshua was following the same order that Paul used in writing to the Romans, beseeching them, "Present [your] bodies a living sacrifice, holy, acceptable unto God, which [is your] reasonable service. And be not conformed to this world: but be ye transformed by the renewing of [your] mind, that ye may prove what is that good, and acceptable, and perfect, will of God" (Romans 12:1–2).

On the basis of verse 14, Joshua was admonishing the people to abandon their sin of idolatry. He was well aware of the seriousness of this abominable sin and made mention of it four times in this chapter. He then added this statement: "If it seem evil to you to serve the Lord then choose this day who you will serve; whether the gods which your fathers served on the other side of the river or the gods of the Amorites in whose land you now dwell; but as for me and my house, we will serve the Lord" (verse 15). He made it clear whom he was serving and was determined to let the people know just where he and his family stood with God. Happy is the man who can speak with such great conviction and assurance, not only for himself but for his whole household as well. Joshua followed this challenge to the people by telling them that they cannot worship a holy God with sin in their lives (verses 19,20).

We can see that Joshua fully realized the difference between the false and the true. To have a false "religion" such as idolatry places one on the broad road leading to perdition. To know the truth of God places one on the straight and narrow road that leads to eternal life and heaven. Joshua knew that he was facing death, that life was short, that death always stands at one's door, and that when God calls, the time is over to make any further choices. Joshua's desire is for this people to "fear the Lord and serve Him in sincerity and in truth," not a god who neither sees, hears, talks, nor walks (verse 14). He wanted them to consider God's being, His power, His holiness, and His justice; by having this clear conception of Him, they could easily serve Him the way Joshua himself was doing—the way he had just described to them.

Joshua could not have given the Israelites the desire of his heart for them to serve and obey God unless he himself had learned lessons of obedience. When he said, "As for me and my house we will serve the Lord," the word *serve* could well be translated *obey.* Some lessons are not always easy to come by, but regardless of our feelings and personal desires, God's way is the best way, it is the right way, and it can only be accomplished by obedience unto Him. What is it to obey?

1. To obey is to do something that we might not want to. If we don't do it when God speaks, we become the losers. An example of not obeying is the rich young ruler's walking away from Christ (Matthew 19:16–22).
2. We must obey although we might want to do something else first. This would make us "me firsters," and these people never get around to doing the will of God (Luke 9:59–62). We can be like Paul who said "that *in me first* . . . I [might be] a pattern to them which should hereafter believe on him to life everlasting" (I Timothy 1:16).
3. We must obey although our actions might contradict common sense. Note Israel's march around the city of Jericho as they shouted, causing the walls to fall down flat (Joshua 6).
4. We must obey even though we think we can do a better job than the Lord. We often make plans and then ask the Lord to put His stamp of approval upon them. Sometimes He might give us *our* answer but will send leanness to our souls (Psalm 106:15). Consider King Saul's experience in I Samuel 15.

THE PEOPLE'S RESPONSE

Evidently, Joshua's message hit the hearts of the people with real conviction. Five times they vowed that they would obey and serve the Lord, making themselves witnesses to these vows by saying that they would not serve other gods, but would obey and serve the Lord *only* (Joshua 24:16,18,21,33,34).

Is there any significance in their saying *five* times that they would serve the Lord? The Bible is full of numbers that often have a spiritual application. *Five* seems to imply *personal responsibility.* The following examples show verses where the number five is mentioned:

1. The man who was given five talents gained five. Because he was faithful over a few things, he was made ruler over many (Matthew 25:20,21).
2. The *five* wise and the *five* foolish virgins (Matthew 25:1,2).
3. It is better to speak *five* understanding words than 10,000 words in an unknown tongue (I Corinthians 14:19).

Five also stands for *victory:*

1. *Five* of God's servants can chase a hundred of their enemies (Leviticus 26:8).
2. David selected five smooth stones as he went out to face Goliath. The extra four were for his four brothers in case they decided to try to get even with him for slaying Goliath (I Samuel 17:40 with 15:16–22).
3. Joshua defeated the *five* kings of northern Canaan to accomplish possession of the whole Promised Land (Joshua 10:5, 14–27).

As we think of these people making such vows in turning to God with a determination to serve Him, I wonder how many vows have been made to the Lord that have not been kept? We, too, who name the name of the Lord, have obligations, and how many times have we made a vow to assume our responsibility and failed to keep it? What are our obligations? Joshua gives us a good example (Joshua 24:14–24):

1. Fear the Lord: verse 14a.
2. Separate unto the Lord: verse 14b. Separation is not how *far* we can get from those with whom we disagree, but how *close* we can get to the Lord.
3. Choose the Lord over all: verse 15.
4. Confess the Lord: verses 16–18a.
5. Serve the Lord: verses 18b, 21.
6. Witness for the Lord: verse 22.
7. Make vows unto the Lord *and keep them:* verse 24.

Whenever we make a vow or pledge unto the Lord, we are not to put off paying it, for God has no pleasure in those who make a mockery of Him. We *must* pay what we vow. It is better that we should not vow than to vow and not keep it (Ecclesiastes 5:4,5).

SEALING THE COVENANT AT SHECHEM

After Joshua had challenged the people and got them to make a vow that they would serve the Lord, he made a covenant with all of them that day and established a statute and an ordinance in Shechem (Joshua 24:25). Since the people had made a vow or covenant with the Lord to abandon idolatry, Joshua set a stone under an oak tree as a lasting testimony of this solemn occasion.

In this celebration of Israel's forsaking idolatry, it is interesting to note where the ceremony and stone-setting took place: in Shechem. For background on this site, we go back to the days when God told Jacob to leave his uncle Laban's house and return to Bethel. While packing for the trip, his wife, Rachel, stole her father's gods, which served not only as his religion but as the title deed to all his property. Anyone possessing them could go to court and claim the property. Rachel probably stole them because Laban had robbed Jacob of many cattle and wages, but especially because her father gave Leah to Jacob and made him work a total of 14 years for her. Three days after they had left, Laban found out what had happened to his gods, overtook Jacob, and searched for the gods, but they were hidden by Rachel (Genesis 31:3–24). Evidently, as Jacob and his family travelled on and arrived at Shechem, Rachel told Jacob that she had stolen the gods (or teraphims), and if Jacob had so desired, he could have laid claim to those idols and been worth a fortune. He knew the truth that Jesus quoted, "What shall it profit a man, if he shall gain

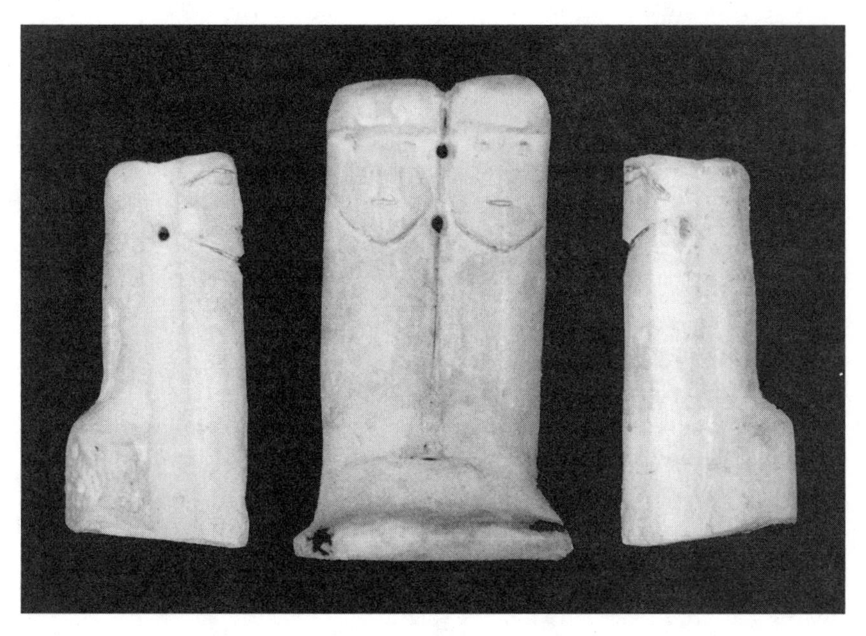

Fig. 19. Family gods: teraphims.

the whole world, and lose his own soul?" (Mark 8:36). The spiritual meant more to him than the material, so he made those in his group bury all their strange gods, rededicate themselves to the Lord, and be clean before their arrival at Bethel. And where did Jacob bury them? "Under the oak [tree] which was by Shechem" (Genesis 35:2–4). How fitting that Joshua mentioned idolatry in his final address at Shechem and erected a monument of victory where Jacob had buried the idols of his group!

JOSHUA'S DEATH AND FUNERAL

There were no newspapers in those days that carried an obituary column, but if there were, I'm sure the article would have read something like this:

> Joshua, the son of Nun, servant of the God of Israel, was a faithful servant all the days of his life. He and his family were God-fearing people. Like his predecessor Moses, he ended his earthly career with dignity and honor. No one could put a finger on one moral blemish in his life. He stands out as one of the greatest characters of all times and is worthy of our admiration and imitation. His influence was such that at the end of his life the children of Israel served the Lord all the days of the elders who outlived him. He was buried in the cemetery on the border of his inheritance in the city of Timnathserah, in Mount Ephraim, on the *north* side of the hill of Gaash. (Joshua 24:30)

Emphasis is placed on the word *north.* In speaking of Mount Zion, the Psalmist said, "Beautiful for situation, the joy of the whole earth is Mount Zion, *on the sides of the north*" (Psalm 48:2). Joshua was buried on the *north* side and north is *up.* He might have been placed six feet under, but he was ready to be caught *up* when the Lord comes back for His own! (I Thessalonians 4:15,16).

Just as we imagined a notice on the obituary page of a local newspaper about Joshua's demise, we can suppose his tombstone looked something like Fig. 20.

POSTSCRIPT

This wonderful account of Joshua shows the faithfulness of God throughout in fulfilling His promises; God's promises had come to pass in Israel's receiving Canaan's land. Joshua's writing stops at his death, and the Bible is silent as to who wrote the last five verses of the book. These verses speak of three burials in the Promised Land: Joshua's, the bones of Joseph that the children of Israel brought back when they made their exodus from Egypt, and that of Eleazar, Joshua's assistant when the land was divided among the Tribes.

Joseph's father, Jacob, had purchased a plot of ground in Shechem; this became Joseph's grave. Before Joseph died in Egypt, he requested that his bones be taken with Israel as they left in their exodus. Upon his death, he was embalmed and put in a coffin (Genesis 50:25,26). As the people left the land of their bondage, Moses took his bones as promised (Exodus 33:19). His body

Fig. 20. Proposal for Joshua's tombstone.

had been "stored" for several centuries, the coffin carried during the wilderness journey and maintained during the time of possession of the land until his burial at Shechem (Joshua 24:32). At the Old Testament site of Shechem there is a monumental building said to be the tomb of Joseph.

Eleazar was the son of Aaron, a Levite. Upon Aaron's death he became the high priest (Numbers 26:28). He had assisted Moses in numbering the children of Israel (26:1,2) and designating the land east of the Jordan River to the Tribes of Reuben, Gad and half of Manasseh (32:28). God appointed Eleazar to help Joshua divide the Promised Land to the Tribes for their inheritance (34:17). Upon his death, he was buried on a hill owned by his son, Phinehas, on Mount Ephraim, not far from Joshua.

CONCLUSION

As we close this period of Israel's inheritance of the land promised to Abraham, the question is raised, What's next for the people of God, the Israelites? When Joshua called to their attention that idolatry was still practiced by some, they all made *five* pledges that they would put away the strange gods of the land and would serve God and Him alone. It is said that they served the Lord as long as the elders lived who outlived Joshua (Joshua 24:31).

Did Israel follow through with her vows to serve the Lord? In the next section of this book we will survey her history through the Old Testament and into the New, as well as events relating to her dispersion after the fall of Jerusalem in A.D. 70 up to the present day.

III

THE JUDGMENTS OF DISOBEDIENCE

12

APOSTASY IN THE NATION

Before we continue our study, we need to consider that there are two groups of Israelites, categorized as the Bible categorizes people: the righteous and the unrighteous, the saved and the lost. In the nation of Israel there were those who were righteous by faith, called the *remnant* (Genesis 15:6; Isaiah 1:9). Then there were those who were recognized as God's people in Israel's nation, but whose heart was far from Him. As we approach this period in Israel's history, we note that the writers, in referring to Israel's sins, speak of Israel as a whole, even though there were those who made up the remnant.

The same could be said of America. Originally known as a Christian nation, over the years a change has taken place and sin has become a reproach to our people. The majority of our population could care less about spiritual matters, and today our country is anything but Christian or Biblical. Yet there is a remnant, a minority of born-again believers, who make up a part of our nation. As a whole, however, just as all Israelites were classified as the Nation of Israel, so all Americans are classified as the United States. This thought must be kept in mind as we read about the nation of Israel: the writers are talking about the vast majority who preferred to live in sin.

It is quite possible that when the people told Joshua that they would obey and serve the Lord, the Holy Spirit reminded them of several things that they were told by Moses in their wilderness journey.

1. There would be untold material and spiritual blessings for them and their descendants if they would obey the Lord and follow Him wholly (Deuteronomy 28:1–14). They were then warned what would happen to them and their seed *forever* if they failed to obey and serve Him (28:15–68, especially verses 46 and 47).

2. They no doubt thought of Moses' command to drive out seven ungodly nations from the land, sparing none, destroying all their idols, making no covenant with them, nor marrying any (Deuteronomy 7:1–5).

3. Possibly they thought of what Moses said they would do after his death, that once they got into the land that flowed with milk and honey, they would turn to other gods, serve them, provoke God, and break His covenant (Deuteronomy 31:16,20).

4. Maybe they thought of God's specific warning not to do after the abominable doings of those in the land of Canaan—adultery, child sacrifice, homosexuality, and bestiality (Leviticus 18:2,3; 20–27).

In spite of their victory in possessing the whole Promised Land, Joshua, in not obeying the Lord fully, permitted the Gibeonites (Hivites) to live (Joshua 9:1–20) even though they were included among the seven nations to be totally destroyed. Tragically, many citizens of these nations were not driven out.

The first chapter of Judges gives an account of the price Israel had to pay for failure to drive out these idolatrous people. Surviving Canaanites, Perizzites, Jebusites, Amorites, and Hittites lived in the territories of Judah, Benjamin, Manasseh, Ephraim, Zebulun, Asher, Naphtali, and Dan (see Map 5 on page 67). Although many battles were fought to drive these people out, many of them remained. One weapon that the enemy had was the "chariot of iron," something new to the children of Israel. These chariots replaced the old wooden ones, which could easily be burned.

When the children of Israel made the vow to serve God, they were rubbing shoulders daily with these idolaters. The question is raised, During the period of time that the elders lived to the time of the Judges, was Israel's vow to serve the Lord real or was it lip service?" "There was a generation who knew not the Lord nor of the work He had done for Israel" (Judges 2:10). Had the parents meant what they vowed, they would have done what Moses taught them to do: "You shall teach your children God's commandments, talk of them in the house or when you are out walking" (Deuteronomy 6:1–7). Evidently, these "vow-making" parents failed to train their children in the way they should go. They must not have realized that they lived in a "glass house" and that their children observed every move they made and every word they spoke. There is an old cliché, "As goes the home, so goes the nation." How true for any people!

Having ignored God's spiritual laws and values and following the example of the earlier inhabitants whom they failed to drive out of their land, the children of Israel "did evil in the sight of the Lord and served Balaam (Baal)." They *forsook* the Lord God of their fathers, who brought them out of the land of Egypt, and followed other gods, gods of the people that were round about them. They bowed themselves unto them and provoked the Lord to anger. They *forsook* the Lord and served Baal and Ashtaroth, an ancient fertility deity (Judges 2:11–13). They had been told by Moses that if they didn't drive out these enemies, the latter would become "pricks in their eyes and thorns in their sides." This is exactly what happened, as Judges brings out (2:2–3 with Numbers 33:55,56). Eventually the Israelites "enjoyed" what they were doing, for they began to dwell among these people, intermarried, and in serving their gods, *forgot* God and served Baal and the groves (Judges 3:5–7). See Baal and Groves in the index.

Since the Israelites had forsaken and forgotten God by doing what they thought was right in their own eyes, God began to do to them what He said

He would do if they failed to drive out the other nations. Doing what one thinks is right in his own eyes is like concocting a way that seems right, but the end is the way of death (Judges 17:6 with Proverbs 14:12). God began to punish them by permitting various nations to take them into captivity. "Whatsoever a man soweth, that shall he also reap" (Galatians 6:7). Although apostasy reigned throughout the nation and God was forced to make Israel reap what she had sown, He was gracious in answering their prayers when they called upon Him for help. Note their oppression by several nations and their deliverance by judges whom God raised up in their behalf.

Oppression	**Delivering Judges**
1. Mesopotamian (8 years): 3:8	1. Othniel: 3:5–11 (peace, 40 years)
2. Moabite (18 years): 3:14	2. Ehud: 3:15–30 (peace, 80 years)
3. Canaanite (20 years): 4:3	3. Shamgar: 3:31
	4. Deborah: 4:1–5:31 (peace, 40 years)
4. Midian (7 years): 6:1	5. Gideon: 6:1–8:32 (peace, 40 years)
5. Apostasy under Abimelech: 8:33–9:57	Abimelech (usurper) (peace, 3 years)
	6. Tola: 10:1,2 (peace, 23 years)
	7. Jair: 10:3–5 (peace, 22 years)
6. Ammonite (18 years): 10:8	8. Jephthah: 10:6–12:7 (peace, 6 years)
	9. Ibzan: 12:8–10 (peace, 7 years)
	10. Elon. 12:11,12 (peace, 10 years)
	11. Abdon: 12:13–15 (peace, 8 years)
7. Philistines (40 years): 13:1	12. Samson: 13:1–16:32 (peace, 20 years)

The above-mentioned judges were raised up on extraordinary occasions to be instruments in God's hands when Israel repented and called upon the Lord. They delivered the people out of the hands of their enemies, protected them, led their armies when needed, settled differences, and administered justice. One detects that the Israelites' was an "elevator life," *down* when they did evil in the sight of the Lord and *up* when they called upon the Lord and were delivered by the judges.

Samson didn't have the best reputation. Although he was the "Superman" of the Old Testament, his fleshly desires got the best of him, and in his flirtation with Delilah, he got a haircut in the devil's barber shop, which brought about his blinding by the Philistines. He also was deprived of the power of God. When he called upon the Lord for help, God came to his rescue, and when he regained his strength, he destroyed the Philistine's pagan temple, but died in the act (Judges 16:13–31).

The last chapters of Judges close with the civil war that almost exterminated the Tribe of Benjamin—all because Israel refused to do that which was right in the eyes of the Lord. They constantly did that which was right in their own eyes (Proverbs 14:12). What a tragic way to end this period in their history!

Fig. 21. Chariot of iron.

There was one bright light during this period, however, a bright light that shone in the midst of the darkness of their apostasy. Found in the Book of Ruth, it shows that there was a remnant that was faithful to the Lord during this time. Ruth and Boaz, her husband, shone forth as a light, and for their faithfulness, both of them are listed in the lineage of Christ (Matthew 1:5).

13

ISRAEL'S UNITED KINGDOM

The books of Samuel, Kings, and Chronicles are, in a sense, a continuation of the Book of Judges. They give us an account of the remaining judges of Israel up to the election of her first king, Saul, and of all the kings of Israel up to the Babylonian captivity.

I Samuel gives us a beautiful picture of a member of the "faithful remnant" family in the person of a woman named Hannah. Being without child and desiring to have a son, Hannah made a vow unto the Lord that if He gave her one, she would dedicate him to God. Her prayers were answered. After weaning him, she took him to the Tabernacle in Shiloh and "loaned" him to the Lord in care of the priest, Eli (I Samuel 1).

Samuel had attentive ears, and when the Lord called unto him, he said, "Speak, Lord, for your servant hears." In due time, he became a judge and a prophet (I Samuel 3). Because the Philistines had made war against Israel and captured the Ark of the Covenant, after 20 years the people cried unto the Lord for help. After defeating the Philistines and reclaiming the Ark, Israel experienced a period of revival.

In spite of their rejoicing, trouble started to brew. As good a man as Samuel was, he appointed his two *unbelieving* sons to be judges (I Samuel 8). They walked not in the way of the Lord, taking bribes and perverting justice. By this time, the people and elders evidently thought that God was not the proper one to rule over them, so they requested that Samuel give them a king—a visible person—to rule over them. They probably figured that they needed someone they could *see* and *talk to* personally to guide and govern them, as well as fight their battles.

When this request for a king was made, Samuel took the only recourse that a child of God should take—he went to the Lord in prayer for wisdom to answer the request. God's answer was that Israel would have to pay a price: they would be subject to the king, their sons would be drafted for army duty, officers would be placed over them to give strict orders, their daughters would become household servants for government employees, they would be taxed to pay employees, they would have to tithe animals and grain for their food, older people would work in the fields, and there would be the possibility of losing property to help support royalty.

In spite of all God told Samuel to say to the people, because they had forsaken Him and were worshipping idols (I Samuel 8:8), the people turned a deaf ear to all these requirements of a *man* king. They "refused to obey Samuel's voice and said *no,* but we will have a king over us that we may also be like all the other nations and that our king may judge us and fight our battles." God then told Samuel to grant their request, to give them a king (8:19-22). These words may seem harsh, but truth is truth—Israel had just dethroned her God—she had rejected her God (10:19). This is just one more case of people doing things that they think are right in their own eyes.

SAUL, ISRAEL'S FIRST KING

It is interesting to note that during Israel's wilderness journey, Moses told the people that once they settled in the Promised Land, they would set up a king over them to be like all the nations around them. Specific instructions were given that he should be one whom God would choose, that he would obey God's commands, and that he would not seek wealth for himself, horses for military service, or multiply unto himself wives for selfish pleasure. Whoever the king might be, he was to make a copy of these instructions and read them all the days of his life as a reminder to fear the Lord and keep the words of His law. By doing this, he had the promise that the days of his kingdom would be prolonged (Deuteronomy 17:14–20). In these verses we find God's standard by which we can judge any of the kings of Israel.

We first learn of Saul in his search for his father's lost donkeys. We see him as obedient to his father in leaving home to find them, concerned and determined to bring them home (I Samuel 9:4,5). Having difficulty in locating them, he sought the man of God (Samuel) for help in his search (9:6). Samuel was told by God that Saul would be the man who would rule over Israel (9:17). The Holy Spirit came upon him to help him serve the Lord and to give assurance that God was with him (10:6). He was anointed as "captain," one who leads his people. Then at Gilgal, the people made him king (11:15). Prior to this event, God had been their King; now that the people had chosen Saul, God set him as king before them (12:12,13).

At the outset, we see this man as an obedient son, with a fine personal appearance (I Samuel 9:2, 10:24), with humility when the people wanted to praise him (10:21,22), and with self-control in not slaying some Amorites when the people requested this of him (11:13). But after having reigned well for two years, his life began to change. His worst fault was being self-willed, choosing to take matters into his own hands. For example, when Samuel was detained in coming to offer a sacrifice before going to battle against the Philistines, Saul usurped the priest's authority and offered the sacrifice himself. He ignored God's law by not trusting in God's power to give victory His way (chapter 13).

Again, in going to battle against the Amalekites, Saul was commanded to destroy everything—the people and the animals. The people were killed, but the king and some good beasts were taken alive. When Samuel questioned Saul as to why they were spared, he blamed the people. Although he acknowledged that he had sinned against the Lord, there was no repentance or asking God for forgiveness (I Samuel 15).

By this time God had had enough of this defiant king. He was grieved for having set Saul up as king. Due to his disobedient actions, Saul was told that his days as king were numbered (I Samuel 15:11). This brought about God's rejection of him (15:23,26).

Not only was Saul self-willed, he was jealous of his son Jonathan and of David, his psychiatrist, who settled his nerves playing the harp. The people praised David for slaying his ten thousands while only giving Saul credit for thousands (I Samuel 18:6–8). On several occasions Saul sought to kill David.

By the end of Saul's reign, the Philistines were ready to do battle against Israel again. Saul sought the Lord for guidance and help, but God's ear was turned against him. He then sought a medium in occult practice for advice from the deceased Samuel (which was forbidden by God: Deuteronomy 17: 3–5), only to learn that he would soon die and Israel would be defeated (I Samuel 28). Having turned his back on the Lord, he was now beginning to taste the bitter dregs of his own life of disobedience. To assure himself that he would not be captured by the Philistines after being wounded in battle, Saul took his own life. When the enemy found his body and the bodies of his three sons, they cut off Saul's head, stripped him of his armor, put it in the house (temple) of the goddess Ashtaroth, and nailed the bodies to the Bethshan city wall (chapter 31). What a sad commentary on the life of this man who was chosen by the people to replace God as king!

Conclusion. If we learn nothing else from Israel's desire to be like other nations, we surely have learned that our ways are not God's ways, neither are our thoughts His. As the heavens are higher than the earth, so are His ways higher than ours and His thoughts higher than ours (Isaiah 55:8,9). In Israel's decision to request their choice of leadership, she was as much as asking God to take a back seat, thinking they were doing right in their own eyes. But it wasn't long before they realized they had asked for the wrong thing. Their sin was confessed, but it was too late (I Samuel 12:20). There was no repentance or asking for forgiveness. There are times we will make known our requests, and too often they are not the best for us, but God will permit it and send leanness into our lives to teach us lessons, always causing us to learn them the hard way (Psalm 106:15).

God allowed Saul to become Israel's king. He gave him in His anger and took him away in His displeasure (I Samuel 9:16,17, 10:1; Hosea 13:11). Although Saul was "tall and handsome," the Lord "looked at the heart and not the outward" (I Samuel 16:7). Saul offered a sacrifice in disobedience, probably out of fear and at the same time to be seen. He was told that "to obey is better than sacrifice" (15:22). Worshipping idols, mentioned by Samuel, was still Israel's besetting sin, and it was compounded by her rejecting her sovereign Leader and replacing Him with a man who was her self-willed and stubborn leader. His reign lasted 40 years (Acts 13:21).

DAVID, ISRAEL'S SECOND KING

As we take into account Israel's choosing Saul to be their king, we must consider this: even though God permits such a thing to happen in relation to His people, He is sovereign, He is still upon the throne, and in due time, we see results for the good. God works in mysterious ways His wonders to perform.

For example, Joseph was hated by his brothers, sold into Egyptian slavery, falsely accused by his master's wife, and imprisoned. Because the Spirit of God was upon him, he interpreted a dream for the Pharaoh; pardoned, he was elevated to a position second only to the Pharaoh himself. Recognizing his brothers who had come to Egypt for grain, he told them that their act of selling him was for a purpose: to save his family from starvation that Jacob's seed might be preserved (Genesis 45:7,8).

In I Samuel we see God setting the stage to choose a young man named David to succeed Saul as king of Israel. In II Samuel, after Saul's death, the men of Judah made David king of the Tribe of Judah. However, one of Saul's sons by the name of Ishbosheth was made king of all Israel by Abner, Saul's captain (II Samuel 2:4–11).

After David had reigned in Hebron for seven years, the elders of Israel came to David and made a league with him to become king over all Israel. He was anointed king of Israel according to the Word of the Lord, and Jerusalem was made the capital of the kingdom (II Samuel 5:1–5; I Chronicles 11:1–3).

When God talks about any of His children, He tells it like it is, never minimizing a few wrong deeds because the good outweighs the bad. We find this to be true as we note several characteristics of David's life.

1. He was an excellent military leader, winning many victories over the enemies of God's people: II Samuel 5:6–10.
2. He was a courageous champion: I Samuel 17:31–50.
3. He was a man after God's own heart: Psalm 89:20; Acts 13:22.
4. He had a desire to build the Lord's house (Temple): II Samuel 7.
5. He was led by passion: II Samuel 5:13; 11:1–27.
6. He listened to Satan: I Chronicles 21:1–7.
7. When he sinned, he repented of it, confessed it, and returned to the Lord. When Saul sinned, he merely said, "I have sinned," possibly because he was caught and the Lord had rejected him. David said, *"I have sinned against the Lord,"* and the Lord put away his sin, receiving him back into fellowship with Him (II Samuel 12:12 with Psalm 51).

David was instrumental in elevating the kingdom to a spiritual plane that honored God. Jerusalem became Israel's most prominent city when the Ark of the Covenant of Zion was installed, the Levite singers were present, and a dedicatory psalm was read (I Chronicles 16). David's leadership was responsible for regaining Israel's territory up to the Euphrates River and for helping Israel gain much rest from war. Of the 150 Psalms, 73 are attributed to David. All of his Psalms are inspiring, but the Twenty-third is the most popular one. He was promised that his kingdom would not be taken away as was Saul's, that his throne would be established forever through the coming Messiah, and that if he sinned, he would be chastened but never forsaken.

Because he was a man of war, he was forbidden to build a Temple for God (I Chronicles 22:8, 28:3). However, his last days were spent in preparation for his son, Solomon, to build it, and he gave generously of material for Solomon's use (28:1–29:19).

Having made preparation for his death, David gave a charge to Solomon, who had been appointed to follow him upon the throne. His last words related to his salvation and the everlasting covenant that God had made with him. "He died in a good old age, full of days, riches and honor, and Solomon his son reigned in his stead" (II Samuel 23:1–5; I Chronicles 28:9–21, 29:26–30). David was buried in Jerusalem, the "City of David," having reigned for 40 years—seven in Hebron and 33 in Jerusalem. He was known as Israel's "versatile king."

Fortunately for Israel, under the reign of a God-chosen king, we find no mention of any of the practices of Baalism. There may have been some who were idolaters, but other events outweighed such practices. To Israel's credit, it appears that enough members of the "remnant" were successful in bringing about a much-needed revival during this period.

SOLOMON, ISRAEL'S THIRD KING

It is the custom in a patriarchal monarchy that the firstborn son of a king succeed his father to the throne. David had several sons who were older than Solomon, but he promised Bathsheba that the son born to her after the death of their first one would be Israel's king. They named him *Solomon,* which means "peaceful" or, in the language of our day, "Shalom." The prophet Nathan gave him the name *Jedidiah,* which means "beloved of the Lord" or "because of the Lord" (II Samuel 12:24,25). This son was of the Lord; the first one was conceived in adultery.

As Solomon ascended the throne, God was with him and magnified him exceedingly (II Chronicles 1:1). While he was offering sacrifices in Gibeon, God asked him what he desired most, and Solomon asked for an understanding heart or wisdom to rule over the people fairly. What an unselfish request this man made! I wonder what you or I would request. God granted him his request, giving him a wise heart of understanding "so that there was none like him before him, neither after him shall any arise like unto him" (I Kings 3:3–9).

Solomon's wisdom was soon put to a test when two women claimed the same child. When he ordered the child to be cut in half and divided between the two, he knew the real mother would ask for the child to be spared, so he gave the child to its real mother (I Kings 3:16–28). His fame began to excel above all the people of the eastern countries and Egypt. He spoke 3,000 proverbs, wrote 1,005 songs, was a forester, botanist, zoologist, ornithologist, and ichthyologist. People from all over the then-known world travelled to Jerusalem to hear him and learn from his gift of wisdom (4:29–34, 5:9–14).

Solomon fulfilled David's desire in building the Temple, a glorious, magnificent building that in today's currency would have cost several billions of dollars, especially when we consider the vast amount of gold and silver that David supplied (I Chronicles 22:14, 29:4,7). Upon completion of the Temple, Solomon brought in the Ark of the Covenant, and God's shekinah glory fell on the place. Solomon's sermon reminded the people that this was the place where God would abide with them, then dedicated the Temple to Him (I Kings 8). It was a place where His people could come and worship Him, but the Temple welcomed strangers (Gentiles) as well (I Kings 8:41–43).

By the time Solomon's fame spread abroad, the queen of Sheba paid him a visit. Having heard of his great wisdom, she asked hard questions of him, and all were answered. Having been shown the city and palace, and especially the Temple, she was convinced that Solomon's God was the true God. Her comment, after all her questions had been answered and she had seen the magnificent buildings, was "The half has not been told." At her departure, she gave Solomon costly spices, 120 talents of gold (equivalent to over $3,000,000), and precious stones (I Kings 10:1–13).

Solomon's Wisdom Turns to Folly. Thus far we have seen Solomon as the wisest man in the then-known world. What a wonderful beginning he had! At this point in his reign, we see him in all of his glory, which even Christ made mention of (Luke 12:27). Despite all the dignity and praise heaped upon him, however, God, who knows the end from the beginning, warned Solomon that if he should not continue to walk with Him, he would soon turn from following the Lord and not keep all His commandments. If he served any other gods and worshipped them, the Temple would become in ruins and the people would be cut off and become a byword among all people (I Kings 9:1–9). It was common knowledge that many were worshipping the Lord at high places because there was no house of God until Solomon built the Temple (I Kings 3:2).

In spite of the fact that God used him mightily, Solomon acted questionably several times at the beginning of His reign. God forbade His people to marry those from heathen nations, but Solomon took to himself the daughter of Pharaoh; this he did before he asked God for wisdom (I Kings 3:1). He was guilty of having his half-brother, Adonijah, killed for seeking the throne; he should have had him exiled (2:13–25). Knowing that it was his privilege to build the Temple for the glory of God, he selfishly spent 13 years building his own house compared to the seven years it took to build the magnificent Temple. He also built a lavish house for himself in the country of Lebanon (6:37–7:12).

Solomon failed to make a book of instructions, as Moses had outlined for kings, and consequently failed to follow any of them (Deuteronomy 17:14–20). He violated God's command in bringing horses out of Egypt and amassing enough for 40,000 stalls with 1,400 chariots and 12,000 horsemen (I Kings 4:26; II Chronicles 1:14). Why did God give such a command? The more horses a king had, the more powerful his nation, and Solomon began to show his trust in horses rather than in God.

God had promised Solomon riches (I Kings 3:13), but he violated the command not to increase unto himself silver and gold (10:14–29). It has been suggested that a talent of gold was worth $30,000. In one year Solomon received 666 talents—120 from King Hiram, 120 from the queen of Sheba, 420 from Ophir, plus many more from the kings of Arabia. These talents alone amounted to almost $40,000,000. Silver was so plentiful that it was like the stones in the land. (Palestine is a *very* stony land.) Solomon's drinking vessels were gold; none were silver. Can you imagine drinking a Pepsi from a gold vessel? "King Solomon exceeded all the kings of the earth for riches and wisdom. And they sought to hear the wisdom that God had put in his heart, and everyone brought presents, vessels of silver and vessels of gold . . . a rate year by year" (I Kings 9:14,28, 10:1–29).

It was bad enough that Solomon was so greedy that he "took it all in for himself and gave nothing out," but instead of sharing his riches with his subjects, he began to inflict heavier taxes on them. The people complained that he had "made their yoke grievous" with such burdensome taxation. Their cry after his death was for taxes to be lighter (I Kings 12:4,5). In spite of hardships at the hands of their king, they needed to be reminded of what Samuel had said would happen if the people chose their own king (I Samuel 8:10–18).

Solomon's worst offense was multiplying wives unto himself—700 of them, plus 300 concubines. The average man can hardly handle one. But Solomon! Why so many wives, and how? Because of his greed for wealth and prestige at the expense of displeasing the Lord, he soon found himself following an international custom practiced by heathen nations, that of "swapping" (exchanging or offering) wives and/or daughters as gifts in order to enhance prestige or keep peace among themselves. Fig. 22 shows a Hittite king giving his daughter to a Pharaoh in exchange for peace.

Solomon started out with an Egyptian wife and then took many others from nations whose God was not Israel's. Moses had said that if a king multiplied unto himself wives, they would turn his heart away from God. This is exactly what happened to this wise king who became foolish: he embraced the god of the heathen women, he built high places for them to worship their

Fig. 22. "Peace" offering of a Hittite daughter.

gods, and he himself burned incense and offered sacrifices to their false gods (I Kings 11:1–8).

It appears that Solomon's problems stemmed from the fact that he simply did not do that which was right in the eyes of the Lord, not only sinning himself but copying what many people were doing (I Kings 11:32,33). The vast majority of the people returned to the old idol-worshipping days of their relatives in the period of the Judges, when every man did that which was right in his own eyes. It would seem that *greed* was Solomon's motive for material things, *power* his motive for collecting so many horses, *lust* his motive for accepting so many wives and concubines, *pride* his motive for welcoming kings from other nations, *blindness* his reason for disobeying the Word and doing right in his own eyes, *authority* his motive for inflicting heavy taxes, *compromise* his motive for embracing idolatry, and *selfishness* his motive for not sharing his wealth with his people. It was his *lack of control* that brought about his unwillingness to continue to live in the wisdom with which God endowed him. He had lost not only his testimony with the Lord but God's good pleasure also, as well as the good standing of Israel among other nations (I Kings 11:9,10). God's anger was greatly kindled against him, and now judgment must be meted out.

Solomon's Punishment. "The Lord said to Solomon, because you are guilty of these sins, especially idolatry, you have not kept My covenant and laws which I commanded of you, I will tear the kingdom away from you and give it to one of your servants. But for the sake of your father David, I will not do it in your lifetime, I will tear it away from your son. However I will not tear away the whole kingdom; I will give your son one Tribe (Judah) for the sake of My servant David and for the sake of Jerusalem which I have chosen." Jeroboam, a servant of Solomon, was told that the kingdom would be torn from Solomon's hands and that he would be given ten Tribes (Benjamin joined with Judah) (I Kings 11:11–13, 31). Solomon sought to kill Jeroboam to circumvent God's verdict, but the servant fled to Egypt and remained there with Egypt's king, Shishak (or Sheshonk), until Solomon's death. Solomon ruled as king over Israel for a period of 40 years and was buried in Jerusalem (11:40–43).

Conclusion. What a sad commentary on this once-famous king of Israel and the people as a whole! What a glorious finish Solomon's reign could have had if he had obeyed the commandments of the Lord, the one and only weapon that could have kept him on the "straight and narrow path"! In the latter part of his reign, he seemed to be an *instructor* rather than an *example:* he simply did not practice what he preached, as much as saying, "Don't do as I do; do as I say." There seems to be no concrete act of repentance on his part, but when he wrote the book of Ecclesiastes in his later years, he seemed to have become reconciled to the fact that all worldly things were a "vanity of vanities" and that if anyone is ever to find and keep favor with God, their whole duty is to "remember their Creator in the days of their youth and *keep* His commandments" (Ecclesiastes 1:1, 12:13,14). Solomon had learned his lesson, but it was too late and he had to reap what he had sown. His sins had found him out (Numbers 32:23).

14

THE DIVISION OF ISRAEL'S KINGDOM

The period of the United Kingdom of Israel lasted 120 years, from about 1050 to 930 B.C. Israel's decline in regard to other nations is seen in the following:

1. Her being *afraid* of other nations when at Kadesh-barnea: Numbers 13:31. This helped to fuel her walking by sight, not faith.
2. Her *mixing* with other nations in Canaan: Judges 1:1–3:7.
3. Her *imitating* other nations after her settlement in Canaan: I Samuel 8:5, 19,20.
4. Her *continuing* to follow heathen nations in worshipping their false gods (I Kings 11:32,33). Although not much is said about the nation as a whole indulging in idolatry during Saul's, David's, and part of Solomon's reign, many had forsaken God, and Ashteroth (the goddess of the Zidonians), Chemosh (the god of the Moabites), and Milcom (the god of the children of Ammon) were being worshipped. Israel as a whole did not do that which was right in the eyes of the Lord in keeping His statutes as David had done.

REHOBOAM SUCCEEDS SOLOMON

Upon Solomon's death, Jeroboam, the servant who fled to Egypt when Solomon threatened his life, returned to Jerusalem and, at the request of the people, spoke to Rehoboam about the high taxes that Solomon had imposed upon them. Rejecting Jeroboam's plea, the new king increased their taxes all the more; the people rebelled and killed the tax collector. On the basis of God's decision to take away the kingdom from Solomon, Jeroboam was made king by the people and given ten of the Tribes (I Kings 12:1–24). This kingdom became known as the Northern Kingdom of Israel, and Rehoboam's became known as the Southern Kingdom of Judah, which included the Tribe of Benjamin.

THE NORTHERN KINGDOM OF ISRAEL

Jeroboam, Israel's First King. Jeroboam had been called and set apart to be the first king of the Northern Kingdom with the full approval of the people (I Kings 11:31). It appears that Shechem was the first capital (12:25). Jeroboam immediately severed relations with the house of David and, afraid that the people would go back annually to Jerusalem to worship, established two centers for worship at the two extremes of his territory—Bethel in the south and Dan in the north (I Kings 12:26–30). He set up altars at each in violation

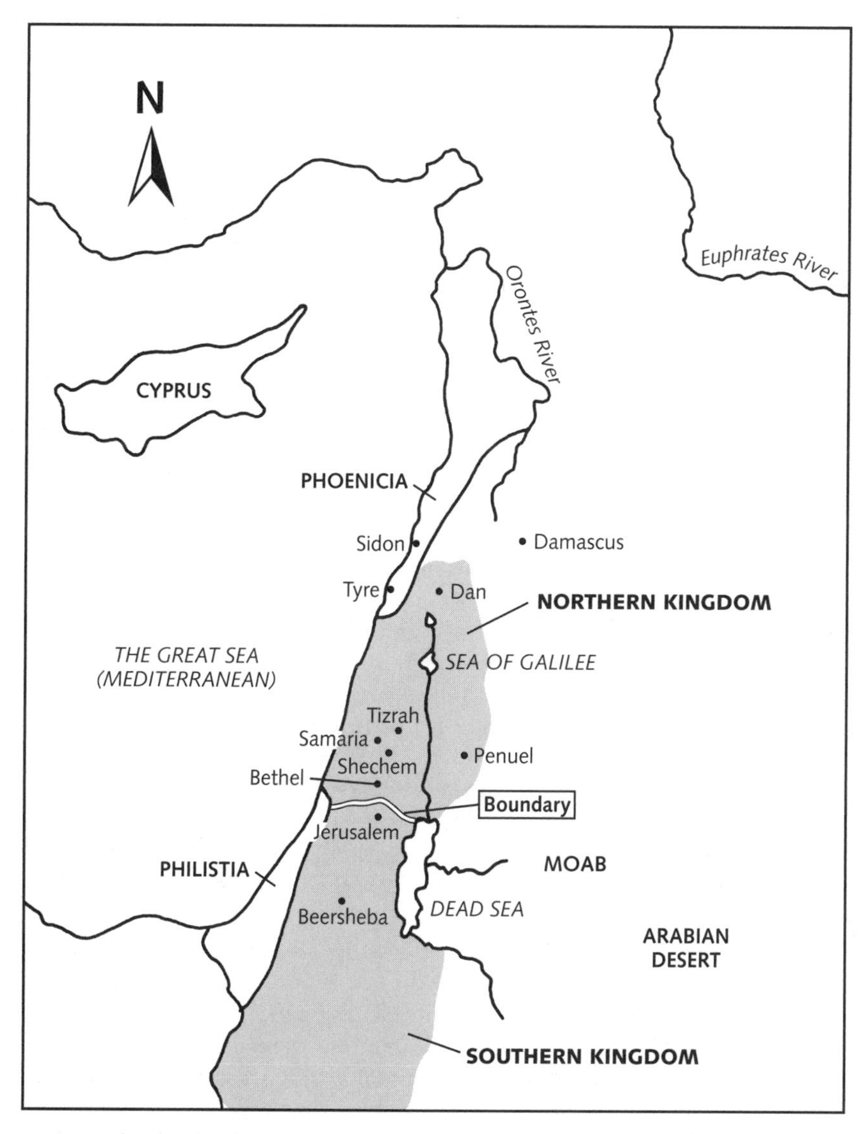

Map 8. The divided kingdoms of Israel and Judah. The northern kingdom is Israel (I Kings 12:16–24); the southern kingdom is Judah (II Chronicles 11:1–12).

of the law that mandated only one place to meet with God: the temple that Solomon built. This was bad enough, but he set up a golden calf (a four-footed beast) at each city, quoting the words that the people used at Mount Sinai: "These are the gods, O Israel, which brought you out of the land of Egypt" (I Kings 12:28 with Exodus 32:4). Godly priests refused to serve at these altars, so Jeroboam took just anyone to serve. He built shrines on high places, changed the date of a feast, and took it upon himself to act the part of a priest (I Kings 12:31–13:1,33). He had expelled the true Levitical priests, who had to leave their possessions and go to dwell in the Southern Kingdom. Many of the people—the true remnant—also left to go worship the Lord in Jerusalem (II Chronicles 11:14–16). Jeroboam sinned greatly himself, making Israel to sin with him, thus provoking the Lord to anger because they had made an Asherah, or grove, a sex object (I Kings 14:15,16).

The prophet Ahijah was used of God twice with this king. First, when Solomon fell into idolatry, Ahijah informed Jeroboam that he would rule over ten Tribes (I Kings 11:29-31). Second, this prophet spoke for God against Jeroboam because in breaking God's commandments he had not been God's servant. He said that Jeroboam "had done evil above all that were before him," had made other gods of molten images to provoke the Lord, and had cast God behind his back. Ahijah told him that this would result in God's smiting Israel and that He would eventually root out this kingdom from the land because he had provoked the Lord (I Kings 14:9,10; 15,16). Truly Jeroboam was evil in the sight of the Lord. Full details of his life can be found in II Kings 11:26–14:20 and II Chronicles 10:1–13:20. He reigned for 22 years.

Ahab, Israel's Seventh King. All 19 kings of the Northern Kingdom did evil in the sight of the Lord. Ahab was branded as "doing evil in the sight of God and that he did *more* evil to anger the Lord than the kings before him" (I Kings 16:30). Some of his evil was marrying an idolatrous woman, Jezebel, whose influence led him to embrace Baal worship, and reviving this worship among his people. He built a house (temple) for this false god, setting up an Asherah (grove) to worship this sex object. Ahab led the people back to the gross worship of Baal as before during the days of the Judges. Jezebel was a Sidonian and participated in licentious orgies as she worshipped the goddess Ashtoreth. She immediately began to murder the prophets of God. To his credit, Ahab got the prophet Obadiah to spare the lives of 100 by hiding them in a cave and feeding them (I Kings 14:4,13).

God had prophesied that if His people stooped to that idolatry, He would withhold rain to keep the land from yielding its fruit (Deuteronomy 11:16–17). Now God was ready to fulfill His Word. The prophet Elijah announced to Ahab that He was going to cause the rain to cease. After three years of drought, Elijah told Ahab that his worship of Baal was the cause of the famine. Elijah called for a showdown among the people over who the true God is—Baal or the God of Israel—saying, "Why halt you between two opinions? If God be God, follow Him. If Baal be God, follow him." Then Elijah set the condition, saying, "The God who answers by fire to consume the sacrifice, let him be God."

The 450 prophets of Baal and the 400 prophets of Asherah called on Baal to hurl down bolts of fire, but to no avail. They screamed for Baal, as god of fire, to perform this action. Elijah mocked them by saying that maybe Baal was on a journey or asleep. This false god of nature failed miserably. Now it was Elijah's turn. Pouring water on the sacrifice and then calling upon his God, the Lord vindicated His name by not only sending down fire to consume his sacrifice but also sending down rain. The prophets of Baal were slain, and the people acknowledged God as the true and living God, but once again, it was mere lip service (I Kings 17,18). Later, Jezebel sought to take Elijah's life, but he escaped (I Kings 19:1–3).

Like Solomon, Ahab had a love for material things and pomp. Ivory was an expensive item, and he boasted of an "ivory house," with ivory carvings on

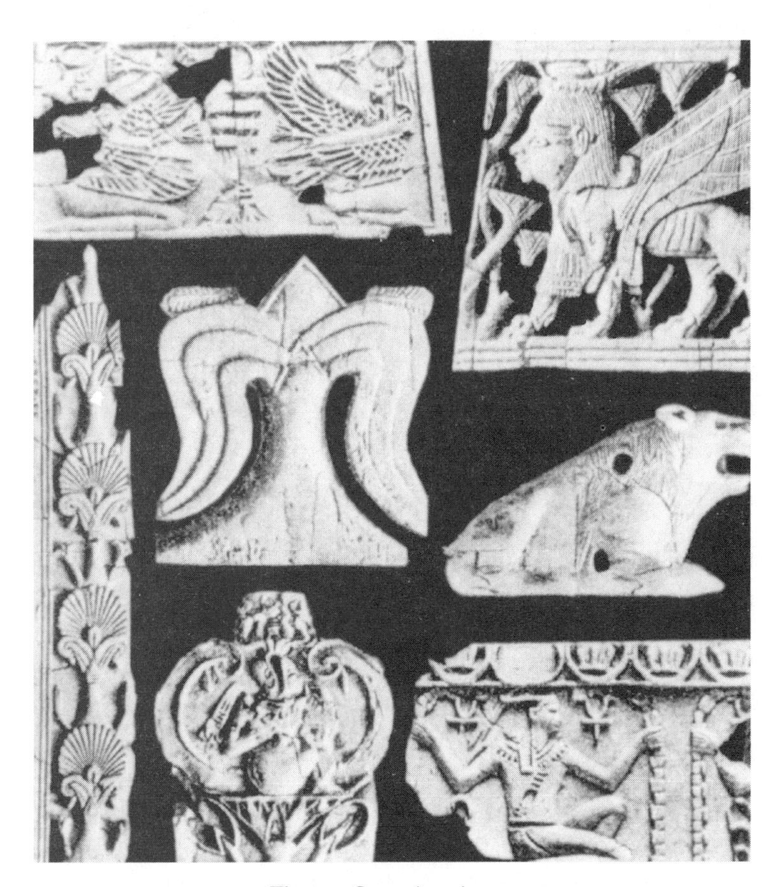

Fig. 23. Samaritan ivory.

the palace walls and ceilings (I Kings 22:39). It was the fad of the day, and the people, following Ahab's example, had "beds of ivory," spending money on that luxury and at the same time robbing God of His tithe (Amos 4:4, 6:4). Thousands of ivory carvings have been discovered at the site of Samaria. Ahab, not content with his own possessions, coveted Naboth's vineyard (property). When Naboth refused to sell his family's inheritance, Jezebel brought false charges against him in the king's name and saw to it that Naboth was stoned to death so that Ahab could have his wish (I Kings 21:1–16).

At the same time that Ahab helped Obadiah protect 100 prophets from being killed by his wife, he also performed a good deed by being at peace with the Southern Kingdom, although he was engaged in war with Syria. Because he had failed to destroy the king of Syria, because he had coveted and accepted Naboth's vineyard after his wife had him slain, because he was intermarried with a heathen woman, and because he had adopted Baalism as Israel's religion, both Elijah and the prophet Micaiah predicted Ahab and Jezebel's deaths. Because Ahab humbled himself, so God did not judge his house until after his death. Struck by a stray arrow, he died in battle (I Kings 20:42, 21:17–29, 22:13–18). In fulfillment of Elijah's prediction, Jezebel reaped what she had sown and died a shameful death (II Kings 9:30–37).

Ahab, Israel's seventh king, reigned for 22 years (I Kings 16:29). The epitaph on his tombstone would probably have read as follows: "There was none like unto Ahab, who did sell himself to work wickedness in the sight of the Lord, when Jezebel, his wife, had led him astray. His acts were abominable in following idols, according to all that the Amorites did" (I Kings 21:25,26).

Jeroboam II, the Thirteenth King of Israel. Jeroboam II walked in the sins of his namesake, Israel's first king, by doing that which was evil in God's sight (II Kings 14:24). Israel had become so sinful by this point in time that God sent *two* prophets to reprimand them, Amos and Hosea (Amos 1:1; Hosea 1:1), both of whom give us a general idea of the depth of Israel's sins.

Accusations by Amos

1. They were mercenary, selling the righteous for silver and the poor for a pair of shoes: Amos 2:6. They also ignored the poor: 5:11a, 12c.
2. They were worshipping Jeroboam's calves: 2:8, 4:4a.
3. They caused Nazarites to break their vows by drinking wine: 2:12a; Numbers 6:1–4 with Habakkuk 2:15.
4. They ordered God's prophets not to prophesy: 2:12b.
5. They were in disagreement with God: 3:3.
6. They were three years in arrears in paying their tithe: 4:4b. In robbing God of His tithe, they were
   - At ease in Zion: 6:1a, 4b.
   - Lying upon beds of expensive ivory: 6:4a.
   - Eating, drinking, and dancing: 6:4c–6.
   - Living in luxurious houses: 3:15, 5:11.
7. They accepted bribes: 5:2.

8. They offered human sacrifices to Molech: 5:25,26a.
9. They indulged in astrology/divination with Chiun: 5:26b; Acts 7:41–43 with Deuteronomy 17:1–5.
10. They put away the day of judgment when advised to "prepare to meet your God": 6:3 with 4:12.

Because their actions were detestable before a holy God, Amos pronounced "woes" or judgments upon them. One was for desiring God's day, which would become darkness for them (Amos 5:18), and the other was for their sin of trusting in natural mountains to defend them from their enemies instead of trusting in God (6:1). Amos reminded them of judgment that had come to other nations, saying that judgment was impending for them also. He said that "for three transgressions, and for four, I will not turn away punishment." This expression was used to show that their cup of iniquity was full and running over, that there was no way they could escape God's punishment (1:3–2:12).

The indictment by Amos was severe enough, but God's love for His sinful people demanded the sending of another prophet. In addition to the sins Amos denounced, Hosea added that because they were guilty of spiritual adultery and worshipping the idolatrous calves of Jeroboam,

Accusations by Hosea

1. They had lost the joy in offering sacrifices unto God and celebrating feast days: Hosea 2:11.
2. They had no truth, mercy, or knowledge of God: 4:1.
3. They were murderous, stealing, swearing, lying people: 4:2.
4. They rejected and forgot the Law: 4:6.
5. They set their heart on iniquity: 4:8.
6. They were drunkards: 4:11b.
7. They offered sacrifices instead of the priests: 4:13a.
8. Sacrifices were offered in the wrong places: 4:13a.
9. They were living in whoredom and adultery: 4:13b.
10. They were backslidden: 4:16.
11. Their priests had become corrupted; they had
    - Entrapped people in error: 5:1.
    - Aided and abetted murder: 6:9a.
    - Committed lewdness: 6:9b.
    - Rejoiced in the idolatry of calf worship: 10:5.
12. They were guilty of pride: 5:5. See I Timothy 3:6.
13. They ignored God and looked to Egypt and Assyria for help: 7:11.
14. They ran from and spoke lies against God: 7:13.

It appears from Hosea's prophecy that the Tribe of Ephraim set a bad example in the nation for her sinful ways. Ephraim is mentioned 37 times in Hosea as a symbol of all the sins being committed in the Northern Kingdom. A summary of these sins may be found in Hosea 4:17–13:12.

Hosea's Plea

1. He urged Israel to return to the Lord: 6:1, 14:1.
2. He urged them to pray: 14:2.
3. He urged them to confess their sins: 14:2.
4. He urged them to consider the promises of God in their behalf. If they returned to God, called upon Him, and confessed their sins to God, He would
   - Heal their backsliding: 6:1b, 14:4a.
   - Love them freely: 14:4b.
   - Give them peace: 14:4c.
   - Refresh them: 6:3, 14:5a.
   - Cause them to grow spiritually: 14:5b.
   - Give them fruit: 14:6a,8.
   - Beautify them: 14:6b with Psalm 149:4.
   - Have fellowship with them: 14:7a with Psalm 91:1.
   - Revive them: 14:7b.
   - Give them fragrance: 14:7c.
   - Lead them: 14:9 with Psalm 23:1,2.

During King Jeroboam II's reign, the Israelites had become defiled in their conduct, and because they followed *self-rule* and refused to heed the prophetic warnings from God, anarchy prevailed (Hosea 4:12, 5:3). God was left completely out of the picture, and it became a matter of Israel versus God, as shown in chapter 11 of Hosea:

God	**Israel**
1. Loved them: verse 1a	1. Worshipped idols: verse 2
2. Called them: verse 1b	2. Ignored God: verse 3b
3. Taught them: verse 3a	3. Refused God's Lordship: verse 5
4. Drew them: verse 4a	4. Followed their own counsel: verse 6
5. Fed them: verse 4b	5. Backslid: verse 7
6. Encouraged them: verse 8	6. Lied about God: verse 12a
7. Assured them: verse 9	7. Lived in deceit: verse 12b

That Israel was God's people and that He was their God account for the forthright preaching that Amos and Hosea did as they approached the king and the people at Samaria, as well as for the jealousy that they exhibited for God's people to return to Him and repent. Because Israel refused to get right with God, however, it was prophesied that the Northern Kingdom would fall and be taken into captivity (Hosea 5:5, 12:6; Amos 13:16).

Before we consider the Northern Kingdom's utter defeat by Sargon, king of Assyria, let us consider one more king and one more prophet. The king is Pekahiah in Samaria, and the prophet is Micah. Messages by Amos and Hosea had fallen on deaf ears; idolatry and murder seemed to be the norm of the day throughout the kingdom. Micah asked the people, "What has God done to deserve all your wickedness?" The Lord certainly had a controversy with His people, and He desired repentance (Micah 6:1–8). Israel needed to be reminded again of her sins, and Micah was the one chosen by God for the occasion.

Accusations by Micah

1. Idolatry: Micah 1:7.
2. Devising iniquity (inventing acts of cruelty): 2:1a.
3. Immorality: 2:1b.
4. Covetousness: 2:2a.
5. Lawlessness, revealing selfishness: 2:2b.
6. Oppression: 2:2c; 6:12a.
7. Being spoiled: 2:4.
8. False prophets: 2:6, 11; 3:5–7.
9. Disobedience to God's Word: 2:7.
10. Injustice—hatred of good, love of evil: 3:1a.
11. Barbaric acts and bloodshed: 3:1b-3.
12. Blindness: 3:6.
13. Astrology/divination: 3:7; 5:12.
14. Bribery: 3:11; 7:3.
15. Dishonest business practices: 6:10,11.
16. Oppression of the poor by the rich: 6:12a.
17. Lying and gossiping: 6:12b.
18. Hatred and strife: 7:2.
19. Treachery among friends, children, and family: 7:5,6.

Micah's Plea. Micah told the people that if they repented, God would have mercy on them, would pardon their iniquity, and would cast their sins in the depths of the sea (Micah 7:18–20). Because they did not accept these promises of God, Micah told the people that God would make them sick in smiting them and desolate because of their sins. He too prophesied their captivity (1:6–16).

Having singled out four kings of the 19, all of whom were evil in God's sight, and the messages of four prophets, we have seen that due to the sins of the majority of the people, God was now ready to fulfill His Word by bringing an end to the Northern Kingdom of Israel and permitting the people to be taken into Assyrian captivity.

God's Indictment Against Israel. Hoshea was the last king of the Northern Kingdom, and it was during his reign that the king of Assyria took Samaria, carrying away Israel into his own country.

> It was all due to the fact that the children of Israel had sinned against the Lord by fearing and worshiping other gods, walking in and practicing the statutes of the nations which the Lord drove out. God's people did impute things that were not right unto the Lord, and they built

> high places in all their cities, setting up pillars (altars) and Asherim (groves) upon every hill and under every leafy tree. There they offered their sacrifices and wrought wicked things like serving idols to provoke the Lord. When God, through the prophets, told them not to do these things, they would not hear, but hardened their necks like their forefathers who would not believe the Lord. They went after the things of nought to become like the nations round about, forsaking the commandments of the Lord in making the molten images of two calves, making an Asherah, worshiping all the hosts of heaven and serving Baal. They caused their sons and daughters to pass through the fire of Molech (human sacrifices), constantly doing evil in God's sight to provoke Him. The Lord was very angry with Israel. He rejected His seed and afflicted them, delivering them into the hands of spoilers until He had cast them out of His sight. He tore Israel from the house of David when Jeroboam was made king. The people walked in the sins of this king; they departed not from them, and the Lord removed Israel out of His sight as He spoke by the mouth of all His servants and prophets. So Israel was carried out from their own land into Assyria.[19]

See II Kings 17:6–41 also about the people of Israel's acts leading up to the exile.

The Northern Kingdom began in 931/30 B.C. under the reign of Jeroboam. Eighteen kings and 210 years later, the kingdom fell prey to the Assyrians in 722/21 B.C. under the reign of Hoshea.

Conclusion. When King Sargon of Assyria defeated the Northern Kingdom at Samaria, he carried 27,290 prisoners back home with him, a figure recorded on a clay tablet discovered in his palace ruins near Nineveh. He left many of the older folks in their homeland; he then repeopled the conquered land with Assyrians and returned an Israelite priest from Assyria to teach them about the true and living God (II Kings 17:24–28). With foreigners in the cities of Samaria, the Assyrians and Israelites intermarried, resulting in a new and heterogeneous people, called *Samaritans,* who lived throughout the former territory occupied by the ten Tribes. Through the priest's efforts, the Samaritans followed the teachings of Moses; they worshipped God in Mount Gerizim in the days of Christ, as we are told when Jesus and the Samaritan woman conversed at Jacob's well. She believed on Christ and told other Samaritans of Him, and they believed when they saw Jesus (John 4:1–43). There is a colony of these people today who still observe the Passover yearly on Mount Gerizim.

The term "The Ten Lost Tribes of Israel" is a misnomer. True, those of these Tribes are "lost" as we understand tribal unity, but we must remember that many members of the ten Tribes fled to Jerusalem when the United Kingdom was divided. When Israel returned from Babylonian captivity, Ezra registered many from the northern Tribes. The apostle Paul mentions that there were those of the whole Twelve Tribes in his day (Acts 26:7), as does James in his Epistle, although he states that they were scattered (James 1:1).

We have no idea how many tens of thousands of Israelites made up the Northern Kingdom over the span of its existence (210 years). More than 27,000 were taken captive to Assyria when the kingdom fell, and many aged and poor people were left in the land. Out of all the sin and debauchery caused by 19 evil kings, Elijah, as one man of God standing against 850 false prophets of Baalism, said that he was the only one remaining who stood for the Lord. God reminded him that there were 7,000 in Israel who had not bowed their knees to Baal and whose mouth had not kissed Baal (I Kings 19:13,14,18). This is a small remnant among multiple people in such a vast territory as Israel had on both sides of the Jordan River—only 7001, counting Elijah! We are reminded of the statement that Jesus made concerning *many* on the broad road leading to destruction, but only a *few* on the road leading to eternal life (Matthew 7:13,14).

THE SOUTHERN KINGDOM OF JUDAH

Fortunately for the Southern Kingdom, of its 18 kings and one queen, some were good.

Rehoboam, Judah's First King. Rehoboam had the distinction of following Solomon as king of the United Kingdom; this lasted for only a short period of time, and Rehoboam became the first king of the Southern Kingdom of Judah.

At the outset of his reign, he and the people walked in the steps of David and Solomon, that is, when David and Solomon were in fellowship with the Lord (II Chronicles 11:17). However, like his father, Solomon, he began to multiply unto himself wives (18) and concubines (60), having a total of 80 children (17:18–21).

At the end of three years, "*he* established the kingdom, strengthened himself, forsook the Lord, and all Israel with him" (II Chronicles 12:1). Rehoboam, as well as the nation, did evil in the sight of the Lord, provoking Him to jealousy because their sins were becoming worse every day. They built high places on every high hill, erected Asherim and houses for sodomites (homosexuals), and embraced all the abominations of the nations that God had cast out (II Kings 14:21–24).

Rehoboam and the people of Judah lived for two years in this vulgar, sexual sin, but their sin soon found them out (Numbers 32:23). God simply raised up Shishak, king of Egypt, to bring multitudes against Rehoboam and Jerusalem because of their great wickedness. It is quite possible that the Pharaoh had learned of the division of Israel's kingdom from Jeroboam, who had visited him when he fled for his life from Solomon (II Kings 10:40). Knowing that the Southern Kingdom was weak, with only two Tribes versus Jeroboam's ten, and fearing no interference from Jeroboam, Shishak and his army struck, capturing many cities throughout Judah. When Shemaiah, the prophet, in-

Fig. 24. Record of Rehoboam's loss on Egyptian temple.

formed Rehoboam that God had raised up Shishak to come against Jerusalem because of Rehoboam's sins and forsaking the Lord, the king humbled himself and God granted *some deliverance.* Jerusalem was delivered when Shishak did not take the city, but he did take away the treasures of the king's house and the Temple, the silver and the gold—*he took all* (II Chronicles 12:2–9).

Amid the precious metal that Shishak took were 300 shields of gold that had been made by Solomon (I Kings 10:16,17). One method of warfare in those days was to position soldiers with such shields on the front lines so that the sun was between them and the enemy. As the enemy approached, the gold shields were turned by the soldiers to reflect the sunbeams directly in the eyes of the enemy. When the enemy soldiers dropped their spears and shields to cover their eyes, the soldiers with these gold shields would step aside while their comrades would rush forward and capture the enemy with a minimum of effort.

These shields of gold could stand for the testimony of a believer who glows and glitters for the Lord. As our lives reflect the light of Christ's countenance, we not only resist the devil, our enemy, so that he flees from us, but we show how Christ enables us to be more than conquerors through His strength (Romans 8:37).

After Shishak took these gold shields, Rehoboam immediately made brass shields (II Chronicles 12:9,10) to have something that would pass for gold from a distance. But there is no substitute for the real thing: we either have a testimony that shines and glows and glitters for the glory of God, or we don't. A shield of brass stands for hypocrisy, which brings out the real character of Rehoboam, even though he humbled himself. Scripture tells us that at the close of his reign "he did evil, because he prepared not his heart to seek the Lord" (12:13,14).

Shishak returned to Egypt with a goodly number of captives. He erected a temple to his god Amon (Amun), inscribing on the wall a list of the cities of Judah that he had captured, with images of Israelite prisoners taken back with him to be his servants. His gold-masked mummy was discovered in 1939 in a sarcophagus of silver and gold. Some have suggested that this burial vault could have been made from some of the gold and silver that he took from Rehoboam's house and the Temple in Jerusalem. What a tragedy that the result of Rehoboam's and Judah's sins have been seen on Shishak's "billboard" temple wall for over 2,900 years!

Asa, Judah's Third King. At last! Asa became the first king (of either kingdom) who "did that which was right in the eyes of the Lord." Met by the prophet Azariah, who encouraged him to follow the Lord (II Chronicles 15: 1,2), Asa took many of the sodomites out of the land and removed the idols that his evil father, King Abijah, had erected. Because his mother also was evil, he removed her as queen and destroyed the Asherim that she had made. Although he did not remove all the high places of idolatry, he did remove them from the cities of Judah and commanded the people to seek the Lord and keep His commandments. He later made sweeping reforms, especially when he removed the abominable idols from the whole land of Judah and Benjamin (I Kings 15:8–14; II Chronicles 15:8–19).

Baasha, the king of Israel, made war against Asa and his kingdom in about the sixteenth year of Asa's reign. The people failed to have complete trust in the Lord, and Asa bribed the idol-worshipping king of Syria to break his alliance with Baasha and draw off his forces from invading Judah. Asa was rebuked by the prophet Hanani for doing this rather than trusting the Lord to fight his battle (I Kings 15:16–22; II Chronicles 16:1–10). Two years before he died, Asa suffered a very great disease and because he sought his physicians instead of praying and trusting God for healing, he died. Asa ruled Judah for 41 years; his finish certainly was not as good as his start.

Athaliah, Judah's Only Queen. A frightening event took place prior to and during the reign of Queen Athaliah. Jehoram, Judah's fifth king, married Athaliah, who was Ahab's and Jezebel's daughter; this was a grave mistake and degraded Judah. Supposed to bring peace between the two kingdoms, the union instead introduced apostasy in the Southern Kingdom and brought reproach, failure, shame, and calamity to the house of David. Jehoram adopted the wickedness and idolatries of Ahab's and Jezebel's Baalism. He became a murderer, killing all his brothers, doing that which was evil in God's sight. But there were groups in the kingdom who revolted against Jehoram's sins: God used the prophet Elijah to denounce him and sent a plague upon him, causing his death. His son, Ahaziah (or Jehoahaz), was thereupon enthroned (II Chronicles 21:12–2:1).

Ahaziah's mother, Athaliah, counselled him to do wickedly, causing him to walk in the way of Ahab's house and do evil in God's sight (II Chronicles 22:1–4). Other wicked counsellors helped him to his destruction. After Ahab's death, as God had said, his household would be destroyed, which included the death of Ahaziah (22:8-10). When Athaliah learned of his death, she killed all of Ahaziah's sons, *the royal seed,* and set herself up as queen, the only woman to rule over either kingdom.

Joash/Jehoash, Judah's Seventh King. Unbeknown to the queen, Jehosheba, sister of Ahaziah and wife of the priest Jehoiada, hid her baby son, Joash, in the house of the Lord for six years. He had been overlooked by Athaliah, and after the sixth year of her reign, Jehoiada gathered the priests, Levites, and the people in the Temple to present seven-year-old Joash and make him king. When Queen Athaliah heard all the people rejoicing, she went to the Temple, saw what was going on, and screamed, "Treason, treason!" She was thrown out of the Temple and slain (II Kings 11:1–29).

God had promised that a "Seed" of a woman would come who would defeat Satan and provide salvation for lost mankind. In spite of all the sins that the people had committed, God had preserved a remnant of believers for the purpose of keeping the lineage open through the Tribe and individuals for the coming of *the Seed Royal.* How frightening it was when all were killed but Joash! It was "nothing but the Providence of God that saved David's line at this time. The whole truth of prophecy and the salvation of the world appeared to be suspended on the brittle thread of the life of a child only one year old."[20] God always knows how to engineer circumstances to accomplish His purpose.

Satan almost won his battle with God when Athaliah tried to wipe out all "the Seed Royal." Had Satan been the victor, the "promised seed" of Genesis 3:15 would never have appeared upon the scene, and where would lost mankind ever have hope for a Redeemer? But God had His Redeemer on deposit, having slain His Son from before the foundation of the world, and our sovereign God's Word *never* returns unto Him void (Isaiah 55:11). Joash was saved, and his lineage was preserved.

Although Joash started out doing good in God's sight, he ended his reign on a sour note. When Hazael, king of Syria, invaded the land of Judah, Joash took all the hallowed vessels of the Temple and palace to bribe Hazael to leave Judah. For his spiritual downfall, forsaking the Lord, and killing Jehoiada's son, God executed judgment upon Joash, inflicting him with a "great disease." His own servants conspired against him for killing the priest's son and killed Joash on his bed (II Kings 12:1–21). He reigned for 40 years.

I sometimes wonder why someone who gets off to a good start with the Lord fails in the end. This is especially true when we think of the goodness of God and His love for those who have been called His chosen people. It is bad enough when an individual king goes astray, but even though the people might be helped when the king is good, they permit his example to influence them to go astray with him, as was the case under Rehoboam's reign (II Chronicles 12:1).

It is also hard to figure out why a son who ascends the throne after his good father dies, turns completely around and dishonors God. King Jotham, who succeeded his father, King Uzziah, did good in God's sight. Although he did not destroy all the high places where some Israelites sacrificed and burned incense in the worship of idols, he did right in the eyes of the Lord because he prepared his ways before the Lord. After Jotham died, his son, Ahaz, became king, did a 180-degree turn, and walked in the idolatrous ways of all the kings of Israel. He made some to pass through the fire, a form of abominable child sacrifice, and sacrificed and burned incense in the high places (II Kings 15: 1–4). He ignored Isaiah's warning that he must have faith in God to be established, and he ignored the Lord (Isaiah 7:10,11). Because Ahaz turned his back on the Lord, Pekah, king of Israel, and Rezin, king of Syria, besieged Jerusalem, and in one day Pekah killed 120,000 men of Judah and carried away 200,000 captives and much spoil. The prophet Oded later secured release of those who were taken captive (II Chronicles 28:5–15).

One might think that this would have turned Ahaz to the Lord, but he still acted treacherously toward the Lord. When the Philistines and Edomites invaded Judah, he sought help from Tiglath-pileser, the Assyrian king, who had come to Damascus. While there, Ahaz worshipped the gods of the Syrians; returning to Jerusalem, he cut the vessels of the Temple, shut its doors, and erected pagan altars throughout the land (II Kings 16:1-20). It is difficult to understand the levels to which some people who know the Lord will stoop.

Hezekiah, Judah's Twelfth King. At the outset of his ascension to the throne, Hezekiah immediately sought to undo the spiritual corruption brought upon the whole nation by his father, King Ahaz. In doing the right thing before the Lord, he removed the high places and broke in pieces the brazen serpent that Moses had made during Israel's wilderness journey (Exodus 21:9). The children of Israel had kept it since that time (about 700 years), and it was being used as an object of idolatry. The people were burning incense to it, thinking it was supposed to possess extraordinary virtue. Hezekiah ground it to pieces (II Kings 18:4). He was also responsible for getting the priests to sanctify themselves for Temple worship, opening the doors of the Temple that King Ahaz had closed, refurbishing the vessels that he had cast away, restoring the offerings and proper sacrifices, reinstating the Passover, and seeing to it that the people paid God what they owed Him, His tithe.

Standing by his side were prophets Isaiah and Micah, spiritual advisors who were a tremendous help in Hezekiah's "doing that which was good, right, and faithful before the Lord, his God. In every work he began in the service of the house of the Lord, in the law, and in the commandments to seek the Lord, he did it with all his heart, and prospered" (II Chronicles 31:20–21). Because of his trust in God and keeping God's commandments, Hezekiah was the most spiritual ruler of Judah (II Kings 18:1–6).

With the help of the Lord, he rebelled against the king of Assyria, Sargon, who had conquered the Northern Kingdom of Israel. Not only was he *the* spiritual leader of his subjects and warrior enough to stand up to any enemy of the kingdom, he was also a brilliant engineer.

When cities were besieged in those days, city gates were closed and water supplies, usually outside the city walls, were not available; many cities had to surrender for lack of water. Hezekiah devised a plan whereby a group of pickmen would start chiselling through solid rock underneath the city at the Spring of Gihon, which was outside the city wall. Another group started digging inside the city wall to meet the other men. This underground tunnel or conduit, which would furnish Jerusalem water in time of war (II Kings 20:20), has been discovered. At the entrance of the tunnel at the Pool of Siloam, this inscription was found:

> This is the story [history] of the excavation. While workmen still lifting up their axe [pick], each toward his neighbors, and while three cubits [four and a half feet] remain [to cut through], each heard the voice of one calling one to another. On the day the workmen struck, axe against axe, to meet his neighbors, waters flowed from the [Gihon] Spring to the [Siloam] Pool, 1,200 cubits [1,800 feet—the length of six football fields], and a hundred cubits [150 feet] over the heads of the workmen.[21]

The 100 cubits "over the heads" indicates the tunnel's depth beneath the city; the actual height of the tunnel averages about seven feet. Entering the conduit at the Spring of Gihon, one notices that the pickmarks are in the direction the men are digging. At the spot marked *X,* it can be seen where the pickmen met, and from there on to the Pool of Siloam, the pickmarks are going in the opposite direction.

Because Hezekiah was so dedicated to the Lord and desired to keep his subjects in tune with God, God came to his rescue when the king of Assyria, Sennacherib, sought to conquer the Southern Kingdom. This king had in-

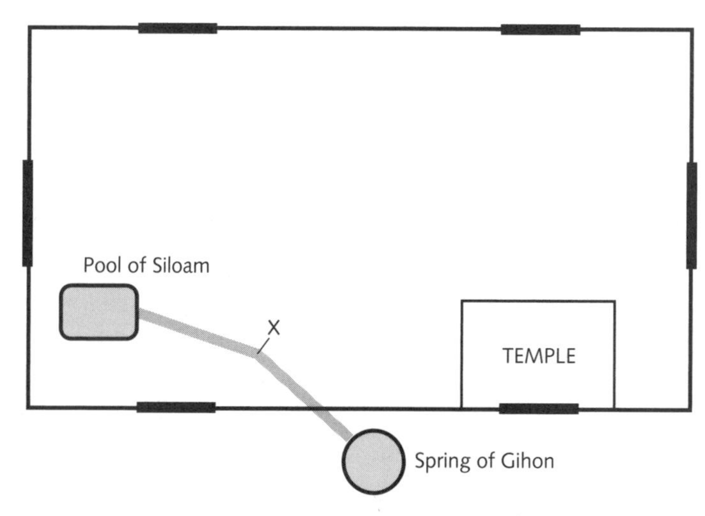

Fig. 25. Diagram of Hezekiah's conduit in the walled city of Jerusalem, as viewed from the Mount of Olives, ca. 700 B.C.

Fig. 26. Conduit entrance at the Spring of Gihon.

Fig. 27. The spot where pickmen met in conduit.

vaded Judah and captured a number of cities, including the stronghold city of Lachish. Jerusalem was next in line. Sennacherib sent a letter to Hezekiah: Surrender or else! Hezekiah got in touch with the prophet Isaiah for advice from the Lord. Taking Sennacherib's letter, Hezekiah fell on his face before the Lord, prayed for help, and in one night an angel of the Lord completely destroyed the Assyrian army. Sennacherib had to return to Nineveh in shame and defeat (II Kings 18:17–19:37; II Chronicles 32:1–22; Isaiah 36:21–37:35).

Kings in those days kept diaries of their deeds and exploits, listing their victories, never their defeats. When Sennacherib had his record inscribed on a clay prism, he made mention of his dealings with Hezekiah by saying: "As for Hezekiah, the Jew, who did not submit to my yoke, forty six of his strong walled cities . . . I besieged and took. Himself [Hezekiah] like a caged bird I shut up in his city Jerusalem and earthworks I threw against him; the one coming out of the city [Hezekiah's messenger saying "no surrender"] I turned

Fig. 28. Sennacherib's prism.

back to his misery." Sennacherib made his defeat at Jerusalem conspicuously absent from his record, and the discovery of this record is archaeological confirmation that he withdrew from Jerusalem without defeating Hezekiah.

Fifteen years before Hezekiah died, he became deathly ill with a boil, or an infected ulcer. Doing what we all do when death is near, he prayed. Upon hearing his prayer, God informed Isaiah to tell Hezekiah that the Lord would add 15 years to his life. A remedy was applied to the boil, and he was healed. When Hezekiah asked Isaiah for a sign that he would not die, he was told the shadow on the sundial would be turned back ten degrees (Isaiah 38; II Kings 20:1–11).

After Hezekiah was given a new lease on life, time marched on. Assyria's power was declining, and Babylon was coming to the forefront. When word spread of Hezekiah's healing, dignitaries from Babylon visited him, bringing gifts. Hezekiah showed them all the gold and treasures of his house that had come his way as a testimony of God's healing him. Isaiah took him to task for revealing all his wealth and exposing his defenses as well, and informed him that one day all these precious articles would be carried away to Babylon as booty, that absolutely nothing would be left, and that even some of Hezekiah's descendants would be taken captive. Here we find a prophetic statement having to do with the downfall of the Southern Kingdom. Hezekiah's other prophet, Micah, prophesied that Zion (Judah) would be plowed as a field and Jerusalem would become heaps or ruins (Micah 3:12). Hezekiah had been blinded by pride, and pride always goes before a fall (II Kings 12:12–20). His reign lasted a total of 29 years, a period of time in Judah's history that shows what a faithful remnant can do as they follow the Lord.

Manasseh, Judah's Most Evil King. During the extra 15 years that God gave Hezekiah, his son Manasseh was born. What shame this king brought to the people during his reign! When Hezekiah's prayer to live longer was answered, he got something that he would have regretted had he lived still longer. Sometimes our prayers backfire, and the answer breaks our hearts (Psalm 106:15).

Manasseh began his reign when he was only 12 years old. Evidently, his tutors had hypocritically professed "religion" but resented Hezekiah's reforms and influence. They led the boy-king back to the old way of Baalism. The exact opposite of his father in doing his evil wickedness in God's sight, Manasseh built up the high places that Hezekiah had destroyed, reared up altars for Baal, made idols as Ahab of Israel had done, and built altars for astrology/wizardry in the Temple. He blasphemed God by setting up an Asherim in the house of the Lord. He made his sons to pass through fire (a form of child sacrifice), provoking the Lord to answer. There were those of the remnant who graciously advised the people to follow all the law that Moses commanded of them, but the people would not listen, and Manasseh seduced Israel to do *more* evil than all the pagan nations that God had told them to destroy (II Kings 21:1–9).

What an awful indictment to make against this king and his people, but they had stooped *lower* in the abominations of all the ungodly nations round about them! God's purpose in raising up prophets was to call His people back to Himself. Because the people did not listen, God brought Assyria's king against them and Manasseh was taken captive in chains to Babylon. While there, Manasseh repented and was brought back to Jerusalem. He made things right with God by repudiating idolatry, and the people sacrificed unto the Lord (II Chronicles 33:9–17).

After King Manasseh, we see a progression leading to the fulfillment of the prophecy that Judah would become captive and cease to exist as a nation. King Nebuchadnezzar of Babylon would soon enter the picture. King Amon, named after an Egyptian god, followed in Manasseh's footsteps, doing evil in God's sight (II Kings 21:18–26). Josiah followed the example of Hezekiah and was the last good king of Judah (22:1–23:23).

The four remaining kings did evil in God's sight, starting with Jehoahaz (II Kings 23:30–34). I suggest consulting Jeremiah's prophecy about this king (Jeremiah 22:10–12). Due to the sins in the land and the pronounced judgment by God, enemies were constantly invading the land. Pharaoh Neco of Egypt had conquered Israel's land as far north as Hamath on the Euphrates River (II Kings 23:29). He made Jehoiakim king and burdened the people with heavy taxes as a tribute to Egypt. Jehoiakim, like other evil kings, did abominable acts in God's sight. The prophet Uriah was raised up to denounce Jerusalem and the nation for its sins. When the king heard of Uriah's accusations, he sought to put him to death. Uriah fled to Egypt but was returned and killed. In contrast, Jeremiah escaped death for his prophesying (Jeremiah 26:1–24). Ezekiel, in describing Jehoiakim, likened him to a "strong (ferocious) lion" who would tear his prey and devour them, and prophesied that he would be put in a cage and taken to Babylon (Ezekiel 19:5–10).

The first invasion of Judah by Nebuchadnezzar was when Neco's power and influence began to ebb. Nebuchadnezzar made Jehoiakim his servant, but after three years he turned and rebelled against him. This encouraged the Syrians, Moabites, and Ammonites to invade Judah in fulfillment of prophecy due to the sins of Manasseh (II Kings 21:10–15). Nebuchadnezzar then bound Jehoiakim and took him to Babylon, along with vessels from the Temple. Many others were taken in the first deportation, including Daniel and the three Hebrew boys (Daniel 1:1–7). Jeremiah summed up Jehoiakim's violence, covetousness, and shedding of innocent blood; he said that Jehoiakim would be so degraded that in dying in disgrace, he would have the burial of a donkey (Jeremiah 22:13–19).

Jehoiachin was Judah's king when Nebuchadnezzar made his second attack on Jerusalem. He stripped the treasures from the palace and Temple and captured 10,000 mighty men of valor, a thousand craftsmen, smiths, officers, the king's mother and wives, and King Jehoiachin himself, taking them all back to

Babylon as captives. Ezekiel was also included in this deportation. Only the poorest of the people were left in the land (II Kings 24:6–16; Ezekiel 1:1,2).

An interesting clay tablet, found in the ruins of Nebuchadnezzar's palace and called the "Babylonian Chronicle," contains a record that he made between the years 605 and 594 B.C. It describes the battle of Carcheimish (Jeremiah 46:2), Nebuchadnezzar's coronation, and removal of Jehoiachin and others to Babylonian exile, and lists their rations. How wonderful that many archaeological discoveries confirm the historical accuracy of God's Word!

Because of God's love for His people, His desire was for them to walk in the old paths of His Word (Jeremiah 6:16). Prophets were raised up to call them to repentance. People can hear truth, but God does not force them to accept it even if they will regret it later. Let us summarize the pleas and accusations that several prophets had to make against God's people, keeping in mind that, even though the prophets' charges were levelled against the nation of Israel as a whole, there were believers, called the *remnant* (Isaiah 1:9a). They had to suffer with the unbelievers, just like Joshua and Caleb suffered in their wilderness journey because the majority of the people disbelieved God.

Fig. 29. Babylonian Chronicle.

We have singled out three prophets who had harsh words about the people of God in the darkness of their sins: Isaiah, Jeremiah, and Ezekiel. So much has been recorded about the Israelites' wicked evil ways that I have condensed the list:

The Prophet Isaiah

The people were in rebellion against God: 1:2.
They did not know God nor consider him: 1:3.
They were a people laden (loaded) with iniquity: 1:4a.
They were a seed of evildoers: 1:4b.
They were corrupters: 1:4c.
They had forsaken and provoked God: 1:4d.
They had gone away backward: 1:4e.
They were sin-sick: 1:5, 6b.
They had no soundness from the sole of their feet to their head: 1:6a.
In spite of a small remnant, they had become like the people of Sodom and Gomorrah: 1:9,10.
They were hypocritical in their worship to God: 1:11–15.
Harlotry, murder, robbery, and bribery prevailed: 1:21,23.
They lived like the heathens, worshipping idols: 2:6,8.
Mighty men, judges, prophets, and the prudent, wise elders had been replaced by those who were immature: 3:2–5.
Their sayings and doings (lifestyle) were against God: 3:8.
They boasted of their sinning like the people of Sodom: 3:9.
Children (immature politicians) were influenced by women: 3:12.
The daughters of Zion were like prostitutes: 3:16–24.
Drunkenness was common: 5:11.
They called evil good and good evil, and changed bitter to sweet and sweet to bitter: 5:20.
They were wise in their own eyes: 5:21.
They justified the wicked and condemned the righteous: 5:23.
They were like a long man in a short bed, having insufficient covering: 28:20.
They had gone astray: 53:6.
Their righteousness was like filthy rags: 64:6.

"Jewish tradition holds that Isaiah was martyred under king Manasseh's reign by being sawed in two."[22]

The Prophet Jeremiah

Their prophets prophesied by Baal: 2:8.
They had forsaken God: 2:13a, 32.
Their works were worthless: 2:13b.
They were spoiled: 2:14c.
God had planted them a noble vine, but they were now turned into a degenerate plant: 2:21.

Their iniquities were marked before God: 2:22.
Their children received no correction: 2:30.
They had dirty garments: 2:34.
They played the harlot with many lovers: 3:1, 6, 8.
God accused them of trusting in lying words, stealing, murdering, swearing falsely, burning incense to Baal, walking after other gods, and boasting that they were delivered to do these abominations: 7:3–11.
They were backslidden: 8:5a.
They held fast to deceit: 8:5b.
They refused to return to the Lord: 8:5c.
They spoke not aright: 8:6a.
They did not repent: 8:6b.
They were ignorant of the times: 8:7.
They were ashamed of the Lord: 8:9a.
They rejected the Word of the Lord: 8:9b.
They had no wisdom in them: 8:9c.
They proceeded from evil to evil: 9:3.
They walked in the imagination of their evil hearts: 11:8.
They refused to hear instructions about the Sabbath: 17:23–27.
They were offering their sons and daughters as burnt offering sacrifices to the god Baal: 19:4,5.
They were persecuting God's prophet: 20:7–12; II Chronicles 36:16; I Chronicles 16:22.
They were following false shepherds: 23:1–4; II Chronicles 36:14.

The Prophet Ezekiel

God's people were rebellious: 2:3.
His people were impudent children and stiff hearted: 2:4.
They were idolatrous because they had idolatrous elders: 6:5, 14:3.
They should turn from all their abominations and repent: 14:6.
They played the harlot: 16:15–17.
They were likened as the sister of Sodom, that Sodom had not done what God's people had done. Israel's abominations were *more* than those of Sodom and Samaria (the Northern Kingdom's sins), and these two ungodly peoples were more righteous than God's people: 16:48–52.

Israel had become the most sinful nation of her day in spite of all the vulgar sins of the heathen nations, simply because she denounced the truth that she had, a truth that the heathen nations did not have. "If therefore the light [truth] that is in thee be darkness, how great is that darkness!" (Matthew 6:23b).

Time was beginning to run out on the Southern Kingdom of Judah. Prophecies had been made about Judah's downfall, and there would be no avenue of escape. When Nebuchadnezzar came up against Jerusalem the second time and captured King Jehoiachin, he appointed Zedekiah king. This king also did evil in God's sight, humbled not himself before the prophet Jeremiah, rebelled against Nebuchadnezzar, and hardened his heart from coming back to the Lord (II Kings 36:10–13).

The Fall of Jerusalem. In the ninth year of Zedekiah's reign, Nebuchadnezzar and his army marched toward Jerusalem for the third and final time to completely conquer and destroy the city. Nebuchadnezzar remained in Riblah in Hamath and sent his officers and army to Jerusalem. When the soldiers built barricades around the city, the people on the inside closed the gates, and as a result, famine spread throughout the city. The soldiers broke through the walls and, showing no compassion, killed people of all ages. Those who escaped were taken captive to the city of Babylon and were made servants for a period of 70 years. Only the poor were left to be vinedressers and workers in the field. Before burning the city and the Temple, the soldiers took the gold and silver and other spoils of victory and carried them off to Babylon, as Isaiah had prophesied to King Hezekiah (II Kings 25:1–25).

In the meantime, Zedekiah, his sons, and what was left of Judah's army fled the city. Overtaken and captured in the plains of Jericho, they were taken to Riblah, where they were presented to Nebuchadnezzar, who decreed that they should die. Before he blinded Zedekiah, he killed his two sons in his presence, and then carried Zedekiah off to Babylon in chains. The last thing that this king saw was the slaying of his own flesh and blood (II Kings 25:4–7). See Fig. 17 on page 83.

THE KINGDOM OF JUDAH FALLS

In the early days of the Southern Kingdom of Judah, God raised up Pharaoh Shishak of Egypt to come against Rehoboam due to his forsaking God's law (II Chronicles 12:1–5). This was about 930 B.C. The next 365 years held a rather dark picture of many of God's people.

> All the officers of the priests and the people committed many trespasses, following all the abominable practices of the nations. They polluted the House of the Lord, which He had consecrated in Jerusalem. The Lord God of their fathers had sent word to them through His messengers daily without fail, for He had pity on His people and His dwelling-place. But they mocked the messengers of God and disdained His words and taunted His prophets until the wrath of the Lord against His people grew beyond remedy [they crossed the point of no return]. He therefore brought the king of the Chaldeans [Nebuchadnezzar] upon them, who killed their youths by the sword in their sanctuary; He did not spare youth, maiden, elder, or graybeard, but delivered all into his hands. All the vessels of the House of God, large and small, and the treasures of the House of the Lord and the treasures of the king and his officers were all brought to Babylon. They burned the House of God and tore down the wall of Jerusalem, burned down all

> its mansions, and consigned all its precious objects to destruction. Those who survived the sword he exiled to Babylon, and they became his and his son's servants till the rise of the Persian kingdom, in fulfillment of the word of the Lord spoken by Jeremiah, until the land paid back its sabbaths; as long as it lay desolate it kept sabbath, till seventy years were completed." (II Chronicles 36:14–21 T)

Another sin can be added: The people chose some of their kings, not all by God (Hosea 8:4).

Isaiah's three words, "Ah, sinful nation," aptly sum up the history of Israel (Isaiah 1:4). She had made the Temple an object of false security in offering her hypocritical sacrifices, made the Law a mockery of justice, turned her calling into a license to sin, made circumcision a fetish, used the Holy Land for unholy, idolatrous practices, exalted her past, flaunted the present, and ignored future judgment levelled at her by her prophets. She was known by her tongue (*sayings*) and *doings* against the Lord and prided herself in sinning like the people of wicked Sodom whom God had to destroy because of their sins (Isaiah 3:8,9 with Genesis 19).

Even if Israel had repented at the point when Nebuchadnezzar came to destroy Jerusalem and took them captive, it would have done no good. Esau found no place for repentance after he sold his birthright to Jacob (Hebrews 12:17). There was no remedy for the people, and her punishment was twofold: she lost her kingdom to the Gentiles and she served a sentence of 70 years in Babylon.

Why 70 years? The children of Israel had been instructed to till the land for six years, then let the land rest the seventh year; God promised a sufficient harvest in the sixth year to carry them through the seventh. This was to be repeated every seven years. Failure to observe this command would result in their being taken out of their land into captivity, one year for every seventh year that they failed to let the land rest. There had been a total of 490 years that they failed to keep this law. By dividing seven into 490, we get 70, the number of years Jeremiah said that the children of Israel would be in captivity (Leviticus 25:1–7, 26:27, 33–35 with II Chronicles 36:20,21).

Much has been said about the Israelites as a whole. It is only fair to those of the faithful remnant to give the testimony of one, which is found in Psalm 121. The background of this portion of God's Word is from Jeremiah 3:23, in which the prophet tried to tell the people that salvation did not come from the hills and the multitude of mountains—where the worshippers of Baal carried out their orgies in the vain hope that Baal would be their salvation. Their whole ritual was a deception, and the true believer whose faith was in the God of Israel prompted this Psalm.

The first verse of Psalm 121 is a bit misleading in our English version since the question is asked whether his help comes from the hills or mountains. The psalmist is really asking, "Is this where my help comes from?" His answer is an emphatic *no,* since he makes the statement, "My help comes from the Lord who made the hills, who made heaven and earth." Baal worshippers believed that Baal was the god of everything, but the believing remnant knew better. The feet of many Baalites stumbled in sin up the hillsides, but verse two assured him that His God never slept, was awake 24 hours a day and He would order His steps in the right path. His life was in God's hands who kept him (verses 3–5a).

Even though astrology was a part of the false religion of that day, many suffered from sunstrokes and a weird belief that the moon could affect the mind. But only the Lord can be the shade for a believer, and so the testimony said that the sun would not smite him by day nor the moon by night (verses 5b and 6). He knew that trust in the Lord would preserve him from the evil, gross sin that many of his friends were doing. He had the assurance that his soul was safe in the Lord's hands. Not only did he have this security, but he knew that God would never leave him nor forsake him, that he would be guarded daily and forever more (verses 7 and 8). This faithful member of the small remnant knew that he was called by God to let others know he was a true believer (Deuteronomy 28:9,10).

15

ISRAEL'S CAPTIVITY AND RETURN TO HER LAND

THE DISPERSION

The dispersion of the children of Israel after the fall of Jerusalem resulted in their settlement in four countries—Judah, Egypt, Babylon, and Persia.

Some Remained in Judah. Nebuchadnezzar did not deport the poorest people of the land; they were left in the rural areas to till the soil and take care of the vineyards (II Kings 24:14, 25:12). Ezekiel mentioned some who inhabited the "waste" areas (33:24). The new governor named by Nebuchadnezzar was Gedaliah. Jeremiah was also included with those left behind. He had been bound in chains and was given a choice by the captain of the guard to either go to Babylon or stay in the land. Jeremiah chose to stay in the land and was told to go to his friend, Gedaliah (Jeremiah 40:1–6).

All seemed to be well for a while, but the king of the Ammonites instigated a plot to conquer them. His captain, Ishmael, killed Gedaliah and many of his subjects, including some Babylonian soldiers. The remainder of the people, fearing retaliation by Nebuchadnezzar, made preparations to flee to Egypt. When Jeremiah heard of this, he vehemently opposed their plan to find safety there, but he was taken with them by force (Jeremiah 39:11–43:7).

Some Fled to Egypt. The Jews who fled to Egypt with Jeremiah settled in the eastern section of the Nile delta (Jeremiah 43:8). This prophet had many messages and prophecies for the people, but Jewish tradition tells us that because of their hatred for him, he died a martyr's death at the hands of his own countrymen. Many Jews settled later on the Island of Elephantine in the Nile River. Under Greek influence, about 285 to 247 B.C., the Hebrew Bible was translated into Greek and called the *Septuagint.* These Jews are credited with two things: they made it possible for the Greek-speaking world to have the Word of God in their language, and there is no evidence that these "Egyptian" Jews ever practiced any Egyptian idolatry.

Some Were Taken to Babylon. During Judah's Babylonian captivity not much is recorded of their history except what we find in Daniel and Ezekiel, who were the two prophets of the Exile. We have already considered Ezekiel's remarks about Israel's iniquities; the other part of his prophecy related to Israel's future. Daniel deals not only with his experiences in relation to Babylonian royalty, but also with future events concerning the first coming of Messiah and events after Messiah's second coming.

During the Jews' 70-year period of captivity, they were given many privileges: they were allowed to build and occupy their own homes, keep servants, and engage in business (Jeremiah 29:4–7). However, in this place of captivity, as they sat down by the river, they were asked by the Babylonians to sing their songs of Zion. They were unable to comply because they were cast out of the place of God's choosing for them (Psalm 137:1–4). But they did have a *song of bitterness,* a song of their own disobedience (Deuteronomy 31:19–22). We have nothing to sing about when we do not walk in the light; we have to follow in the steps the Lord orders (Psalm 119:133).

One hundred fifty years before the birth of Cyrus the Persian, Isaiah prophesied that he would come upon the scene and subdue nations. He was to be God's *shepherd,* God's *anointed,* who would give the Jews permission to go back to their motherland and rebuild the Temple and their city (Isaiah 44:28, 45:1). Isaiah prophesied the downfall of Babylon, saying that the Medes would overtake it and that "Babylon, the glory of kingdoms, the beauty of the Chaldeans' excellency, shall [later in its history] be as when God overthrew Sodom and Gomorrah" (Isaiah 13). This would bring joy to Israel because it

Fig. 30. King Darius.

would lead to her release (14:23). Jeremiah also prophesied about Babylon's downfall (Jeremiah 50:1–51:58).

Daniel gives us a firsthand account of Babylon's overthrow under the rule of Belshazzar when Darius the Mede conquered it (Daniel 5). Darius made Daniel first president of this new kingdom, and while studying the Word of God, Daniel realized that the 70-year captivity of Judah was coming to a close. He then began to petition God for the restoration of divine favor to His people (Daniel 9:1–19). The alliance of the Medes and Persians gave Cyrus precedence over Darius. Having become acquainted with Daniel, no doubt, because of his high position under Darius, Cyrus was shown passages in Isaiah where he is mentioned by name and his exploits and conquests are mentioned (Isaiah 44:28, 45:1). When he found himself thus distinguished by the God of the Jews, being called God's "shepherd" and His "anointed," he was anxious to give God proofs of gratitude in return. Cyrus referred to the Lord as the "God of heaven" and gave credit to Him for having "given him all the kingdoms of the earth" (Ezra 1:2).

As a result, Cyrus issued a most unusual proclamation. Most of the Eastern kings delighted in persecuting their captives, never liberating prisoners of war. Cyrus' decree was music to Israel's ears—a "freedom" act that included all captives, but the Jews in particular. They would not only be allowed to return and rebuild their Temple and city, but were to be given the gold and silver vessels that Nebuchadnezzar had taken from the Temple when he destroyed Jerusalem (Ezra 1:1–4, 5:14,15). In Isaiah's prophecy regarding Cyrus and his decree to let Israel return to their beloved city, we see that her sovereign God knew the *when* of their release and He designated Cyrus as the one to carry out the fulfillment of his Word and purpose. No law of the Medes and Persians could be revoked (Daniel 6:8).

Fig. 31. Decree of King Cyrus.

ISRAEL RETURNS HOME

Israel's recorded Old Testament history ends with the historical books of Ezra and Nehemiah, and the prophetical books of Haggai, Zechariah, and Malachi. The period of time covered by these books is approximately 138 years.

When King Zedekiah died and Judah was taken into captivity, Israel lost her kingdom status. There has not been a Hebrew king on David's throne up to this day. From their return from exile through the intertestamental period, Gentile powers have ruled—Persian, Greek, and Roman. Her deportation took place in three stages, and with Cyrus' release, her return home was in three stages. From a chronological standpoint, the postexilic books should be read in the following order:

1. First return under Zerubbabel, about 543 B.C., 49,897 people.
   Ezra 1–4 with Haggai.
   Ezra 5:1 with Zechariah.
   Ezra 5,6 with Esther.
2. Second return under Ezra: 7:1, 8:1.
3. Third return under Nehemiah: 1:5–11, 13:6,7.
   Ezra 7–10.
   Nehemiah.
   Malachi.

The Priesthood of Ezra. Ezra could not serve as a priest during captivity, but in giving his time to the study of Scripture, he became a "ready scribe in the Law of Moses" (Ezra 7:6). He was the "census taker" as the people returned to record the name of the Tribe to which they belonged. This was done so that it might be known the Tribe and family through whom Messiah was to come (Ezra 2). Ezra's delight was in his proclaiming God's Word to the people so that they would not make the mistakes they had before captivity. Next in order was the building of the Temple. In Babylon they had lost their song, but now they sang together as they praised the Lord. Some were even weeping (Ezra 3:8–13; Psalm 126:1,2).

Anytime there is the working of God in the midst of His people, it seems that the devil begins to work overtime. Some Jews (adversaries), having married Assyrians when the Northern Kingdom fell, sought to hinder the rebuilding of the Temple. These people, known as the "Samaritans," followed Sanballat and Tobia in this effort. (Nehemiah had the same problem when rebuilding the city wall: 2:10.) These enemies persuaded the Persian king, Artaxerxes, to issue a "stop work" order. At the encouragement of the prophets Haggai (1:1) and Zechariah (1:1), a letter was sent to King Darius, who confirmed the decree of Cyrus. Work resumed on the Temple until it was completed and dedicated, and the Passover restored (Ezra 3:8–6:22). Another such problem existed in the matter of returning the gold and silver vessels of the Temple, and a letter was given confirming Cyrus' decree (7:11–28).

The Laws of the Medes and Persians. The laws of the Medes and Persians could *never* be altered, once made (Daniel 6:8). Regardless of events that transpired before or after issuance, or the personalities involved, once issued, these laws were binding. In spite of the personal feelings Darius had for Daniel, his decree forced him to cast Daniel in the lion's den (6:1–24).

When God prophesied that Cyrus would permit Israel to return to Jerusalem after their captivity, He knew that his decree could not be altered. This assured Israel of her return to her land. When adversaries sought to stop the building of the Temple, and they did succeed temporarily, King Darius wrote a letter confirming the unchangeable decree of Cyrus. Work resumed until the Temple was completed and dedicated (Ezra 4:1–6:18).

After this problem was settled, Ezra faced another critical one. There were some among the returnees, including priests and Levites, who had intermarried with heathen women of the Canaanites, Hittites, Moabites, Jebusites, Perizzites, Ammonites, Egyptians, and Amorites and were going after their abominations. As a result, the "holy seed" was mixed with unholy seed. They had not separated themselves from these ungodly people (Ezra 9:1–2). It is mentioned in Nehemiah that in this unholy relationship the children of these couples had lost the mother Hebrew tongue, that they spoke the foreign tongue of the heathen parent. In judging the people, Solomon was offered as the sinful illustration of marrying heathen women, which proves God's Word that the sins of the fathers are handed down from one generation to another (Nehemiah 13:23 with Numbers 14:18). Ezra had to force the offenders to divorce their wives (Ezra 9:1–10:44).

Ezra's spiritual success with the people was based on the fact that he prepared his heart to seek the Law of the Lord, to *do* it by his example, and to *teach* it to the people (Ezra 7:10).

Nehemiah's Ministry. Ezra's job with Zerubbabel was to build the Temple; Nehemiah's was to repair the city walls that Nebuchadnezzar's men had torn down. He had been the king's cupbearer in captivity, which gave him a close relationship with King Artaxerxes of Persia. Nehemiah's heart was with God, His people, and His city. After much prayer, he influenced the king to give him permission to go to Jerusalem and undertake the task of rebuilding the city. Permission was granted, and the king gave him much timber for his own house, the palace, and especially the city gates (Nehemiah 2:1–8).

Arriving in Jerusalem, Nehemiah viewed the ruins and immediately headed up a team of workers who had "a mind to work." They repaired the wall, going from gate to gate (Nehemiah 1:1–6:19). When Nehemiah dedicated the wall, there was evidence of a revival among the people. Ezra reminded them of the commands of God's Word and the people publicly confessed their sins, promising the Lord that they would obey His Law, support the Temple, and give Him His tithe (Nehemiah 10). Ezra and Nehemiah offer a good spiritual principle for us. The people worked on the Temple *first,* then rebuilt the city wall. The *inner* was repaired before the *outer,* which shows that if the heart (the inner) is cleansed first, all else (the outer) will be right.

In relation to the city wall and gates that Nehemiah and the people repaired (Nehemiah 3), there are some spiritual lessons for us relating to our Christian life. We can rest assured that Nehemiah made sure that there was a solid foundation that speaks to us of Christ, who is our Foundation (I Corinthians 3:11). As each gate was finished, the workmen would repair the wall to the next gate.

The Gates of Jerusalem (chapter 3 of Nehemiah)

1. The first gate was the "Sheep Gate," where the sheep were brought to the priests for sacrifices. This speaks to us of Christ, the Lamb of God being sacrificed for us (verse 1 with John 1:29).
2. The second was the "Fish Gate," the marketplace. As we enter the Fish Gate, we follow Christ and become "fishers of men" (verse 3 with Matthew 4:19).
3. The third was the "Old Gate," which speaks to us of the established path of God for His children to tread in their daily walk with Him (verse 6 with Jeremiah 6:16). This path enables us to grow in grace and knowledge of our Lord and Saviour, Jesus Christ (II Peter 3:18).
4. The fourth was the "Valley Gate," which speaks to us of humility in our service to the Lord (verse 13 with I Peter 5:5,6).
5. The fifth was the "Dung Gate," through which city waste was taken. It speaks to us of separation from the world, the flesh, and the devil, being cleansed from the filth of the flesh (verse 14 with II Corinthians 6:14–17).
6. The sixth was the "Gate of the Fountain," which speaks to us of being filled with the Holy Spirit, a spring of living water overflowing in us for thirsty souls (verse 15 with Ephesians 5:18b; John 7:38).
7. The seventh was the "Water Gate," which speaks to us of the desire for the "water of the Word," the only thing that will quench our spiritual thirst (verse 26 with Ephesians 5:26; Matthew 5:6).
8. The eighth was the "Horse Gate," which speaks to us of battles that we have to fight and will endure as "a good soldier of Jesus Christ" (verse 28 with II Timothy 2:3,4; Ephesians 6:10–18).
9. The ninth was the "East Gate," which speaks to us of Christ's second coming (verse 29 with John 14:1–3; I Thessalonians 4:16,17).
10. The tenth was the "Miphkad Gate," where the elders sat to make decisions and pass judgments, which speaks to us of assignment or appointment (verse 31). This represents the "Judgment Seat of Christ," where we will learn the *yes* or *no* of our rewards (II Corinthians 5:10; II Corinthians 3:11–15). When this gate was finished and the wall was completed to the next gate, it was the Sheep Gate, which speaks to us of our being in glory

with our Shepherd and being just like Him (I Thessalonians 4:16–18; I John 3:2)

Esther, Queen of Persia. The Book of Esther has little or nothing to do with the exodus of the Jews and return to Jerusalem from captivity. King Ahasuerus demanded that his wife embarrass herself before the men of the court, but she refused to obey his order. Getting rid of her, he made Esther, a Jewess, his queen. Officer Haman, who hated the Jews, concocted a plan to exterminate them from the Persian empire. Esther was persuaded by Mordecai to approach the king to persuade him to overrule Haman. Persian law forbade anyone under penalty of death to approach the king uninvited; the person could be killed unless the king held out his golden sceptre, which he did to Esther. The king granted her request for the Jews to be spared. As a result, Haman was hanged and the Jews celebrated by instituting the thanksgiving feast of *Purim.* It is said of Esther that "she had come for such a time as this" (Esther 4:4, 11–17). This could also be said about believers today. Moses said that a "Sceptre shall rise out of Israel," meaning Messiah (Numbers 24:17). Just as Esther could not approach her king unless his sceptre was extended to her, neither can we approach God unless His "Sceptre, Jesus Christ" is offered to us to approach His throne.

The Prophets Haggai and Zechariah. Haggai and Zechariah, contemporaries of Ezra and Nehemiah, filled in the condition of the hearts of the people in their daily living. It has been said that Zechariah was a "visionary with his head in the clouds," while Haggai was a "realist with his feet on the ground." As a priest, Zechariah concerned himself both with the spiritual condition of the people and with the glory of God's people in the future.

Haggai's ministry lasted four months, during which he delivered four messages, each dated (Haggai 1:1; 2:1,10,20). The problem that he set forth is that the people were selfishly constructing their own houses while the house of the Lord was in waste (1:3–4,9). Their crops were bad, their wages were very low, they were dissatisfied, and they were simply putting off until tomorrow what they were supposed to be doing today (1:6). Haggai's message was threefold: (1) consider your ways (1:5,7), (2) consider judgment (1:4), and (3) be strong and work (2:4). He revealed the promises of God to encourage them:

1. God will take pleasure in them if they obey: 1:8.
2. They will be assured of his presence: 2:4.
3. He will give them confidence: 2:5a.
4. He will eliminate fear: 2:5b.
5. He will flood them with His glory: 2:7b.
6. His peace will permeate the Temple: 2:9b.

The people were content to build their own houses first before building God's house. They were not *considering their ways.* Haggai sought to show them that what they were doing was the *enemy* of the one thing that they should be doing—helping to repair the house of the Lord. What they were doing was needful, *good,* but good is always the enemy of the *best.* They needed to realize that first things come first. We must always put Him *first,* for He has a job for each of us to do *today,* not tomorrow.

God's Job for Me[23]

The Lord had a job for me,
But I had so much to do
I said, "You get somebody else
or wait till I get through."
I don't know how the Lord came out,
I suppose He must have got along;
But I had a feeling—sneaking like,
That I'd done God wrong.

One day I needed the Lord,
Needed him right away;
But He never answered me at all.
I could hear him say,
Way down in my accusing heart—
"My child, I've got too much to do,
You get somebody else,
Or wait till I get through!"

Now, when the Lord has a job for me,
I never try to shirk;
I drop what I have on hand
And do the good Lord's work.
My affairs can run along,
Or wait till I get through,
'Cause nobody else can do the work
That God wants me to do.

The Prophet Malachi. From the time of Israel's return from Babylon to the end of Malachi's day was about 75 to 100 years. Still under Persian rule, Israel returned to her old sinful ways. Zechariah made mention that the high priest, Joshua, was backslidden and was setting a bad example for the people. They were a lying people (Zechariah 8:16a) and were imagining evil against their neighbors (8:10). He pleaded with them to remember the sins of their fathers (1:1–6, 7:8–14), speak the truth (8:16b), and think good of their neighbors (8:19). Apparently, they were cured of idolatry but were extremely prone to disobedience. After Haggai and Zechariah had disappeared off the scene, the Israelites had become complacent. Hypocrisy and irreverence characterized their social life, and so we find Malachi listing a number of indictments against them:

1. They questioned God's love: Malachi 1:2.
2. They were dishonoring God: 1:6a.
3. The priests were unfaithful and deceitful; they
   - Despised the name of the Lord: 1:6b.
   - Offered polluted bread on the altar: 1:7.
   - Would not listen to the Lord: 2:2.
   - Departed from God's way: 2:8a, 9b.
   - Stumbled at the Law: 2:8b, 9c.
   - Corrupted God's covenant: 2:8c.
4. They dealt treacherously against each other: 2:10.
5. They committed abomination: 2:11a.
6. They profaned God's holiness: 2:11b.
7. They were unequally yoked with unbelievers: 2:11c. Nehemiah had this same problem years before (Nehemiah 13:23–27).
8. They had marital problems: 2:14.
9. They were hypocrites: 2:13,17.
10. They were trying to cover up violence: 2:16.
11. They were involved in sorcery: 3:5a.
12. They were guilty of adultery: 3:5b.
13. They bore false witness: 3:5c.
14. They cheated employees: 3:5d.
15. They mistreated widows and the fatherless: 3:5e.
16. They were not hospitable to strangers: 3:5f.
17. They were like their sinning fathers: 3:7a.
18. They were disobedient: 3:7b.
19. They were thieves: 3:8, 9.
20. They used stout language (rude, obstinate, contemptible, insolent—saying *no* to a holy God): 2:13,14.
21. They were proud: 3:15a; 4:1a.
22. They were wicked: 3:15b; 4:1b.

Malachi was burdened for his kinsmen and pleaded with them to beseech God and remember the Law of Moses (Malachi 1:1,9, 4:4). He was anxious that they face their own sins and then face or look to God. Several promises were given by God to the people through this prophet:

1. Return unto Me and I will return unto you: 2:1–3.
2. Quit robbing Me and tithe so that the windows of heaven might be opened for your land to be productive again and that nations might call you blessed: 3:10–12.
3. If you fear the Lord, you will be remembered as jewels in the book that God is keeping: 3:16,17.

It is heartbreaking as we look at the last Book of the Old Testament and see how Malachi described the people of God. The record of all their "sayings and doings" (Isaiah 3:8) must have broken His heart innumerable times. It is shocking to see that Israel had become a backsliding people. Having returned from Babylonian captivity and enjoying the blessings of God in rebuilding the Temple and Jerusalem, the Israelites should have been encouraged by the messages of Ezra, Nehemiah, Haggai, and Zechariah. What happened to these people during the years after their return up to Malachi's day? Evidently, parents had not assumed their responsibility, and a new generation arose who ignored the claims of God upon them, like those after the death of Joshua (Judges 2:10). Parents must have been totally ignorant of the laws that Moses gave them concerning family devotions (Deuteronomy 6:6–25). "Righteousness exalts a nation but sin is a reproach to any people" (Proverbs 14:34). "As goes the home, so goes the nation."

CONCLUSION

Several lessons can be learned from Israel's failure to be known as a people called by God's name. The end result of disobedience is found in the words of their wisest king, who became the most foolish—"vanity of vanities, all is vanity" (Ecclesiastes 1:2). Solomon is referring to the emptiness of life apart from God, living as though there were no tomorrow or eternity. He revealed all this and then repeated, "Vanity of vanities, all is vanity" (12:8). But he added some important advice by saying, "Let us hear the conclusion of the whole matter: Fear God and keep His commandments, for this is the whole duty of man. For God shall bring every work into judgment, with every secret tiling, whether it be good, or whether it be evil" (12:13,14).

To be fully blessed of the Lord, one must stay in God's will according to His Word, His commandments. It *must* be according to a "thus saith the Lord," *period.* We need to be aware of the record that He is keeping of our thoughts, our words, and our deeds. This will prompt us to speak often of Him, and then when we stand before Him as He opens the books, we might be numbered among his jewels (Malachi 3:16,17).

In looking back to what Moses said God would do if His people obeyed Him, we can better understand why so much happened because of Israel's refusal to walk in obedience to His commandments. Deuteronomy lists the blessings that God would give if His people obeyed Him (Deuteronomy 28: 1–14), and the rest of the chapter spells out the consequences if they disobey. This we have seen throughout our study of their history. Never was love so little regarded, never was mercy so lightly esteemed, never was goodness so little appreciated, and never was righteousness so greatly despised as by those who refused to be numbered among God's remnant. In this study of the Jews of the Old Testament, we have seen the majority of God's chosen people "rise to shame." Oh, to think that it could have been "Israel's Rise to Spiritual Fame!" (Psalm 106:32–43)

16

INTERTESTAMENTAL AND NEW TESTAMENT PERIODS

Israel's history was by no means over. The Old Testament not only records the way God's people lived and the manner in which He dealt with them, but many prophecies were made concerning this nation's future, especially about Messiah's coming to this earth. The period of time from the end of Malachi's prophecy to the New Testament era is often referred to by those of the Christian faith as "The Four Hundred Silent Years" because there was no prophet of God on the scene. This period ended with the coming of John the Baptist, who was spoken of by the prophet Isaiah, saying, "The voice of one crying in the wilderness, Prepare ye the way of the Lord, make his paths straight" (Matthew 3:1–3 echoing Isaiah 40:3).

While Daniel was in Babylonian captivity, he mentioned four ruling Gentile powers, three of which would hold Israel subject during these silent years. In a dream of Nebuchadnezzar, which Daniel interpreted it for him (Daniel 2:32–40), Nebuchadnezzar saw a huge statue in the form of a man, 90 feet tall. The head was pure gold, representing Nebuchadnezzar as king of *Babylon,* the

Fig. 32. Seal of Nebuchadnezzar.

Head of GOLD
King Nebuchadnezzar
BABYLON (Daniel 2:32a)

Chest and arms of SILVER
Cyrus/Medes—Darius/Persia
PERSIA (2:32b)

Stomach and thighs of BRASS
Alexander the Great
GREECE (2:32c)

Legs of IRON, feet of IRON and CLAY
The Caesars
ROME (2:33)

Fig. 33. Daniel's interpretation of Nebuchadnezzar's dream in terms of four Gentile nations.

first Gentile kingdom under which Israel was subjected (ca. 586–516 B.C., 2:32a). The chest and arms were silver, which represented the second Gentile power ruling over Israel, *the Medes and Persians* (ca. 516-332 B.C., 2:32b). The belly and thighs were bronze, representing the third power, *Greece* (ca. 332–145 B.C., 2:32c). The legs were iron and the feet were iron and clay mixed, representing *Rome,* the fourth kingdom. (ca. 145 B.C.–A.D. 476, about 621 years). It is said that the strength of iron can smash gold, silver, and bronze, showing Rome's mighty power throughout its empire. When iron and clay are mixed, the substance becomes brittle and shows that no matter how powerful a kingdom may be, it will sooner or later fall. History proves this, and the period is referred to as "the rise and fall of the Roman Empire": "Iron and clay" simply did not hold up for Rome.

GREEK RULE

After Babylonian and Persian rule over Israel had come to an end, Alexander the Great came upon the scene in 333 B.C., defeated the Medes and Persians, and became a world conqueror and ruler. The lifestyle of the Jews was about the same, although exhibiting certain religious practices. After Alexander's death, his empire was divided among five of his generals. By the year 165

B.C., a general by the name of Antiochus Epiphanes IV became ruler of Syria. He invaded and took control of Palestine.

This Greek ruler had one desire, to convert his kingdom to speaking Greek and adopting Hellenistic culture. Since the Jews had their own culture as well as their own religion and priests, Antiochus' title was changed from "Antiochus the Illustrator" to "Antiochus the Madman." Determined to take his anger out on the Jews, he entered the Temple and took out the golden altar, the candlestick, and all the costly vessels. He damaged the Table of Showbread, massacred a number of the people, and bragged about his actions against God's people. He forbade the Jews to circumcise their sons, observe feast days, or offer any sacrifices in the Temple. Altars to Zeus and other Greek gods were set up in the Temple, plus an Asherim. To add insult to injury, he even offered a pig (swine) sacrifice on God's altar. The Books of the Law in the Temple were ripped to shreds and burned. Anyone caught with a scroll or any portion of the Law was put to death, and any woman who circumcised her son was killed and the baby was hanged by the neck. Then they rifled their homes. In the words of the prophet Daniel, to the Jews this was the "abomination of desolation" (Daniel 11:31–36).

The Maccabean Revolt. In spite of Israel's past history of sin and dishonoring God, there were those who made up the faithful remnant, and they still stood for the ordinances, feasts, ceremonies, laws, and customs that distinguished them as Jews. What Antiochus did was incite them to rebellion under a priest named Mattathias. He undid all that the Greek ruler had done to the Jews in his desecration of the Temple and ignited a defiance among the people.

After Mattathias' death, Judas, whose surname was Maccabee (the "hammer"), became the leader, fought against the Syrians, and won. Antiochus sent another army, and in 165 B.C. the Maccabeans achieved complete victory over Greek supremacy. The Temple was cleansed, order was restored, sacrifices began to be offered, feasts were celebrated, and the "Feast of Dedication," or *Hanukkah,* was instituted.

As time marched on, the "Maccabean house" took advantage of a power vacuum and became the political as well as religious leaders. The authority of the Levitical priesthood was usurped, and the loyal priests found themselves in fierce opposition to the Jerusalem authorities. According to Josephus, they revolted; at least 800 of them were martyred at the hands of the Maccabees. The survivors fled from the "City of Blood" (Jerusalem) to the "City of Salt" (Qumran) in the desert near the Dead Sea. These priests became known as the *Essenes,* and their purpose was fourfold:

1. To preserve the unity and purity of the priesthood.
2. To hold to Moses, the Psalms, and the Prophets.
3. To practice their beliefs daily.
4. To make copies of the Word of God for posterity.

These were the people who hid the now-famous Dead Sea Scrolls, among which was found the entire scroll of Isaiah, which corresponds with our King James Version. The only differences are various synonyms explaining the same truth. What Jesus read from Isaiah 61:1,2b is the same as we have in our Bible. We can thank the Lord for preserving His truths down through the centuries.

After the persecuted priests escaped to Qumran, there was much division in the family of the self-appointed priests in Jerusalem. During this period much emphasis was placed on Jewish writings and Sabbath laws.

Jewish Writings

1. The *Torah,* the five book of Moses, which were followed by the Jews in general as the foundation for God's laws, along with the Psalms and the Prophets.
2. *Targum,* or *Targums,* renderings of the Old Testament in Aramaic. This language became common after Israel's Babylonian captivity.
3. The *Talmud.* The Old Testament claims for itself to be the Word of God. The Talmud, or oral laws, does not claim for itself this distinction. It is merely a commentary on the Old Testament and, being comprised of oral laws, it is nothing more than a commentary on a commentary, making it the word of man, and man has a reputation of being wrong at times. The *man-made* laws were practiced by the Jews in the days of Christ, who referred to them as the "traditions of your fathers [the elders]." Christ asked them, "Why do ye also transgress the commandment of God by [or for the sake of] your tradition?" Later He told them, "Ye do err, not knowing the scriptures" (Matthew 15:1–6, 22:29). Even the apostle Paul boasted that before he was saved, he was "exceedingly jealous of the traditions of my fathers" (Galatians 1:14). Clinging to the traditions is one reason why the Jews failed to recognize Jesus as their Messiah, or "Anointed One."

The Jews say that the Talmud, or oral law, is equal to the "written Torah" because it goes back to the "Revelation at Sinai." They claim that some of the laws in the Talmud were given to Moses, but not written down in the Torah, or Pentateuch. The doctrine of the oral laws was the harvest of the "seed" that was planted when the original laws were given on Mount Sinai. Their *seed,* of course, is definitely *not* a "thus sayeth the Lord" seed.

One manifestation of the love that the remnant had for the Torah was the erection of a "fence" around it for protection against any changes. Evidently, the fence that the rabbis have built around the Torah to protect it has turned out to be a fence to keep one from taking the Torah at face value. The Talmud has become a substitute for their Scriptures.

Sabbath Laws. Scripture lays down the general law that no manner of work is to be performed on the Sabbath. In building a fence around the Torah, rabbis turned attention from the plain, simple law to a Talmudic treatise that explains what *they* think does and does not constitute a desecration of the Sabbath. Notice how they stretch the truth[24]:

"He who spills any liquid in a place where the soil is apt to produce something is guilty of violating the law against sowing on the Sabbath. . . .

"If there be any dirt on a garment or the like, one may wipe it with rag or the like, but he is not permitted to spill water thereon, because the putting on of water is analogous to washing it. . . .

"Mud on one's garment may be scraped off with a nail or with a knife if it still be moist, but if it be completely dry it may not be scraped off, for it is equivalent to the act of grinding. . . .

"It is forbidden to shake off snow or dust from a black garment. . . .

"It is forbidden to carry a covering as a protection from the sun or from the rain, which commonly is known as an umbrella, because it is considered as making a tent."

Jesus had a confrontation with the Jews of His day when His disciples were taken to task for picking and eating grain on the Sabbath (Matthew 12:1–8). The Pharisees saw several sins committed in the disciples' actions:

1. *Harvesting* as the disciples picked the grain.
2. *Sifting* as they rubbed the grain in their hands to separate it from the chaff.
3. *Winnowing* by blowing the chaff away.
4. *Grinding* by crushing the wheat to eat it.

Jesus needed only to remind them that in the law Moses gave permission to eat from one's field or vineyard (Deuteronomy 23:24,25) and the priests to work on the Sabbath day (Matthew 12:1–8). In relation to eating, the Talmud states that "Whosoever eats bread without previously washing his hands is as though he had intercourse with a harlot, and whoever makes light of washing hands [before and after a meal] will be uprooted from this world." When Jesus healed a man on the Sabbath and reminded them that if a sheep fell in a ditch on the Sabbath they would pull it out, it went in one ear and out the other, and they held a council to decide how they might destroy Him (Matthew 12:9–14). A Jew could walk just so far on the Sabbath day (Acts 1:12).

In addition to the rabbis' interpretation of harvesting, sifting, winnowing, and grinding on the Sabbath day, the Jews could not sow, plow, knead, bake, sheer the sheep, bleach, dye, spin, weave two threads, separate two threads, sew, hunt, kill an animal and flay it, write two letters of the alphabet, kindle a fire, transfer one object from one place to another, strike with a hammer, and so forth. Orthodox Jews today are not allowed to turn on lights, amplify voices with a microphone, or even push buttons of an elevator on the Sabbath. These Sabbath laws are but samples of the interpretation that rabbis have given to laws found in the Talmud. All this is simply an example of the blind leading the blind (Matthew 15:12–14).

Fig. 34. Stone indicating end of a Sabbath day's journey.

GROUPS AND SECTS

Prior to and during the intertestamental period, several groups came into existence who played a role during the New Testament era.

1. The *Scribes,* or lawyers, whose main responsibility was to copy the Scriptures. They were more concerned with the *letter* of the law than the spirit. They also taught the Scriptures (Nehemiah 8:2–8).
2. The *Sanhedrin.* This word does not appear in Scripture, but it means "judges" or "council." The Sanhedrin, presided over by the high priest, was comprised of 70 men who acted as the "supreme court" in matters of decision and trials. This group probably originated under the rule of King Jehoshaphat, about 800 B.C. (II Chronicles 19:4–11).
3. The *Samaritans.* See page 116.
4. The *Pharisees.* It is believed that this group came into existence during the Maccabean revolt. Refusing to bow to Antiochus Epiphanes and for a time standing true to the Law, the Psalms, and the Prophets, the Pharisees "graduated" into becoming legal separatists and ultimately trusted more in the "traditions of their fathers" than they did in their own Scriptures. In some of the confrontations that Jesus had with them, he called them "blind leaders of the blind" and "blind guides" (Matthew 15:14, 23:16).
5. The *Sadducees.* Worldly minded or rationalistic, the Sadducees were priests who obeyed the letter of the Law but conformed to the culture of their day. They were called a "generation of vipers" by John the Baptist. They hated the Pharisees, but were their allies in opposition to Christ (Matthew 3:7; Acts 5:17). They denied the resurrection (Luke 20:27); this is why they were "sad you see."

Fig. 35. "Seat of Moses," chief seat in the synagogue.

ROME CONQUERS PALESTINE

After the Maccabeans had won their freedom from the Greeks around 165 B.C., they enjoyed this freedom a little over 100 years. They were settled in their groups and the traditions of the oral laws of the rabbis. Although Rome had defeated the Greeks in ca. 145 B.C., it wasn't until 63 B.C. that they conquered Jerusalem. The full record of the Maccabees is found in two books of the Apocrypha named for them, along with several other books that are not accepted as part of either the Jewish Scriptures or Protestant versions as being inspired by God.

CONCLUSION

In this four-hundred–year period the Jews have freed themselves from the idolatry of Baal and other gods, so common in their previous history. However, anything can become an idol if it comes between one's self and the Lord. It could be a child, house, car, television, money, denomination, cult leader, traditions that contradict the Word of God, and so on. We are admonished by the apostle John to "keep yourselves from idols" (I John 5:20,21).

As we approach the New Testament period, we find that the "idol" of the "tradition of the rabbis" replaced the Word of God. This was the stumbling block that kept the Jewish leaders so blinded to the coming of their Messiah, who was so plainly prophesied in their Scriptures. This was the idol that they worshipped, ultimately leading them to reject Jesus Christ. They ignored the Word of God, deprived it of its authority, believed *man,* and followed the traditions of the oral laws instead of "thus saith the Lord" (Matthew 15:2,3,6). As we approach the introduction to the life of Christ, thank the Lord that those of the remnant, such as Simeon and Anna, believed what God said in their Scriptures! (Luke 2:25–38).

17

MESSIANIC PROPHECIES

Christ took the Jews to task for not taking their Scriptures at face value, but instead accepting the "tradition of their fathers" in place of the Scriptures (Matthew 15:3–6). They will swear by the Torah, which is the first five Books of Moses, yet follow the Talmud, which is a collection of over 600 oral laws that rabbis have written to interpret the Law as given by Moses in the Torah. Many of these laws will be discussed in Chapter 19.

A review of these oral laws makes it easy to see how the Jewish people have ignored the wonderful promises of Moses in the Torah itself, in the Psalms, and in the prophecies relating to Messiah. Since they do not accept their own Scriptures concerning Messiah, we can better understand why they do not see the fulfillment of many prophecies pointing to Him in the New Testament. It is amazing how they interpret the portions that relate to Him. One who has accepted the New Testament as God's inspired Word, on the other hand, easily sees how many Old Testament prophetic references are literally fulfilled in the One who presented Himself as Messiah over 1,900 years ago.

How do we deal with Jews when witnessing about Christ, the Messiah? One rabbi said that although Jesus was a wonderful man, His followers *made him* the only begotten Son of God. He accuses Christians of reading one type of book (the New Testament), for Christians to believe that Jews would accept Jesus as the Messiah is absolutely ridiculous. Since they do not "see" in their Scriptures who the true Messiah is, how can we, apart from their Bible, portray *their* Messiah or Anointed Prince? To get a true picture, we will consider the following as a build-up to His identity.

1. Is the God of the Old Testament "one" God or a "triune" God?
2. Who is the "Seed" promised as Messiah?
3. Through whom will He be born?
4. What is the significance of blood sacrifices?
5. Where will He be born?
6. When will He be born?
7. Who will introduce Him?
8. What will His mission be?
9. How will He be treated and suffer?
10. Will He die and live again?
11. Will He at His first coming restore David's throne?

ISRAEL'S GOD: "ONE" OR "TRIUNE" GOD?

The Jews claim that there is only *one* God: "Hear, o Israel, the Lord our God, the Lord is One," and that He is eternal and everlasting (Deuteronomy 6:4, 33:27; Genesis 21:33). This monotheistic view of God is one of their main tenets. This verse referring to *one* God is taken literally, while many, many others are explained away with oral laws.

Rabbi Stanley Greenberg of Temple Sinai in Philadelphia has written, "Christians are, of course, entitled to believe in a trinitarian conception of God, but their effort to base this conception on the Hebrew Bible must fly in the face of the overwhelming testimony of that Bible. The Hebrew Bible affirms the one God with unmistakable clarity. Monotheism, an uncompromising belief in one God, is the hallmark of the Hebrew Bible, the unwavering affirmation of Judaism and the unshakable faith of the Jew."[25]

We appreciate the rabbi's consideration that Christians are entitled to their opinion of a trinitarian God. He, too, has a right to his opinion, but opinions must be based on facts, and since we are using three versions of the Jewish Bible in our discussion of Israel's history and beliefs, we must evaluate his statement that "Hebrew Scriptures are clear and unequivocal on the oneness of God [and] the Hebrew Bible affirms the one God with unmistakable clarity."

To get the meaning of the word *God,* we need to explore the Hebrew language. In the Torah, the word *God* is used numerous times. Various titles are used in connection with His name, for example, *Jehovah-jirah* ("the Lord will provide") (Genesis 22:13,14), *El-Shaddai* ("I am that I am") (Exodus 3:14,15), *Jehovah* ("the Lord that healeth") (Exodus 15:26), and *Adonai-nissi* ("the Lord our banner") (Exodus 17:15). The word for *God* that is so emphasized by the Jews in Deuteronomy 6:4 is *Elohim.* This word is a *plural* noun, not singular as is claimed. From Genesis 1:1 through Deuteronomy 33:27, *Israel's Torah,* the name *Elohim* is used no fewer than 743 times!

We learn in Genesis 1:1 that *God* (*Elohim*) said, "Let us"—not "Let *me* [singular]," but "Let *us* [plural] make man in *our* [plural] image." How can we explain the concept of "one" God in view of this "plural" connotation? Are there two Gods, three, four? The best answer is that there is but one true and living God, but a God who is more than one as a personage, more than one who makes up the Godhead.

God, the Father. In our consideration of Scripture speaking of God as *Elohim* (plural), it is interesting to note that God is referred to as "Father." He is Father as the "Creator" (Isaiah 64:7; Malachi 2:10), Father as "Provider" of Israel's inheritance of the land (Jeremiah 3:19), and Father as "Redeemer" (Isaiah 63:7). There is no doubt that "God the Father" is *One* in the Godhead.

God, the Holy Spirit. When God's "Spirit" moved in His act of creation of the earth, was the Spirit a Person or an "it"? (Genesis 1:2) Nehemiah said that God gave His Spirit to instruct Israel in the wilderness (Nehemiah 9:28). Was this "Spirit" a thing, a ghost, a wind, or a Person? Nehemiah also said that

God testified against His people by the Spirit *in* the prophets (9:30). When David confessed his sin with Bathsheba to God, he asked God to "take not Thy Holy Spirit from me" (Psalm 51:11). It appears that God's Spirit is a part of His Person, not only in helping in creation, but in instructing His people, being *in* His prophets, and being possessed by a man anointed of God (Psalm 89:20). Isaiah mentioned that in Moses' day Israel rebelled against God and *vexed* His Holy Spirit. A *thing* or an *it* cannot be vexed, but *a person can.* It is also mentioned that God's Spirit was "in him [Moses]" (Isaiah 63:10,11). It is difficult not to see that the Spirit of God *is* a Person in the Godhead.

God, the Son (Messiah). So far the Hebrew Scriptures have accounted for *two* Persons in the Godhead. Are there more? I believe we can account for one more. The Psalmist makes mention of the Lord—God—speaking to *My Lord,* saying, "Sit Thou at My right hand until I make Thine enemies Thy footstool" (Psalm 110:1–4). In this verse we have two "Lords," one speaking to the other. The Psalmist also mentions rulers of the earth taking counsel against the Lord and against His "Anointed," who appears to be "My begotten Son" of Psalm 2:7. "Begotten" implies lineage, which traces "Son" to God Himself.

This "Son," who is associated with God, is a "Priest *forever* after the manner of Melchizedek" (Psalm 110:4). The Levitical priests lived and died. This Priest lives forever—which can only apply to God, or one in the Godhead. We find Him making an appearance to Abraham (Genesis 14:18–20). God is occasionally called *Jehovah,* which means the "self-existent" or "eternal" One. If the Son is a Priest *forever* and being begotten of God's lineage, He, too, is Jehovah, a Person of the Godhead.

IDENTIFYING ISRAEL'S MESSIAH

The One whom Christians call "Messiah" is called the "Anointed One," the "Anointed Prince," or the "Anointed Leader" in the three different versions of the Hebrew Bibles. The King James Version and other modern translations of the Bible use "Messiah." Some bibles, like the New International Version, use the "Anointed One," and the Catholic version uses "Christ." The Greek word for "Anointed" is *Christ,* and it is amazing that in the English translation of the Greek Septuagint, "Christ" is used for "Anointed" in Daniel 9:25. "Christ" is also used for "Anointed" in I Kings [I Samuel KJV] 2:10, 35; Psalms 2:2, 19:6 [20:6 KJV]; and Amos 4:13. The reference in Daniel 9:25 is considered later in this chapter.

What do the terms "Messiah" and "Anointed" mean to Jewish people? Many feel that it means a person who will come to set up a utopia to establish peace, to deliver them from oppression, to establish peace throughout the world with David's kingdom and Temple worship restored. This is the general view of Messiah's mission, a view held at the beginning of the New Testament era when the Jews were looking for a leader who would break the yoke of Rome and give them independence for their own kingdom again. Such a Messiah is portrayed as a Person, none can truthfully deny.

THE SEED ROYAL

Throughout the Old Testament emphasis has always been on a "Seed." Jews apparently look at a "seed" as descendants of Abraham, Isaac, and Jacob in reference to the Promised Land and the Jewish nation. However, their Bible also refers to the *Seed of promise* or the *Seed Royal* as the coming Messiah. When Adam and Eve sinned due to Satan's temptation, God said to the serpent, "Because *thou* hast done this . . . I will put enmity between thy seed and her seed, they [her seed] shall bruise thy head and thou shall bruise [her seed's] heel" (Genesis 3:14,15). This was God's ultimatum to the originator of sin concerning the "Seed Royal," who would come as a woman's child to defeat the enemy of men's souls. This verse has little or no meaning to Jews in general, but it is the springboard to many, many verses that follow, up to the fulfillment of Daniel's prophecy concerning the "Anointed One" (Daniel 9:24–27).

The preservation of the "Seed Royal" was one battle after another between God and Satan due to Satan's determination to stamp out the lineage. When Eve bore Cain, she said, "I have gotten a man from the Lord." When Abel was born, Satan was confused as to which was the "Seed" from the Lord. Since Abel's sacrifice was accepted by the Lord and Cain's was rejected, Satan enticed Cain to kill Abel, thinking he was *the* Seed, but God raised up Seth to continue the line (Genesis 4:1–8,25,26). By the time of Noah, Satan had so polluted the minds of men that their evil deeds brought about the judgment of the flood. Noah, however, so lived for the Lord that he and his family found grace in the sight of the Lord, and only eight souls were spared while the rest of the human race perished (Genesis 6–9).

With the beginning of a new race of people through Noah, man again turned from God and sought to "reach heaven on his own" by building a great tower. God brought the work to nought and confused the tongues of the people, which brought about the beginning of the different nations. Finally, Abraham was selected to be the head of a people who would preserve the lineage. His son Isaac became the "Seed of promise" (Genesis 17:6–8, 15–19). From Isaac came Jacob, who fell heir to this heritage (28:1–4,14). When Jacob called his sons together to predict their future, the Tribe of Judah became the lineage (49:1,2,8–10). This continued on to include the "house of David" (II Samuel 22:51; I Kings 2:33). None of those of the Northern Kingdom of Israel were in this line (II Kings 17:21).

Queen Athaliah of the Southern Kingdom of Judah tried to kill all of the "Seed Royal," but the babe Joash was spared, he being the only one left of the "Seed Royal" through his father, Ahaziah (II Kings 11:1–3). This lineage continued through the Tribe of Judah, many of whom returned from Babylonian captivity (Ezra 1:5, 10:9). We do not expect to find the genealogy of Messiah listed in the Jewish Old Testament, but we do find it recorded in the New Testament in Matthew (1:1–17) and Luke (3:23–38). When one considers all the opposition that Messiah received from the Jews, it is interesting that not once is it recorded that they ever questioned His genealogy.

THE SEED—BORN OF A VIRGIN

Through the prophet Isaiah, God elaborated on His promise of a Seed who would come for the purpose of being His "Anointed One." He spoke of a *sign,* a young woman who would conceive, bear a son, and call his name "Immanuel" (Isaiah 7:14). The "sign" was of a prophetic nature, even though it may appear to be linked to Isaiah's period. There are two important points in this verse:

1. The word *virgin* does not appear in any of the Jewish Bibles, although we do find it in the King James Version. In the Jewish Bible the word *woman* is used, meaning "almah," or "virgin." There are two words for virgin in Hebrew, *almah* and *bethoolaw.* The root meaning of *almah* is *alam,* which means "conceived, covered." Applied to a virgin, it signifies a young woman who has never known a man. She is "concealed" or "covered" to this relationship. The account of Rebekah being chosen for Isaac provides a good illustration of this truth. She was a "virgin who had never known a man" (Genesis 24:16). The word used here for virgin is *bethoolaw,* meaning "a young woman," or even a young bride, one just married. In verse 43 Rebekah is called a virgin using the word *almah,* which shows that even though she was a young woman, she was a "virgin who had never known a man" until she married. Isaiah was pointing out that such a son would be born to a young woman who was a virgin.

2. A son born to a newly married virgin is no *sign.* This has happened down through the centuries. What makes Isaiah's prediction a sign is that the seed of this virgin will be called "Immanuel," meaning "God with us" or, better yet, "with us is God." Any seed born to a human father and human mother would have been conceived in sin, and no sinner could ever be God (Psalm 51:7 [51:5 KJV]). But to be born of a virgin without a human father would be a miracle and would be God in the flesh—a true Messiah. This is what makes Isaiah's "sign" different from the natural order of birth.

Isaiah also stated, "For a child is born unto us, and a son is given unto us; and the government is upon his shoulder. His name is called Pele-joez-el-gibbor-Abi-ad-sar-shalom [Wonderful in Counsel is God the Mighty, the Everlasting Father, Ruler of Peace], that the government may be increased, and of peace there be no end, upon the throne of David and upon his kingdom to establish it and to uphold it through justice and through righteousness from henceforth forever" (Isaiah 9:5,6 [9:6,7 KJV]). These verses definitely have to be a prophecy concerning a child born as of Isaiah 7:14, and a *son* born as the "Son of God" (Psalm 2:7). Who else but the Son of God would be called a child born and be called "Wonderful, Counselor of the Mighty God, of the Everlasting Father, Prince of Peace," and whose government shall be *forever*?

THE SIGNIFICANCE OF BLOOD SACRIFICES

A cardinal truth in the Torah is that "For the life of the flesh is in the blood, and I have assigned it to you for making expiation for your lives upon the altar; it is the blood, as life, that effects expiation" (Leviticus 17:11 T), or "For the life of the flesh is in the blood: I have given it to you upon the altar to make atonement for your souls: for it is the blood that maketh an atonement for the soul" (Leviticus 17:11 KJV).

Not only has emphasis been put on the fact that Messiah is a person, a "Seed," but also on the fact that a blood sacrifice will be an integral part of Messiah's ministry. Blood sacrifices began in Eden after Adam and Eve sinned against God. An animal was slain to provide "garments of skin" for a covering to give our first parents standing again with God (Genesis 3:21). Abel met God's approval with a slain animal as a blood sacrifice (4:4). Noah's first act upon dry ground was to build an altar and make a burnt-offering sacrifice (8:20).

Abraham's offering of Isaac is a classic example of a blood sacrifice pleasing to God, a sacrifice done by faith. God, seeking to test Abraham's faithfulness, told him to take Isaac, the "Seed of promise," and offer him as a sacrifice. Abraham made preparation but made no resistance, acting solely on faith according to God's command, and he and Isaac headed toward the place where an altar would be erected. Isaac questioned where the lamb was for the sacrifice, to which Abraham replied, "My son, God will provide Himself the lamb for a burnt offering." Note that he did not say that God would "provide *for* Himself the sacrifice," but that God would "*provide Himself the sacrifice.*" What faith Abraham had to believe that God would provide a substitute for his son! When he went so far as to bind Isaac, place the wood in order to burn Isaac as the sacrifice, and then raise the knife to slay him, God intervened with a ram that had been caught in the thicket, and the ram became the sacrifice instead of Abraham's son. Although Isaac was Abraham's son of promise, he was not a type of Messiah as a substitute; only the ram caught in the thicket was. Instead of Isaac dying, the ram did—a true picture of God making the necessary sacrifice—a substitute. If Isaac had been a type of Messiah, there would have been *two* available substitutes, and there can only be *one* substitute, or Messiah. Abraham rightly saw Messiah's day when he recognized that God Himself would be the one and only Messiah by saying, "God will provide Himself the sacrifice" (Genesis 22:1–13 with John 8:56).

It is no wonder that Abraham called the name of that place *Jehovah-jirah,* meaning "God will provide" (Genesis 22:14). God has supplied, and always will supply, man's need, but it must start with the proper blood sacrifice, and it is man's faith that appropriates it, which faith is counted for righteousness. It took faith for those who sprinkled blood on the doorposts to be spared when God pronounced judgment on the firstborn in Egypt (Exodus 12:7).

Like a scarlet thread, blood sacrifices run throughout the Old Testament for atonement for sin. Israel's worship set forth God's pattern for forgiveness of sin: it was not their *works* of the rituals and sacrifices that produced the necessary results, it was their *faith* in obedience in performing these offerings that counted with God and enabled Him to count them righteous.

When Israel lived in sin, their offerings and sacrifices became null and void simply because no faith was involved. God said He hated such (Isaiah 1:11–18) and predicted through Moses that Israel would be a treacherous breed in whom there was no faith (Deuteronomy 32:20). Without faith it is impossible to please God. It wasn't that the blood of bulls and goats and lambs could save them or forgive them or enable them to be counted as righteous before God as sinners, but *faith* to believe that without the shedding of blood there was no remission of sin and that "it is the blood that maketh atonement for the soul" (Leviticus 4:20, 17:11). See Cheap Sacrifices in the index.

THE PLACE OF MESSIAH'S BIRTH

"But thou, Bethlehem Ephrathah, thou that be little among the thousands of Judah, yet out of thee shall come forth unto Me that is to be the Ruler of Israel, whose going forth are from old, from everlasting" (Micah 5:1 [5:2 KJV]). "From everlasting" definitely implies someone who has always existed and certainly must apply to a member of the Godhead. Who else but Messiah is the One who comes as the "mighty God" to rule in the hearts of men?

THE FORERUNNER OF MESSIAH

Isaiah 40:2–3 foretells of One who will come to bring comfort for sins and pardon and that He will be announced by one who heralds His coming by saying, "Hark, one calleth, Clear ye in the wilderness the way of the Lord, Make plain in the desert a highway for our God [implying God as Messiah, or Anointed One]." The prophet Malachi also said, "Behold, I will send My messenger and He shall prepare the way before Me [God], and the Lord [Messiah], whom ye seek, shall suddenly come to the Temple, even the Messenger of the covenant" (Malachi 2:7).

THE TIME OF MESSIAH'S COMING

"If therefore the light that is in thee be darkness, how great is that darkness!" (Matthew 6:23b). Israel, in her blindness to the bulk of her Scriptures, is in darkness concerning the *one* portion of God's Word that tells them *when* their Messiah will come and what His mission will be. Their prophet Daniel gave a full description of this momentous event. His timetable starts with the issuance of a "command to rebuild Jerusalem *until* Messiah appears to accomplish His mission on earth." He said,

> Seventy weeks are determined upon thy people and upon thy Holy City, to finish the transgression, and to make an end of sins and to

> make reconciliation for iniquity, and to bring in everlasting righteousness, and to seal up the vision and prophecy, and to anoint the Most Holy. Know therefore and understand, that from the going forth of the commandment to restore and rebuild Jerusalem shall be seven weeks, and during threescore and two weeks it shall be built again, with street and trench, even in troublous times. And after threescore and two weeks shall the anointed be cut off, and there shall be no more to succeed Him. (Daniel 9:24–26b)

Of the 70 weeks mentioned by Daniel, only 69 weeks have to do with the issuance of a command to rebuild Jerusalem after Babylonian captivity until Messiah accomplishes His mission. "Weeks" in Hebrew means a period of *seven* years. Seven weeks total 49 years, so "threescore and two weeks" (62) equals 434 years, or a total of 483 years from the command to rebuild Jerusalem to Messiah's making a reconciliation for sin and bringing in everlasting righteousness.

When Nehemiah learned of the ruins of the city of Jerusalem (Nehemiah 1:1–4), he requested permission of King Artaxerxes to return to his beloved city and rebuild it. He was granted permission to return *at the word* of the king, and the king gave letters to secure passage out of the country. Not only were letters given for safe passage, but the king also gave Nehemiah timber to be used for the palace, for the city wall, and for his new house (2:1–8). The "word" spoken by the king is *dabar,* which means "a spoken word that can be taken as a command."

Some say that the command or decree is the one that Cyrus issued in 535 B.C. at the end of the 70-year Babylonian captivity of Israel. His decree was to build the Temple, the house of the Lord (Ezra 1:2–5). Subtracting 483 years from this date would put the mission of reconciliation of sin by the "Anointed Prince" at about 52 B.C., which would make Messiah's birth about 85 B.C. while the Greeks were still in power. We note, however, that Daniel's prophecy says that the period of time began "from the going forth of the word [command] to restore and build *Jerusalem* unto the Anointed One," not to *build* Jerusalem and the Temple. Artaxerxes' issuance of this "word" for Nehemiah's return was dated in the month of Nisan, in the twentieth year of the king's reign, ca. 445 B.C. By subtracting 483 years from 445 B.C., we arrive at A.D. 38. Due to calendar changes of anywhere from four to six years, this would be just about the time that Messiah, or the Anointed Prince, would be 33 years old. According to Numbers 4:35, one who served the Lord in His house had to be 30 years old. This Anointed One of whom Daniel prophesied—Christ, Messiah—started His ministry at the age of 30 after being introduced by His forerunner, John the Baptist (Matthew 3:21-23). Christ attended at least three yearly Passovers and one annual feast (John 2:23, 5:1, 6:4, 13:1). This adds at least three more years to His life, making Him 33 when He fulfilled Daniel's prophecy at the end of 483 years.

How true the Word of God! If only the Jewish people would believe their God—not the rabbis—and believe what God said through their prophet Isaiah, who reminded them:

> For My thoughts are not your thoughts, neither are your ways My ways, saith the Lord. For as the heavens are higher than the earth, so are My ways higher than your ways, and My thoughts than your thoughts. For as the rain cometh down and the snow from heaven, and returneth not thither, except it watereth the earth, and make it bring forth and bud, and give seed to the sower and bread to the eater; so shall My Word be that goeth forth out of My mouth: It shall not return unto Me void, except it accomplish that which I please, and make the thing whereunto I sent it prosper. (Isaiah 55:8–11)

How wonderful it would be if the Jews would just

> Seek the Lord while He may be found, call upon Him while He is near. Let the wicked forsake his way, and the man of iniquity his thoughts; and let him return unto the Lord, and He will have compassion upon him, and to our God, for He will abundantly pardon. (Isaiah 55:6,7)

Not only would they humble themselves and call upon the Lord while He is near, they would also accept the New Testament and discover how many of their Old Testament prophecies relate to the fulfillment of their Messiah's coming.

JESUS CHRIST, GOD'S TRUE MESSIAH

In witnessing to Jewish people about fulfilled prophecy in Messiah's coming and His mission, we need to show them these prophecies in their Bible and then point out what the New Testament says about their fulfillment. For example, the custom in crucifixion was to break a bone to see if the victim was really dead. In Christ's case no bone was broken since it was determined that He had already expired; hence we read, "These things were done that Scripture might be fulfilled, a bone of Him shall not be broken" (Exodus 12:43,46; Psalm 34:20 with John 19:35,36). The same is true when His hands and feet were pierced in crucifixion and when a soldier pierced His side (Zechariah 12:10 with John 19:34,37). Christians use many, many Old Testament verses in relation to fulfilled prophecy in Messiah's mission, but some are not backed up with the statement "that the Scriptures might be fulfilled." For example, Psalm 22 paints a vivid picture of a person being crucified, even though crucifixion was unheard of when this Psalm was written. Many statements in the New Testament relating to the crucifixion of Christ refer to verses in Psalm 22, but very, very few refer to this Psalm as "fulfilled Scripture," such as piercing His hands and feet, staring at His bones and not breaking them, and parting His garments (Psalm 22:14–18 with John 19:34–37; Matthew 27:35).

There are a number of New Testament verses, such as Luke 18:32 and Matthew 26:67, that speak of Messiah's sufferings, such as being spit upon and stripped naked. Isaiah tells us of one's giving his back to the smiters and his cheeks to them that plucked off his hair, hiding not his face from spitting (Isaiah 50:6), about his visage being marred more than any man (52:14). All this corresponds to what Christ endured when He was sentenced to die by crucifixion. But none of these events are referred to as prophecy being fulfilled when they occurred.

PROPHECIES FULFILLED IN CHRIST, THE MESSIAH

If any Jew wants to ignore verses that correspond to some Old Testament sayings, declaring that they are not prophecy simply because the New Testament does not make the explicit claim of prophecy being fulfilled, he will have much difficulty in honestly disbelieving the following verses that relate to Christ, the Messiah:

1. His advent—for Jews and gentiles: Genesis 3:15; Isaiah 9:6 with Galatians 4:4,5.
2. Being born of a virgin: Isaiah 7:14a with Matthew 1:22,23; Luke 1: 26–35, 2:5–7.
3. His Divinity—named *Immanuel* ("God with us," or "with us is God"): Isaiah 7:14b. Born as a child—physical birth by a virgin, *given* as the *Son,* God in the flesh who is "Wonderful, Counsellor, the Mighty God, the Everlasting Father, the Prince of Peace": Isaiah 9:6.
4. Being born of the Tribe of Judah: Genesis 49:10 with Hebrews 7:14; Revelation 5:5.
5. Being born in Bethlehem: Micah 5:2 with Matthew 2:6. Out of the thousands of villages in Asia, Europe, and Africa in Christ's day, one obscure village named Bethlehem is chosen to be the birthplace of Messiah. But there are two Bethlehems in Palestine, one in Zebulun's territory (Joshua 19:15) and the other south of Jerusalem in the land of Judah, Bethlehem Ephratah. How specific was Micah to prophesy that God's everlasting Ruler, or Messiah, would be born in "Bethlehem Ephratah of Judah" and not the other Bethlehem! *Bethlehem* means "house of bread," and how fitting that it was *this* Bethlehem where the "Bread of Life" was born! *Ephratah* means "fruitful," and how fitting this name, the place where all the fruits of salvation began! (Luke 2:1–20).
6. Herod's determination to slay all babies, including Messiah (Matthew 2). Mary and Joseph were told to take the babe Jesus to Egypt (Matthew 2:12,13). This was in fulfillment of Hosea 11:1, when God said

that He would call His Son out of Egypt (Matthew 2:15). It also fulfilled Jeremiah's prophecy about Jewish mothers weeping due to Herod's slaying all males two years of age and under (Jeremiah 31:15 with Matthew 2:16–18).

7. The child adored by great persons: Psalm 72:10 with Matthew 2:1–12. Since this psalm speaks of One greater than Solomon, it is no wonder that the Magi came with gifts worthy of God incarnate.
8. Being announced by a forerunner, John the Baptist: Isaiah 40:3 with Matthew 3:3; John 1:29.
9. His message and mission: Isaiah 61:1,2 with Luke 4:14–19; Acts 10:38.
10. Preaching in Galilee: Isaiah 9:1,2 with Matthew 4:12. He came not to destroy the Law, but to fulfill it: Matthew 5:17.
11. Taking our infirmities: Isaiah 53:4 with Matthew 8:16,17.
12. Speaking in parables: Psalm 78:2 with Matthew 13:34,35.
13. His zeal for the Lord: Psalm 69:9 with John 2:17.
14. Performing miracles: Isaiah 29:18,19 with Matthew 11:4–6.
15. Riding into Jerusalem upon an ass, lowly, and bringing salvation: Zechariah 9:9 with Matthew 21:1–11. How humiliating such an act was to a Jew who thought his Messiah would come as a "king" and enter Jerusalem in pomp and royalty! Yet Messiah was predicted as One who would come lowly, riding upon an ass *bringing salvation,* or coming to perform reconciliation for iniquity and bring in everlasting righteousness, as Daniel had prophesied (Daniel 9:25,26a).
16. Being betrayed by a friend in dipping the sop at the Passover: Psalm 41:9 with Matthew 26:20–25.
17. Being silent before His accusers: Isaiah 53:7 with Matthew 27:13,14.
18. Being smitten: Zechariah 13:7 with Matthew 26:31.
19. Being cut off—crucified, His garments and vesture (mantle) parted: Psalm 22:18; Isaiah 53; Matthew 27:35. This event fulfilled Daniel's prediction that at the end of 483 years from the command for Nehemiah to rebuild Jerusalem, the "Anointed One" will be cut off in making reconciliation for sin and bringing in everlasting righteousness by His death upon the Cross (Daniel 9:24; see also Isaiah 53:5–8, 10,11). Christ's crucifixion and death for all sinners was God's will for His Son: Psalm 110:6–8 with Hebrews 10:6–8. His death was for a purpose—a substitutionary atonement: Isaiah 53:11,12; Daniel 9:24 with Romans 3:23–26; II Corinthians 5:21, 15:3,4; Hebrews 9:11–15, 24–28.
20. Praying for His enemies: Isaiah 53:12b with Luke 23:34.
21. Being crucified between two thieves—with transgressors: Isaiah 53:12a with Matthew 27:38; Mark 15:28.
22. Being thirsty, given vinegar to drink: Psalm 69:21 with John 19:28–30.
23. Having no bones broken after death: Psalm 34:20 with John 19:31–36.
24. Having His side pierced: Zechariah 12:10 with John 19:34,37.

25. Dying: John 19:30. He fulfilled all that the prophets had said would come to pass regarding His sufferings: Acts 3:18; I Corinthians 15:3, 4a.
26. Being in the grave three days and three nights: Matthew 12:40 with Jonah 1:17.
27. With no corruption of His body; His resurrection: Psalm 16:10 with John 20:9; Acts 2:29–32, 13:33; I Corinthians 15:4b.

CONCLUSION

After His resurrection, Christ berated the two on the road to Emmaus for their unbelief in what the Scriptures had said about His death, burial, and resurrection. He said, "'O fools, and slow of heart to believe all that the prophets have spoken: Ought not [the Anointed One] Christ to have suffered these things, and to enter into His glory?' And beginning at Moses and all the prophets, he expounded unto them in all the scriptures the things concerning himself. . . . And their eyes were opened, and they knew Him; and he vanished out of their sight. And they said to one another, Did not our heart burn within us, while he talked with us by the way, and while He opened to us the scriptures?" (Luke 24:25–27,31,32).

Having purged our sins with His own precious blood (I Peter 1:18–19) and come forth from the grave with the keys of Hell and death as the victorious Redeemer (Revelation 1:18), Christ spent 40 days with His disciples before He went back to heaven to be with His Father (Acts 1:9). He is now seated on the throne with His Majesty (Father) on high (Hebrews 1:3, 10:11,12; Revelation 3:21). He is now the *one* Mediator between God and man, and ever lives to make intercession for us. He is now our High Priest after the order of Melchizedek. Because He shed His blood for the remission of our sins, a new and living way has been opened unto us to approach His throne boldly to find grace and mercy in time of need (I Timothy 2:5; Hebrews 4:14–16, 5:6, 10: 19,20). His finished work at Calvary assures us everything we need in this life and for godliness, plus a home in heaven with Him. And to think that all this was done because He loved us and preserved His Seed through His chosen people, so that we might know this Redeemer personally and have fellowship with Him through all eternity!

18

THE JEWS' RESPONSE TO THE NEW TESTAMENT MESSIAH

In the previous chapter we showed how many Old Testament portions of prophecy were linked to fulfillment in New Testament events relating to Daniel's "Anointed One" (Daniel 9:25,26a). Since the Hebrew people have thus far rejected their Scripture's Messiah, foretold according to a clear-cut timetable of events, we can ask the same question Christ asked on one occasion, "What think ye of Christ?" (Matthew 22:41-46). The fact that the Jews have rejected Him shows that they have the attitude "Our mind is made up concerning what we think of Him. Don't confuse us with facts," or as someone else said, "Their mind was like cement—thoroughly mixed and permanently set."

HISTORY CONFIRMS THE PERSON OF CHRIST

One of the Jews' most authoritative historians was Josephus, born in A.D. 37, about four years after the death, burial, and resurrection of Christ. The name of Christ was known at that time throughout the whole region of Palestine, as well as throughout Asia Minor and Europe during Josephus' lifetime. He heard and learned much about this well-known Person. He mentioned John the Baptist, a preacher of virtue who baptized proselytes, and James, the brother of Him who is called Jesus. Of Christ Himself he wrote these words: "Now there was about this time Jesus, a wise man, if it be lawful to call him a man; for he was a doer of wonderful works, a teacher of such men as receive the truth with pleasure, He drew over to him both many of the Jews and many of the Gentiles. He was [the] Christ; and when Pilate, at the suggestion of the principal men amongst them, had condemned him to the cross, those who loved him at the first did not forsake him, for he appeared to them alive again on the third day, as the divine prophets had foretold these and ten thousand other wonderful things concerning him; and the tribe of Christians so named for him, are not extinct at this day."[26]

Even Roman historians recognized the historicity of Christ. Tacitus, who recorded the persecutions of the emperor Nero, remarked that the people called

"Christians" derived their name "from one Christus who was executed in the reign of Tiberius by the procurator of Judaea, Pontius Pilate."[27] Elsewhere in his *Histories,* Tacitus refers to Christianity when alluding to the burning of the Temple of Jerusalem by Titus in A.D. 70. Christ, as an historical figure, is also mentioned by other Roman historians—Celsus, Suetonius, Severus, and Lucian the Cynic. In writing to the Emperor Trajan, Pliny the Younger made mention of the treatment given Christians by Romans, and testified of their piety and allegiance to their founder, one Christ.

Valleus Paterculus, whose writings have been verified by Priscian and Tacitus, said that he met a man in Judaea called Jesus of Nazareth, one of the most remarkable characters that he had ever met. He recorded that this Jesus cured all manner of diseases and raised the dead, and that when He cursed the orchards or fruit trees for their barrenness, they instantly withered to their roots. In referring to His wonderful works, Valleus said that Jesus did not abuse anyone with it but was always inclined to help the poor. According to Valleus, as Jesus preached and ministered, the Jews were divided in their opinion of Him, the poorer class accepting Him and the upper class hating and cursing Him behind his back, calling Him an Egyptian necromancer, although they were afraid of Him and the crowd.

PILATE'S REPORT TO CAESAR REGARDING CHRIST'S CRUCIFIXION

It only stands to reason that every governor, king, and procurator appointed by the Caesars to govern the provinces of Rome, would demand reports from time to time about situations in these areas. Logic would demand such a report from Pontius Pilate regarding the upheaval of the trial of Jesus Christ and the demand for His crucifixion by the Jews in his territory. According to Valleus Paterculus' writings, such a letter was sent to Caesar by Pilate, and it is believed to be located in the multitude of documents in the Vatican Library in Rome.[28] I will quote only the highlights of this lengthy letter.

> To Tiberius Caesar. Emperor of Rome.
>
> Noble Sovereign, Greeting: The events of the last few days in my province have been of such a character that I will give details in full as they occurred, as I should not be surprised if, in the course of time, they may change the destiny of our nation, for it seems of late that all the gods have ceased to be propitious. I am almost ready to say, "Cursed be the day I became governor of Judaea, for since then my life has been one of continual uneasiness and distress."

Pilate's letter goes on to explain the difficulty that he was having with the Jews, especially in regard to certain of their laws as opposed to the laws of Rome. Fearing insurrection, Pilate mentioned how he was ever on guard to have his soldiers ready to force the Jews into submission.

His letter ends with an account of the Jews' "forcing" themselves upon him in their demand to try one called "Jesus, the Christ" for blasphemy and for His desire to make Himself a king. He wrote:

> Three powerful parties had combined together at this time against Jesus: the Herodians, the Sadducees, and the Pharisees. All hated the Nazarene and were impatient with the Roman yoke. Jesus had been dragged before the High Priest and condemned to death. It was then that the High Priest, Caiaphas, performed a divisory act of submission and sent his prisoner to me to confirm his condemnation and secure His execution. Since Jesus was a Galilean, I sent Him to Herod, but this wily tetrarch refused to take any action.
>
> My wife came to me, weeping and throwing herself at my feet said to me: "Beware, beware, touch not this man, for He is holy. Last night I saw Him in a vision. If you will not listen to your wife, dread the curse of a Roman Senate; dread the frowns of Caesar."
>
> By this time the marble stairs groaned under the weight of the multitude. The Nazarene had been brought back to me. In asking in a severe tone what they demanded, they replied, "The death of the Nazarene." "For what crime?" "He has blasphemed; He has prophesied the ruin of the Temple; He calls Himself the Son of God, the Messiah, the King of the Jews." "Roman justice," said I, "punishes not such offences with death." "Crucify Him! Crucify Him!" cried the relentless rabble. The vociferations of the infuriated mob shook the palace to its foundations.
>
> There was one who appeared to be calm in the midst of the vast multitude, the Nazarene. After many fruitless attempts to protect Him from the fury of the merciless persecutors, I adopted a measure which at the moment appeared to me to be the only one that could save his life. I proposed, as it was their custom to deliver a prisoner on such occasions, to release Jesus and let him go free, that he might be the scapegoat, as they called it, but they said Jesus must be crucified. I reminded them of all their laws, their inconsistencies in their trials, crucifying one on the same day of judgment, but to no avail. I urged all these pleas, hoping they might awe them into subjection, but they still cried, "Crucify him! Crucify him!"
>
> I then ordered Jesus to be scourged, hoping this might satisfy them, but it only increased their fury. I called for a basin and washed my hands in the presence of the clamorous multitude, thus testifying that in my judgment Jesus of Nazareth had done nothing deserving death, but in vain. It was his life these wretched thirsted for.
>
> Often in our civil commotions have I witnessed the furious anger of the multitude, but nothing could be compared to what I witnessed on this occasion. It might have been truly said that all the phantoms of

the infernal regions had assembled at Jerusalem. The crowd appeared not to walk, but to be borne off and whirled as a vortex, rolling along in living waves from the portals of the praetorium even unto Mount Zion, with howling screams, shrieks, and vociferations such as were never heard in the seditions of the Pannonia, or in the tumults of the forum.

The day darkened . . . such as had been at the death of the great Julius Caesar. I, the governor of a rebellious province, contemplating the dreary gloom these fiends dragging to execution the innocent Nazarene. Jerusalem had vomited forth her indwellers through the funeral gate. A loud clamor was heard proceeding from Calvary, which, borne on the winds, seemed to announce an agony such as was never heard by mortal ears. Dark clouds lowered over the pinnacle of the Temple, and setting over the city covered it as with a veil. So dreadful were signs that men saw both in the heavens and on earth that they are reported to have exclaimed, "Either the author of nature is suffering or the universe is falling apart." There was a dreadful earthquake which scared the superstitious Jews almost to death.

The crowd was returning from Golgotha, and I knew the sacrifice was over. Those who betrayed and sold him, those who testified against him, those who cried, "Crucify him, we have his blood," all slunk off like cowardly curs, and washed their teeth with vinegar. An old man, who said he was Joseph of Arimathaea, begged to have his body to bury this Jesus of Nazareth. A few days after the sepulchre was found empty, His disciples proclaimed all over the country that Jesus had risen from the dead, as he had foretold. I had been told that Jesus taught a resurrection and a separation after death. I had placed guards around the sepulchre to secure his burial but there was great excitement when it was found empty. Questioning the officer in charge, he testified that on that morning when women came to embalm him, he was gone. The officer said the priests offered them money to say they had fallen asleep and his disciples had stolen his body, but there were those who had seen him.

I have heard many things about this man, how he could convert water into wine, change death into life, disease into health, calm the seas, still the storms, call up fish with a silver coin in its mouth. Now, I say, if he could do all these things, and many more, as the Jews all testify, and it was doing these things that created this enmity against Him—He was not charged with criminal offenses, nor was He charged with violating any law, nor of wronging any individual in person, and all these facts are known to thousands, as well as by His foes and by His friends. I am almost ready to say, as did Manulus at the cross, "Truly this was the Son of God."

Now, noble Sovereign, this is as near the facts in the case as I can arrive at, and I have taken pains to make the statement very full, so that you may judge my conduct upon the whole, as I hear that Antipater has said many hard things of me in this matter. With the promise of faithfulness and good wishes to my noble Sovereign:

I am your most obedient servant,
Pontius Pilate
Jerusalem of Judaea

That Jesus Christ was an historical Figure, none will deny. Both the Jewish Scriptures and the Christian New Testament, along with secular history, confirm His existence. It is indeed difficult for the critic, or anyone else for that matter, to prove the non-existence of Jesus Christ, the Son of God. Have you ever wondered why those who deny the existence of Christ always date their checks and letters after His birth?

MESSIAH OFFERED TO THE JEWS, AND REJECTED

It is difficult to find any portion of the New Testament that Jesus came to offer the Jews a restored, literal, Davidic kingdom with Himself upon the throne as their king. This is what the Jews looked for in a Messiah, but when they heard His messages, followed His mission, and saw His lifestyle, opposition to His presence grew. One wonders what would have happened if in fact a Davidic kingdom had been offered and accepted. There would have been an enthroned "Anointed One" (Christ), the "King of the Jews"; but can you imagine what would have happened when prophecy was fulfilled in His crucifixion, death, burial, and resurrection—being dethroned to suffer a rejection, and then placed back on the throne after the resurrection? This is what would have happened if a kingdom had been offered and accepted.

There is a popular teaching in Christian circles today that says that God had two plans for Christ's appearing: Plan A, in which the Jews would be offered an earthly, Davidic kingdom, and Plan B, in which, if Plan A was rejected, Christ would have to be crucified. C. I. Scofield wrote, "Jews should have believed on Christ in the flesh as King of the Jews, but as such could be no proper object of faith to the Gentiles. . . . For Gentiles the corn of wheat must fall into the ground and die; Christ must be lifted up on the cross and believed in as a sacrifice for sin, as Seed of Abraham, not David"[29] (John 12:20-24). This sounds like Plan A and Plan B.

The evidence of Scripture is that Jesus was born to die as the Lamb of God—the Lamb slain before the foundation of the world (John 1:29; Revelation 13:8). The angel told Joseph that Mary's baby would be called "Jesus: for he shall save his people from their sins" (Matthew 1:21). There is no mention here of deliverance from Rome and a Davidic kingdom. When Simeon saw the eight-day-old baby in the Temple, he said, "Mine eyes have seen thy salvation [the salvation of the Lord]" (Luke 2:25–32). Anna, the prophetess, recognized the babe as "*redemption* in Jerusalem" (Luke 2:36–38). God the Father introduced Him at His baptism as His "Son" (Matthew 3:16,17; John 1:34). John the Baptist made straight the way for Him, calling Him "Lord" and later introducing Him as "the Lamb of God, which taketh away the sin of the world" (John 1:23,29). Jesus made it known that He had come to offer eternal life (John 3:16), that He came not as king to rule but as a servant "not to be ministered unto, but to minister, and to give his life a ransom for many" (Matthew 20:28), and that He came "to seek and to save that which was lost" (Luke 19:10). He emphasized the fact that He must suffer and die (Matthew 16:21).

When Jesus stood trial before Pilate, He was asked if He was a king. Jesus replied, "Thou sayest that I am a king. To this end was I born, and for this cause came I into the world, that I should bear witness unto the truth" (John 18:37). However, He prefaced this reply to Pilate's question with these words: "My kingdom is not of this world; if my kingdom were of this world, then would my servants fight, that I should not be delivered to the Jews: but now is my kingdom not from hence [or 'not from this realm']" (18:36).

Two things are involved in Jesus' defense: (1) Yes, He is King, but not of an earthly kingdom; otherwise, He would have presented Himself as Israel's King, son of David, and Israel would have accepted Him as such. This means that the Jews never would have instigated a trial of their King before Pilate. (2) When Daniel spoke of four world powers, Babylonian, Persian, Greek, and Roman, he mentioned another kingdom that would be set up sometime during the period of these kingdoms—"a kingdom the God of heaven shall set up, a kingdom which shall never be destroyed; and the kingdom shall not be left to other people, but it shall break in pieces and consume all the kingdoms, and it shall stand forever" (Daniel 2:44). The "kingdom" over which Christ is King is the "kingdom of heaven/God," His spiritual kingdom that resides in the hearts of those who have received Him as Messiah, the kingdom that shall *never* be destroyed, a kingdom that shall stand *forever.* This could not be a millennium kingdom, simply because such a kingdom would have a beginning and an ending; the kingdom of which Christ is now King has a beginning, yes, but no ending.

If there is a "kingdom of heaven/God" now in this dispensation, there must be a ruler over such a kingdom, and Jesus said He is King over such a kingdom. What we have now does not rule out the *future* reign of Christ as King on earth in what has been called the "millennium." What we (and all Jews) need to see is the *why* of Messiah's *first* coming—to be their Saviour from sin, to offer forgiveness, to give eternal life, to place them in His spiritual kingdom, and to be King (Master) of their daily lives—their living in obedience to His commands, which their forefathers had failed to do. This Jesus mentioned to those of Emmaus that He must suffer *first* (Luke 24:26).

The apostle Paul nowhere recognized Christ as having come to be Israel's King in order to deliver them from Roman tyranny. Instead, he said, "This is a faithful saying, and worthy of all acceptation, *that Christ Jesus came into the world to save sinners . . .*" (I Timothy 1:15). God's will was for Christ to be man's substitute for sin, to fulfill the Law, to do away with the Old Covenant, to establish a New Covenant in the forgiveness of sins by offering Himself as the sacrifice *once and for all* (Hebrews 10:1–10). When Jesus met the Samaritan woman at the well, He told her that "salvation is of the Jews" (John 4:22). The Greek renders this expression as "salvation is *from* the Jews," meaning that it came through the Jewish Messiah. The prophetic Scriptures of Messiah were given to the Jews, but this Samaritan woman, who was part Jew, understood that the Jewish Messiah, or "Anointed One," would be the Christ who would come (John 4:25). Christ explained to her that He was the Messiah and opened the door of salvation to those other than regular Jews (4:39). Furthermore, Jesus also declared that *other sheep,* not of the Jewish fold, would also be added to the flock of the Messianic Shepherd (10:16). This vision should not have been strange to Jews familiar with their Scriptures: God had stated through their prophet Isaiah that Messiah would "be a light to the Gentiles" and that His plan of salvation would spread to the ends of the earth (Isaiah 49:6, 60:1–3).

When Jesus sent the Twelve to preach to the house of Israel but not to the Gentiles, they were not going out to offer a literal, earthly, Davidic kingdom to them. They were going out to "the *lost* sheep of the house of Israel" (Matthew 10:5,6). There is only one message for "lost sheep," and that is one of repentance—salvation—the kingdom of heaven/God is at hand (Matthew 3:2; Mark 1:14,15). This expression, "the lost sheep of the house of Israel," implies that not all Jews were saved just because they were Jews. Even the apostle Paul said, "For they are not all Israel, which are of Israel" (Romans 9:6). On one occasion, when Christ had a confrontation with the Jews, they bragged that Abraham was their father. Christ said that if they were the children of Abraham, they would do the works of Abraham; since they were unbelievers and hypocrites, He added that since God was not their Father, they were of their father the devil (John 8:44).

The apostle Paul, noted for being a "Hebrew of the Hebrews" before he was saved, recognized that his Bible pointed to the coming of Messiah; hence he said, "This is a faithful saying . . . that Christ Jesus came into the world to save sinners; of whom I am chief" (I Timothy 1:15). He also wrote "that Christ died for our sins according to the scriptures, And that he was buried, and that he rose again the third day" (I Corinthians 15:3,4). Jews in general deliberately blinded themselves to this truth, and when Jesus did come, "He came unto his own, and his own received him not" (John 1:11).

19

WHO CRUCIFIED CHRIST?

The Jews were blind to the prophecies that related to Messiah and His mission. Instead of rejoicing and saying, "Praise the Lord," "Amen," or "Hallelujah," their cry was "Crucify him, crucify him!" Of Calvary it was said, "There they crucified Him" (Luke 23:33).

Did the Jews actually kill or crucify their Messiah, as so many people, including Christians, have said down through the centuries? To give a definite answer, we must, of necessity, consider the background of an actual crucifixion, events relating to the "Man" Christ Jesus, including His betrayal by Judas, the accusations made against Him by the Jewish leaders, the Jewish and Roman trials, and, in particular, the demand by the Jews that He must die, that he must be sentenced by Rome.

THE "MAN" CHRIST JESUS

It is wise that we look at Christ the *Man* to get a better understanding of just who was rejected by the Jews, betrayed by a friend, and arrested. He was tried three times by the Jews, three times by the Romans, and then crucified—all in a period of less than 20 hours.

Linking Old Testament prophecy with New Testament fulfillment, we have seen that Christ's birth in Bethlehem was not His origin, but His incarnation. His birth did not establish His origin—it gave evidence of His coming as a Man in the flesh at a certain point in time. He was the combination of human and divine. He pre-existed His birth—He *is* a Person of the Triune Godhead. His birth did not introduce His beginning but it revealed His appearance in fulfillment of Old Testament Scriptures. He was revealed as God's Man at God's appointed time (Galatians 4:4,5). If He is not God, He is not the Creator and Redeemer.

> Greek learning and culture, Roman law and Roman roads, Jewish monotheism and Jewish synagogues . . . and Jewish apocalyptic and Messianic hopes prepared the world for the coming of Christ and Christianity. Divine providence can be traced everywhere in the long interval between the Testaments. The goal was the incarnation and birth of the long awaited Messiah and Savior of the world, prophesied

> so often in the [Jewish] Old Testament. To this great event all preceding centuries of world history, especially Jewish history, pointed.[30]

After the birth of Christ by the virgin Mary and His growth into manhood, He Himself acknowledged His prior existence, telling His hearers, "I came out from God. I came forth from the Father, and am come into the world" (John 16:27,28). He spoke of the glory that He had with the Father before the world existed (17:5). Every other human being entered earthly life born of natural parents and as a new person, but Jesus had neither beginning of days nor end of life (Hebrews 7:3). The Old Testament prophet Micah told us that this One who would be born in Bethlehem would be from old, from everlasting (Micah 5:2), so we have it in "black and white" from the Jewish Bible that the Messiah would have no beginning.

We see in this Man something that had never been seen in any other creature. Whatever He needed to be on any given occasion, He was. His character was complete. He would always go where people needed help, whether women, men, or children. He had no preferences. He never sought advice from anyone, for He knew all things that were in man (John 2:24,25). He never had to retract a statement that He made, for He always spoke the truth. He never had to ask for forgiveness, and never once did He confess sin, for in Him was no sin (8:46). He never had to say, "I'm sorry," for anything that he ever did or said. We find no evidence that He ever exhibited a guilty conscience or that He feared judgment. He never requested prayer for Himself. His life was an open book. This is why He could look His Father straight in the face and say, "I do always those things that please him" (8:29). Given His perfect, sinless, spotless life, He could tell the Jews to "search the Scriptures; for . . . they . . . testify of me." He did not say, "search the traditions of your fathers," but "search the Scriptures." He let them know that Moses, whom they trusted, wrote of Him, and if Moses wrote of Him and He is in their Scriptures, as well as in their midst, they should believe His Word (5:39–47). It was promised in Moses' writings that God would raise up a Prophet like unto him who would speak God's Word, and we find this fulfilled in Christ (Deuteronomy 18:15–19 with John 1:45, 6:14; Acts 3:22,23, 7:37).

Not only did the "Man" Christ Jesus give evidence of His Messiahship as the Divine Son of God, but so often He demonstrated "agape" (Divine) love for all human beings and sought to meet their needs. He would weep with those who were bereaved (John 11:35). He would feed the hungry, cure the lame, restore sight to the blind, cast out demons, raise the dead, eat with sinners, forgive sin, deliver the guilty, and give peace in the midst of storms. His life centered on others. He became weary, hungry, thirsty, and lonely, and although foxes had holes and birds of the air had nests, He had no place to lay His head (Luke 9:58). His mission was to minister unto others, not to be ministered unto (Matthew 20:28). There were times when He exhibited righteous indignation, but for a good reason. God's house (the Temple) had been made into a den of thieves, and Jesus had to forcefully drive out the money-changers (John 2:13–17). The Scribes and Pharisees had become so hypocritical that He called them serpents, a generation of vipers, and blind leaders of the blind (Matthew 23).

In summary, Jesus Christ, the perfect Man, is God's greatest gift to fallen mankind, and "whosoever believeth in him should not perish, but have everlasting life" (John 3:16; II Corinthians 9:15).

Plotting Christ's Life. Jesus came into the world as prophesied and lived and taught as no other man (John 7:46,47), but the Jewish leaders, in their unbelief in their own Scriptures, failed to recognize Him as Messiah, and they received Him not (John 1:11). Even as the common people heard Him gladly (Mark 12:37), the religious Jews constantly found fault in Him and brought numerous accusations against Him (Matthew 12:10; Luke 11:54, 23:2, 10). After Caiaphas, their high priest, informed them that Jesus was truly the Messiah, the ruling Jews, from that day forward, took counsel to put Him to death (John 11:49–53). What charges could they bring against this innocent Man? He had, for over three years, under the anointing of the Holy Spirit, gone about doing good and healing all who were oppressed of the devil, for God was with Him (Acts 10:38).

Jesus knew that He had been born to die for sin. When the Jews asked for a sign after He had cleansed the Temple, He said, in speaking of His body, "Destroy this temple, and in three days I will raise it up" (John 2:13–21). On one occasion when going up to Jerusalem, He said, "The Son of man shall be betrayed unto the chief priests and unto the scribes, and they shall condemn him to death, And shall deliver him to the Gentiles [Rome] to mock, and to scourge, and to crucify him: and the third day he shall rise again" (Matthew 20:17–19). On two occasions when the Jews sought to lay hands on Him, He said that His "hour [of death] was not yet come" (John 7:30, 8:20). In approaching the observance of His last Passover, He once again spoke of His death, illustrating it with the planting of a grain of corn (or wheat), dying but bringing forth much fruit. With this timely illustration, He said, "The hour is come, that the Son of man should be glorified . . ." (John 12:20–33). The *hour*—time—for Messiah's betrayal, arrest, trials, and crucifixion was at hand.

The Passover and the Lord's Supper. Nothing could point more fittingly to Christ's death, the shedding of His blood for sin's deliverance, His burial, and His resurrection from the grave than the fulfillment of His observing Passover and establishing the "Lord's Supper." The Passover originated in Egypt in connection with God's tenth plague of death to the firstborn upon Egypt, to induce Pharaoh to let the children of Israel make their exodus from the land of bondage. Any dwelling that had the blood of a lamb sprinkled on its doorposts, the death angel would "pass over," thereby sparing the life of the firstborn within (Exodus 12). The whole episode speaks of deliverance. Jesus applied the Passover to His body being offered and His blood being shed for deliverance from sin. His body is symbolized by bread, and His blood is symbolized by "the

Fig. 36. Silver coins typical of those received by Judas for betraying Christ.

cup" or the "fruit of the vine"—"this cup is the new testament in my blood, which is shed for you" (Luke 22:7–20). *Unleavened* bread was used, since *leavened* bread is a type of evil. *Wine* is not used because of fermentation and the impurities that result from it. Only the words *vine* or *cup* and *unleavened* bread were used, because His body was sinless and His blood was without blemish (I Corinthians 5:7b).

Judas, the Betrayer. Judas, called the "son of perdition" (John 17:12), was identified by Christ after the Passover as the one who would betray Him. Upon being identified, Judas, being motivated by Satan, immediately made a hasty exit to go to the religious Jews for the betrayal price of 30 pieces of silver (John 13:21–27; Matthew 26:14–16).

Jesus in Gethsemane. After Judas left the upper room and Jesus had instituted the Lord's Supper, the disciples sang a hymn and went out. Jesus took three of them and went to the Garden of Gethsemane to pray, fully aware of the events that were to immediately follow. He asked His heavenly Father for deliverance from this hour, knowing that God could call legions of angels to help Him escape. He had previously asked to be saved "from this hour" (Matthew 26:39; John 12:27).

Save Me From This Hour[31]

Save Me from the hour of loneliness in the Garden when My disciples sleep.
Save Me from the hour of drinking the bitter dregs of this sin-cup.
Save Me from the hour of betrayal by one of My friends.
Save Me from the hour when all My disciples will forsake Me and flee.
Save Me from the hour of Peter's denial—from hearing one of My very own curse and swear at the mention of My name.
Save Me from the hour when the Jewish rulers accuse Me of blasphemy.

Save Me from the hour when I hear My own people say, "Crucify Him."
Save Me from the hour when My own people reject Me for a condemned criminal.
Save Me from the hour of Pilate's blindness to truth.
Save Me from the hour of the brutal lash of the scourge.
Save Me from the hour of those who mimic My kingship by placing a crown of thorns on My brow, clothe Me with a scarlet robe, and put a reed in My hand.
Save Me from the hour when I am identified as a criminal between two thieves.
Save Me from the hour when I must bear in My body the sins of the whole world.
Save Me from the hour of humiliation on the cross when those I came to save mock Me.
Save Me from the hour when My own Father turns His back on Me.
Save Me from the hour of tasting death for every man.

Yet, in His pleading to be saved from this hour, He fell on His face and passionately, but graciously, prayed, "O my Father, if it be possible, let this cup pass from me: nevertheless not as I will, but as thou wilt" (Matthew 26:39).

Jesus Betrayed and Arrested. After praying, Judas appeared on the scene to betray Christ with a kiss, followed by a great multitude—people, soldiers, chief priests, and elders of the Jewish hierarchy. We find the account of this dastardly, malicious act recorded in Matthew 26:47–50; Mark 14:43–46; Luke 22:47,48; and John 18:1–5.

Judas was willing to sacrifice Christ to a mob bent on killing Him, but he was a victim sacrificed to the curse of money—the love of money being the root of all evil (I Timothy 6:10). Money carries with it, together with the filth of the hands that have clutched and handled it, a contagious desire for crime. Its desire is more deadly than all the diseases combined, and it is no wonder that some have called it filthy lucre. But this is what Judas wanted, and this is what Judas got, when he betrayed the Son of God into cruel hands. Actually, Judas did not offer himself as a cutthroat criminal, but as a merchant doing business in blood. This is the same Judas who had been chosen among the Twelve to carry the Gospel to the world. Over three years Jesus had kept him with Him, had him in all His travels, had eaten, slept, and prayed with him. He had washed and wiped his feet in the upper room. But at the table the die was cast—money meant more to Judas than being a friend to the One who had so lovingly treated him as one of His own.

It was night when Judas left the upper room to go to the chief priests for the betrayal money, and it was night, in the glow of the mob's lanterns and torches, when Judas planted the betrayal kiss upon Jesus. From this moment the betrayer knew no peace. He had gone out in darkness to be paid for betrayal, and it was in darkness that he turned his back on Jesus. He "stood" with the crowd, and to stand with the crowd is to betray Christ. The last word of Jesus to Judas was "friend." The guilt of the "betrayer" so bore on his conscience that he went back to the chief priests, repented, cast down the 30 pieces of silver, saying "I have betrayed the innocent blood," departed, and went out and hanged himself (Matthew 27:1–8). It is no wonder that Christ said of this man, "Woe unto that man by whom the Son of man is betrayed! It had been good for that man if he had not been born" (26:24).

The Jewish Trials of Jesus. After Judas gave the betrayal kiss, Jesus was arrested, bound, and taken to the house of Annas. Although Caiaphas was the high priest, his predecessor Annas still retained it (John 18:12–14). The Sanhedrin certainly felt that they had the right and jurisdiction to try Jesus because of the charge brought against Him, namely blasphemy. He had claimed to be one with the Father (John 10:30), He had forgiven sin, the prerogative of God alone (Mark 2:7–11), and He had said that He was the Christ, "the Son of the Blessed" (Mark 14:61,62).

The purpose of the trial of Christ was capital punishment. The Jews wanted Christ killed, and to condemn Him, their own ecclesiastical trial had to take place first. Knowing that under Roman law they did not have the power to inflict this penalty, they first had to convict their "criminal" before presenting Him to the Roman authorities. Knowing also that Jesus had many followers, they planned to capture, try, and convict Him so that all would be done after sundown and before daybreak. How true the saying, "Men loved darkness rather than light, because their deeds were evil" (John 3:19). The only ones who would know what was being done were the conspirators, and the execution would be left to be carried out after sunrise the same day (a day being reckoned from sundown to sundown).

Just as any civilized nation has rules and regulations for an orderly trial, so did the Jews, according to their Talmud. There were a number of steps that had to be followed in a Hebrew trial, especially if the accused was guilty of a crime worthy of death.[32]

A court could not meet for capital punishment during feast days (Matthew 26:4,5). When a trial was in order, before anything else was done, the morning sacrifice had to be offered.

All the Sanhedrin (judges) needed to be assembled in the appointed place—the Temple, in this case. The Sanhedrin, the highest tribunal of the Jews, was comprised of 70 men: 23 priests, 23 scribes, 23 elders, and the presiding officer, the high priest (see Numbers 11:16,17).

Once convened, the Sanhedrin examined all the witnesses. No one could speak against the accused until someone had spoken in his favor. All evidence had to be heard. Testimony of the witnesses had to agree, and all evidence had to be established in the mouths of two or three witnesses (Deuteronomy 17:6, 19:15); if not, the testimony was rejected. Each witness was required to give evidence separately and in the presence of the accused, and the evidence needed to be corroborated *both times.* No witness could be bribed to testify. The accused could testify on his behalf but was not compelled to do so, nor could he be compelled to testify against himself. A confession alone was not acceptable as a basis for conviction.

Afterward, there was a debate and balloting on the innocence or guilt of the accused. If any member of the Sanhedrin had a preconceived idea about the guilt or innocence of the accused, the case was thrown out of court. The youngest voted first, then the next youngest, then the juniors, and last the seniors. This was done so that the younger members would not be influenced by the elders. If the defendant was acquitted, he was freed immediately. If convicted, the court met again the *next day,* discussed all the evidence again, and took another vote (the second trial was like an appeal). If a judge voted "not guilty" in the first trial, he could not change his vote to "guilty" in the second trial. But if he voted "guilty" the first time, he could change his vote to "not guilty" after due consideration of all the evidence. The verdict of the court could not be unanimous: A simultaneous and unanimous verdict of guilt on the day of this trial had the effect of an acquittal. If found guilty both days, there was no delay in the execution of the person (if the sentence was death). The execution was at sundown, and the guilty person was stoned to death, which was the Jewish method of capital punishment (Leviticus 24:16).

In their haste to condemn Christ, the Jewish leaders broke almost every existing rule of the law of Moses, the Mishna, and their customs. Justice was abused and disregarded. They actually raped their own judicial and ecclesiastical system, with the result that His trial was illegal from start to finish.

To begin with, the Sanhedrin decreed that Jesus should be killed (Matthew 26:1–5). This was pre-trial judgment. "No judge could sit in judgment if he had been at enmity with the accused or if he had formed a preconceived idea concerning him."[33]

The arrest was made without the issuance of a legal warrant. It was not the result of a legal mandate from a court whose intention it was to conduct a legal trial.

His arrest was effected through the information of a traitor, which violated Moses' code: "Thou shalt not go up and down as a talebearer among the people: neither shalt thou stand against the blood of thy neighbor" (Leviticus 19:15–18 with Luke 22:1–6, 47–53).

Jesus was arrested by members of the Sanhedrin (Luke 22:52–54).

His arrest took place at night (Mark 14:17,27,32,43–66).

All the Sanhedrin were not present in Annas' house (Numbers 11:16,17).

Jesus was struck physically by a member (John 18:22) and was spit upon (Matthew 26:67).

He was judged and bound over to the high priest (John 18:24).

The trial before Caiaphas, the high priest, took place before the morning sacrifice.

The witnesses could not agree (Mark 14:56).

Jesus testified against Himself (Mark 14:56, 60–63).

The high priest rent his clothes (Matthew 26:65). An ordinary Israelite could tear his garment as a sign of grief, but priests were forbidden to do so because their vestments were made according to specific instructions from the Lord and were figurative of their office.

The trials before Annas and Caiaphas were in their houses, not in the proper place, the Temple (Luke 22:54). The sentence of condemnation also had to be pronounced in the Temple.

The high priest could never say that the accused was innocent or guilty. Yet Caiaphas did (Matthew 26:65).

Jesus was never afforded the opportunity for someone to speak in His favor (remember that all the disciples had forsaken him: Mark 14:50).

He was found guilty upon his own uncorroborated testimony.

He was condemned to death by *all* the Sanhedrin (Mark 14:64). Not only were Jews good at twisting their own laws to suit their desires, but they were shrewd politicians as well. They knew Pilate would reject decisions that they had made on religious grounds, so they changed the charge from blasphemy to sedition, knowing Pilate must seriously consider this false allegation (Luke 23:2). When Pilate was approached, he asked, "What accusation bring ye against this man?" They made it clear that they were more anxious for him to confirm their judgment of death than to dispense justice. Pilate advised them to go away and judge Him by their own law (John 18:28–31a). But they pressed the issue all the more since they wanted Jesus dead. Pilate then requested a formal incriminating charge. These shrewd religious politicians brought not only one, but three: (1) Jesus had perverted the nation, (2) He had prohibited paying tribute to Caesar, and (3) He had claimed to be their King (Luke 23:2). Pilate ignored the first two, but considered their accusation that Jesus claimed to be a king, since this would be treason against Rome. Trying to get Jesus to incriminate Himself, which was contrary to Roman law, he failed and said to the Jews, "I find in him no fault" (John 18:34–38). Jesus should have been released immediately, but when the Jews accused Jesus of stirring up the people in Judea and Galilee, Pilate sent Jesus to Herod, who was in charge of the Galilee province and was in Jerusalem at the time (Luke 23:7). Herod, failing to find any legal evidence for a death sentence, sent Him back to Pilate. Pilate again sought to release Him (John 19:12a).

Luke tells us that "the same day Pilate and Herod were made friends together" (Luke 23:12). Pilate and Herod had not gotten along before, but now they were friends. They were both conspirators against Caesar, and the Jews knew this. Immediately the Jews said to Pilate, "If thou let this man go, thou art not Caesar's friend" (John 19:12b). Pilate knew that if he released Jesus, the Jews would file charges against him before Caesar and Pilate himself would be condemned to death. Though warned by his wife to have nothing to do in this matter, Pilate tried once more to free Jesus by releasing a prisoner at the

Passover. The Jews demanded the release of the criminal Barabbas, and when Pilate asked, "What shall I do then with Jesus which is called Christ? They *all* say unto him, Let him be crucified" (Matthew 27:15–22).

Pilate Washes His Hands.[34] On three occasions Pilate said, "I find no fault in this man" (Luke 23:4, 14; John 18:38). "When Pilate saw that he could prevail nothing, but that rather a tumult was made, he took water, and washed his hands before the multitude, saying, I am innocent of the blood of this just [righteous] person" (Matthew 27:24). What was the significance of this act by Pilate? All governors of Rome had to be trained in the religion, culture, and customs of those over whom they would rule, and Pilate knew God's law as found in Deuteronomy 21:1–9. Where there was murder and no criminal to blame, Israel's elders would gather where the body was and, confident that there was no guilt upon the village, wash their hands in token of the innocence of the people.

What a stinging rebuke this must have been to the accusers of Christ when Pilate called for water to wash his hands. They understood exactly what he was saying: "This is murder—I am innocent. If you crucify Him, you are acknowledging your own law and *you* are guilty of murder." But they cried, "His blood be on us, and on our children." Every Jew in that throng who joined in that utterance, as well as every Jew who heard it without protest, was familiar with Numbers 35:33, where, in no uncertain terms, the Lord God Jehovah stated that He would bring retribution upon those who shed innocent blood. They were equally familiar with Moses' law, where the God of justice and holiness said, "There is no sanctuary for such that shed innocent blood" (Deuteronomy 19:10–13). They also knew the utterance of God that the "blood of the innocent will surely fall upon the heads of those who slay such" (Joshua 2:19). There was not a single Jew in that throng but who understood that God's Word taught that it is death to slay the Lord's Anointed (II Samuel 1:16). They had been told that Christ was God's Messiah or Anointed (John 11:49–52), but with a knowledge of truth and with an understanding of God's stern and righteous judgment, they willfully lifted their voices in the face of an outraged heaven in that awful cry, "Let him be crucified. . . . His blood be on us, and on our children" (Matthew 27:25). God heard them, their wish was granted, Pilate had Jesus scourged, and they led Him away to be crucified (27:26).

Pilate's washing his hands was adding insult to injury. But he was not through with the Jews yet. Although he gave permission for the Roman soldiers to crucify Christ, he also showed his malice toward the Jews by placing upon the cross of Jesus the title, "JESUS OF NAZARETH THE KING OF THE JEWS" (John 19:19). How irritating and chafing this must have been to the Jews as they watched Him die! Instead of a moment's reflection upon what Caiaphas had said regarding His death (John 11:43–52), the chief priests just sat there, and as they watched him agonize in pain and die, they had the audacity to mock Him (Matthew 27:33–43).

Fig. 37. Calvary, Place of the Skull.

Not once is it recorded in the New Testament that any Jew among those guilty of demanding His death ever repented, attesting to His innocence. But some unbelievers attested to His innocence:

Judas did, saying, "I have betrayed the innocent blood" (Matthew 27:3,4).

Pilate's wife did, calling Jesus "that just man" (Matthew 27:19).

Pilate did, calling Him "this just person" (Matthew 27:24) and saying, "I find in him no fault" (John 18:38).

Herod did, saying that He had done "nothing worthy of death" (Luke 23:15).

The thief on the cross did, saying, "This man hath done nothing amiss"; he became a believer in Jesus (Luke 23:39–43).

The Roman centurion, having seen what was done, "glorified God, saying, Certainly this was a righteous man" (Luke 23:47).

Jesus Was Forsaken. What an awful indictment—Jesus crucified and forsaken! To be lonely is a tragic thing to experience, but to be forsaken is far worse. *To forsake* means "to leave, to utterly abandon." Jesus was forsaken to a degree that no other man has ever known, or will know. He was utterly forsaken

- By the world He created: John 1:3 with 1:10.
- By the nation from which He sprang. He was from the Seed of Abraham, the Tribe of Judah, the family of David. He was a Jew according to the flesh, but when He came to His own people, they received Him not: John 1:11.
- By His own village, Nazareth, where He spent His childhood. When He preached His first sermon, they sought to kill Him, and He never returned to do mighty works there, because they did not believe in Him. No prophet is accepted in his own country: Luke 4:16–30.
- By His own brothers. Yes, He had half-brothers and sisters. Joseph "knew not [Mary]" *until after Jesus was born* (Matthew 1:25). His siblings did not believe on Him: Matthew 13:55,56; John 7:5. Evidently, they believed on Him after His resurrection, for they were with their mother, Mary, awaiting the descent of the Holy Spirit on the Day of Pentecost: Acts 1:14.
- By the disciples whom He trained: Mark 14:50 with Zechariah 13:7.
- By His own eternal Father when He hung on the cross and God "spared Him not": Matthew 27:46 with Romans 8:32.

He was forsaken in a way that you and I, through faith in Him, need never be. "Lo, I am with you *alway*" and "I will never leave thee, nor forsake thee" (Matthew 28:20; Joshua 1:5). He is present *in* every believer (Colossians 1:27).

DID THE JEWS CRUCIFY CHRIST?

After all the evidence presented in both the Jewish and the Roman trials, there is but one answer to the question, Did the Jews crucify Christ? Christ answered the question for us: "The chief priests and . . . the Scribes [Jews] . . . shall condemn [Me] to death, and . . . the Gentiles [Romans] shall mock, scourge, and crucify Me" (Matthew 20:17–19). The Jews did not perform the act of crucifixion. They did not drive the spikes through His hands and feet and erect the cross upon which He died. But they were the instigators of the whole dastardly act. They were guilty by association, just as King David was guilty of Uriah's death when he wrote the letter instructing Joab to send Uriah into the thick of battle that he might be killed (II Samuel 11:14–17). There is absolutely no way that the Sanhedrin can plead innocent of their crime.

Christ had come unto His own, and they rejected Him. They chose Barabbas instead, and in their demand to have Jesus crucified, they proved their guilt by saying, "His blood be on us, and on our children" (Matthew 26:15–25; Mark 15:6–14; Luke 23:13-24; John 18:28–19:16). This desire of the Jews to have the blood of Jesus upon them and their children has been literally fulfilled down through the centuries. Because of this, the Jew has known no peace, has had no Temple or sacrifice, has had no home until recently, and is being trodden down, blinded (hardened) in part, until the fullness of the Gentiles comes in or, to put it another way, until the full number of Gentiles is saved (Romans 11:25). One portion of their Scripture that the Jews have never seemed to learn is "Be sure *your* sin will find *you* out" (Numbers 32:23). The New Testament counterpart is "Be not deceived; God is not mocked: for whatsoever a man soweth, *that* shall he also reap" (Galatians 6:7).

DID THE ROMANS CRUCIFY CHRIST?

Let us take everything into consideration: Pilate's capitulation to the Sanhedrin's demand that Christ be put to death (we must accuse the Romans of the actual act of crucifixion), the scourging, driving the spikes into Christ's hands and feet, and erecting the cross. Although this was Rome's method of capital punishment, and although the Jewish leaders saw to it that Rome carried out this cruel performance, the fact remains that these *two—the Jewish religious leaders* and *Pilate*—are guilty: *both* are responsible.

WHO REALLY DID CRUCIFY CHRIST?

We have just accused both the religious leaders of the Jews and Pilate of being the culprits who crucified Christ. Is there another party responsible, another guilty party involved? Yes, there is. *I* crucified Christ! *You* crucified Christ! *The whole human race* crucified Christ! "Christ died for *our* sins according to the scriptures" (I Corinthians 15:3). No sinner could ever atone for his sins (Ephesians 2:8,9). No human being by any means could redeem his own brother (Psalm 49:7). We "all have sinned, and come short of the glory of God" and "the wages of sin is death" (Romans 3:23, 6:23a).

Ever since Adam disobeyed God, the human race has been contaminated with sin (Romans 5:12, 19). Only a blood sacrifice can atone for sin (Leviticus 17:10). God, who is sovereign and who knows the end from the beginning, provided a substitute for lost mankind through "the Lamb slain from the foundation of the world" (Revelation 13:8). All blood sacrifices ordained of God for sin in the Old Testament were but "shadows" (a foreshadow of the *real* sacrifice to come) (Hebrews 10:1–10). The blood of bulls and goats could not purify, but the *Fulfiller* of the "shadows" did by shedding His own blood for the forgiveness of sins (Ephesians 2:7; Revelation 1:5).

Christ's death for lost sinners was in the foreknowledge and plan of God from eternity past (Acts 2:23,24). We "were not redeemed with corruptible things, as silver and gold, . . . but with the precious blood of Christ, as of a lamb without blemish and without spot, Who verily was *foreordained* before the foundation of the world, but was manifest in these last times . . . *for* [*us*]" (I Peter 1:18–20; Titus 3:5). The instruments that God used to fulfill His plan of salvation for lost human beings were the Jewish leaders and the Roman government. The rejection of Christ by the Jews and His crucifixion by Pilate did not affect the purpose of the coming of Messiah, because He was ordained to come and finish what God had planned for redemption, righteousness, and eternal life. "But those things, which God before had shewed by the mouth of all his prophets, that [His] Christ should suffer, *he hath fulfilled*" (Acts 3:18). No matter how much one wants to blame the Jews or Pilate, for Christ's crucifixion, all he or she needs to do is look in the "mirror of God's Word," and there will be seen the real crucifier of Jesus Christ.

CONCLUSION

Although Jews in general reject the New Testament as God's inspired Word, *nowhere* does it contradict a single Old Testament prophecy relating to Messiah (Christ). Even secular history is on the side of the New Testament writers. Josephus, a Jewish historian himself, confirms Christ's existence and His works. He even mentions John the Baptist as a preacher of virtue who baptized proselytes and James, the brother of Him who is called Jesus.

THE MISSION OF CHRIST AND THE PURPOSE OF HIS COMING

1. To fulfill prophecy: Matthew 1:22,23.
2. To manifest God's love: John 3:16; I John 4:9.
3. To defeat the devil: I John 3:8; Hebrews 2:14.
4. To bear witness to the truth: John 18:37.
5. To reveal the Father: Matthew 11:27.
6. To fulfill the law: Matthew 5:7.
7. To bring about redemption: Titus 2:14.
8. To redeem those under the curse of the Law: Galatians 4:4,5.
9. To seek the lost: Luke 19:10.
10. To call sinners to repentance: Luke 5:32.
11. To save sinners: I Timothy 1:15.
12. To give His life a ransom for many: Matthew 20:28; John 1:29.
13. To die as our sacrifice for sin: I John 4:10.
14. To taste death for every man: Hebrews 2:9.
15. To provide a new deliverance: Galatians 1:4; II Corinthians 5:17.
16. To pave a new way to approach God: Hebrews 10:19,20.
17. To lead us to righteousness: II Corinthians 5:21.
18. To secure a new acceptance to God: Hebrews 4:16; I Peter 3:18.
19. To give us everlasting life: John 3:16, 10:10a.
20. To lay a base for a new fellowship: I Thessalonians 5:10.
21. To provide an abundant life: John 10:10b; II Peter 1:3.
22. To involve the believer in a new life: Galatians 2:20.
23. To empower believers by the Holy Spirit: John 14:16,17; Acts 1:8.
24. To build His Church: Matthew 16:18; Ephesians 5:25.
25. To win a new Gentile family: Matthew 12:18; Acts 15:14; I Peter 2:9,10.
26. To promote humility: Philippians 2:5–8.
27. To beget love: I John 3:16.

28. To encourage believers to put Him first in their lives: Matthew 10:32–42.
29. To become Lord of their lives: Romans 14:9.
30. To give us an example to live by: I Peter 2:21.
31. To be to the praise of His glory, having trusted in Him: Ephesians 1:12.
32. To herald a message of hope after death: I Thessalonians 4:13–18.
33. To make a new home in heaven for believers: John 14:1–3; I Peter 1:3–5.
34. To assure us that we will be like Him when we see Him: I John 3:2.
35. To provide the riches of His grace for all eternity: Ephesians 2:7.

Though He was tried unfairly and illegally, and judged unjustly, the outcome fulfilled God's plan for man's redemption, as outlined in the Jewish Old Testament. Before the Jews He died because He claimed to be (and was) the Son of God and Messiah, and before Pilate He died as King of the Jews. He died for all our offenses, but glory be to God, He was raised the third day for our justification! (Romans 4:25). God would not allow His son to see corruption, so, according to the Old Testament Scriptures that the apostle Paul used, "Christ died . . . was buried . . . and rose again the third day (I Corinthians 15:3–4). Christ now has become our great High Priest:

> God, who at sundry times and in divers manners spake in time past unto the fathers by the prophets, Hath in these last days spoken unto us by his Son, whom he hath appointed heir of all things, by whom also he made the worlds; Who being the brightness of his glory, and the express image of his person, and upholding all things by the word of his power, when he had by himself purged our sins, sat down on the right hand of the Majesty on high; Seeing then that we have a great high priest, that is passed into the heavens, Jesus the Son of God, . . . being come an high priest of good things to come, . . . by his own blood he entered in once into the holy place, having obtained eternal redemption for us. So Christ was once offered to bear the sins of many; and unto them that look for him shall he appear the second time without sin unto salvation. (Hebrews 1:1–3, 4:14, 9:11,12,28)

20

FROM CALVARY TO THE ACTS OF THE APOSTLES

When Jesus said "It is finished" on the cross and died, Joseph of Arimathaea, a Jew and secret believer in Christ, boldly came out of hiding and asked Pilate for permission to take the body of Jesus from the cross and bury Him. He was joined by another secret Jewish believer, Nicodemus, who then stood up for Jesus and helped Joseph prepare Jesus' body. Nicodemus had brought spices, and the two prepared the body, wrapped Him in grave clothes, and laid Him in Joseph's newly hewn tomb. A seal was placed over the opening to assure all that the body was there (John 19:38–42; Matthew 27:57–61).

When the Jewish leaders looked on Him who was pierced, they remembered that they had heard Jesus speak of His coming forth from the grave after being in it three days and three nights. Jesus told them of this when they asked for a sign and He referred to Jonah being in the belly of the fish for that period of time (Matthew 12:38–41). Fearful that His body might be stolen, they went to Pilate, saying they remembered that *this deceiver* had said that He would be in the grave for that period of time, and requested that a watch be set to see that there would be no resurrection. They were told to take care of the matter themselves, so they sealed the rolling stone. After Jesus arose, the guard found the tomb empty. They reported it to the elders, who bribed the soldiers to say that the disciples stole the body while they slept (Matthew 27:62–66, 28:11–15).

CHRIST'S RESURRECTION AND ASCENSION

Without a shadow of a doubt, Christ's resurrection is God's stamp of approval on His death for man's sins. Paul assured us that if Christ be not risen, our faith is in vain and we are still in our sins (I Corinthians 15:12–17). Christ gave assurance of His resurrection to the women at the empty tomb and to His disciples (even though Thomas doubted at first), and on one occasion He appeared to over 500 people at once (15:6). Christ's death, burial, and resurrection has established once and for all the validity of the Old Testament Scriptures that the "Seed of the woman" promised in the Garden of Eden *would be fulfilled* and that the Lamb slain from before the foundation of the world would provide a salvation for any who would take God at His Word and trust in Christ as their very own personal Saviour (Genesis 3:15; Revelation 13:8b; John 5:24).

After Christ came forth from the grave, He spent 40 days primarily with His disciples, giving instructions to follow after He returned to His Father in heaven. His most important challenge was the "Great Commission," going forth to preach the Gospel to every creature, to baptize the new converts, and to teach the babes in Christ to observe all the things that He had taught them during His earthly ministry (Matthew 28:18–20).

THE DAY OF PENTECOST

Just before He was caught up into heaven, His believers were told to return to Jerusalem and wait for the promise of the Father, the descent of the Holy Spirit upon them to empower them as they went forth to witness for Him (Acts 1:4,5,8). This they did, and while they were in the upper room praying, the Holy Spirit descended and all were filled with the Spirit of God. As they spoke in other national tongues, the thousands of different nationalities marvelled as they recognized their own language and asked, "What does this mean?" Peter took advantage of their interest and stood up to preach, saying that this was the fulfillment of the prophecy of Joel and that the time had come for God to pour out His Spirit upon any and all who would trust in His only begotten Son, Jesus Christ (Joel 2:28–32). As Peter continued his sermon, he played the role of evangelist in reminding the Jewish listeners how Christ had come in fulfillment of God's determinate counsel and foreknowledge, and how the local Jewish people cried out for their Messiah's crucifixion. But Peter hastened to add that this same Jesus came forth from the grave as both Lord and Christ.

When the local and foreign Jews had heard Peter's message, they asked "What shall we do?" They did not ask, "What must we do to be saved?" It sounds like they wanted to know what they had to do to get the filling of the Holy Spirit. So Peter gave an evangelistic invitation to repent of their sins, proving that they meant it by renouncing their present religious beliefs, and to be baptized as an outward act that they were going to serve the Lord; then they would receive the gift of the Holy Spirit. This is God's promise to all who call upon the name of the Lord (Acts 2:1–41).

What a sermon, and what results! About 3,000 Jews accepted Christ as Saviour and were added to the fellowship of believers, God's faithful remnant. Those who remained in Jerusalem continued in the apostle's doctrine and had fellowship together, in breaking of bread and in prayers. Those who returned to their homes in their various countries did likewise, making the Gospel known to others (Acts 2:42–47).

THE ACTS OF THE APOSTLES

So much has been said about the *unbelieving* Jews, but as we leave the wonderful happenings after Peter's sermon, we take up the apostles' ministry and the response they got from preaching the resurrection of Christ. To the credit of many rank-and-file Jews, there was acceptance of Christ as Messiah prior to Christ's crucifixion, even among many of the chief priests (John 11:45, 12:42). Not only were these Jews identified with Christ, but all the apostles were Jews. In addition to the almost 3,000 saved on the Day of Pentecost, Peter had occasion to preach again to a multitude of people, and about 5,000 were saved (Acts 4:4).

Anytime there is a great movement of God among His people, the devil will do all in his power to stop it. He will employ any method of evil to downgrade God and His people. No sooner had Peter's preaching brought almost 8,000 people to Christ, than the Pharisees and the chief priests picked up where they had left off mocking Jesus at the cross and accusing the disciples of stealing His body from the grave. After Peter finished his second sermon, they were so filled with indignation that the apostles were arrested and warned to stop preaching about Jesus. Peter boldly told the Jewish hierarchy that in order for them to be right with God, they needed to accept Christ as their Messiah, that there was no other name under heaven by which they might be saved (Acts 4:12). They were incensed, ordered the Apostles not to preach again in His name, and released them. Peter, having told his accusers that he had to obey God rather than man, just kept on preaching about Jesus. They were arrested again, and there was a debate about killing them. Gamaliel, a Hebrew teacher, persuaded the Pharisees to calm down, reminding them that if God was in what the apostles were doing, it would be impossible for the Pharisees to stop their efforts, since they would be fighting against God. They agreed with Gamaliel, beat the apostles, and again commanded them not to speak the name of Jesus in public (5:17–42).

Stephen, a devout Christian Jew, was stoned to death because he dared tell those of the synagogue and the high priest concerning the unbelief of Israel (Acts 6:8–7:60). Saul of Tarsus, Hebrew of the Hebrews, consented to Stephen's death and made havoc of the Church, entering into houses of believers and arresting them. Wherever he went, he boldly breathed out threatenings and slaughter against Christ's disciples (8:1–3, 9:1). When King Herod had killed James, he arrested Peter to kill him too, because it pleased the Jews (12:1,2).

After Saul of Tarsus "saw the Light" and trusted Jesus, he knew that the One whom he had persecuted was Messiah. Yielding to Him, he became Paul the Apostle (Acts 9:1–20; I Corinthians 15:6–9). What a rude awakening he received when, no sooner had he been converted from Judaism and began to testify of Christ, than the principle of "sowing and reaping" was applied to him (Galatians 6:7). The Jews of Damascus took counsel to kill him. He was detained by the governor of Damascus, but was befriended by fellow believers and managed to escape over the city wall in a basket (Acts 9:20–25; II Corinthians 11:32,33). From that moment on, his life was filled with threats and persecution by his fellow kinsmen. As a proud Jew, due to his heavenly experience, he was given a "thorn in the flesh" to buffet (torment) him lest he become conceited (II Corinthians 12:1–7). His "thorn" was not an eye problem, contrary to popular belief. He had *good* vision ("set his eyes on": Acts 13:9; "beheld": 17:23). "Thorn in the flesh" is an Old Testament expression that refers to *people* (Numbers 33:55; Joshua 23:13; Judges 2:3). Paul's thorn was a "messenger of Satan," meaning individuals or a collection of people to oppose his preaching the Gospel.

Satan used Paul's own kinsmen, the Jews, to hinder his ministry since he was determined "not to know any thing among [men], save Jesus Christ and him crucified." Paul said that the Jews scourged him five times, each time with 40 stripes minus one, and that three times he was beaten with rods. He was often in perils by his brethren (II Corinthians 11:24–26). In his missionary travels, he would usually go to the Jewish synagogues first, but Jewish opposition was always ready to meet him, sometimes threatening his very life. At Lystra, Jews from Antioch and Iconium stirred up the people, who stoned Paul and left him for dead (Acts 14:19). In Thessalonica, the Jewish leaders incited a riot and sought to seize him, but failed (17:5–9). When he visited Jerusalem and took a Greek into the Temple, the mob almost lynched him (21:27–31). He was buffeted, persecuted, reviled, defamed, made the filth (the scum or garbage of humanity) of the world, and became the offscouring (dregs) of all things (I Corinthians 4:11–13). There was no easing of opposition against this saint by the Jews. From his arrest in the Temple to his imprisonment in Rome, his life was always in peril because of the hatred that the Jews had for him because of his conversion to Christianity (Acts 21:1–28:29).

As in the case of believers and unbelievers, many Jews did trust Christ as God's promised Messiah, but there were those who did not. Paul's heart was broken for their unbelief when he had to tell them these last words: "Well spake the Holy Ghost by Esaias the prophet unto our fathers, Saying, Go unto this people, and say, Hearing ye shall hear, and shall not understand; and seeing ye shall see, and not perceive: For the heart of this people is waxed gross, and their ears are dull of hearing, and their eyes have they closed; lest they should see with their eyes, and hear with their ears, and understand with their heart, and should be converted, and I should heal them. Be it known therefore unto you, that the salvation of God is sent unto the Gentiles, and that they will hear it." (Isaiah 6:9,10 with Acts 28:24–28). This prophetic portion of Isaiah ties in closely with Paul's statement concerning most of the Jews in this age—"blindness in part is happened to Israel" (Romans 11:1–10,25). One cannot deny, according to the New Testament, that many, many Jews of Christ's day and the early New Testament period of the Church were definitely anti-Christian. *But thanks be to God for the believing Jews,* the faithful remnant who ignored the oral laws and helped to preserve the Word of God that we might have it today!

The early Church was comprised mostly of Jews, who gave us sound Biblical doctrine as they continued in the teachings of the Apostles (Acts 2:42).

They did not follow the "traditions of their fathers." The Bible points out that salvation is *from* the Jews, having been prophesied in their Old Testament Scriptures and fulfilled in the Jewish Messiah, Christ. Thus Christians of all races should be grateful to those Jews who had a part in this "so great salvation" that has been provided for all fallen, lost mankind. It is apparent that the Jews were predominant in the success of the early Church period.

SALVATION FOR GENTILES

When the chief priests and elders of the people questioned Christ's authority, He gave them a history lesson about their forefathers. Israel was to have been God's "vine," a fruit-bearing nation. Having been brought out of Egypt, God planted them in the Promised Land (Psalm 80:8). Instead of bearing fruit, she bore *wild grapes* and became an *empty vine* (Isaiah 5:1,2; Hosea 10:1) and a *degenerate plant* (Jeremiah 2:21). Having sent servants (prophets) unto them for fruit, they beat some, killed some, and stoned some (Jeremiah 20:2, 26:20–23; II Chronicles 24:2). The owner of the vineyard (God) finally sent His Son to them for fruit, but they killed Him. At this point, Jesus asked them what should be done to those who killed the heir, the Son of God. They said that the lord of the vineyard "will miserably destroy those wicked men, and will let out [lease] his vineyard unto other husbandmen, which shall render him the fruits in their seasons." Then Jesus replied, "Therefore say I unto you, The kingdom of God shall be taken from you [the Jews], and given to a nation bringing forth the fruits thereof. . . . And when the chief priests and Pharisees had heard his parables, they perceived that he spake of them" (Matthew 21:33–45).

These Jews were absolutely right—he was speaking to them as the representatives of the Jewish people. Having come to His own and having been rejected, Christ now turns to *anyone* who would receive Him (John 1:11,12). Blinded, Jews in general were "spared not," and God "did visit the Gentiles, to take out of them a people for his name" (Romans 11:21a; Acts 15:14). This is not to say that a Jew cannot be saved. *God forbid!* Anyone who calls upon the name of the Lord, no matter what nationality he may be, can be saved (Romans 10:12,13).

With the establishment of the Church and the inclusion of Gentiles apart from any Jewish ritual, an entirely new order began at Pentecost. Gentiles had previously been called the "uncircumcised." They were "without Christ, being aliens from the commonwealth of Israel, and strangers from the covenants of promise, having no hope, and without God in the world" (Ephesians 2:11,12). In Old Testament times, a Gentile could become a proselyte—he could embrace the Jewish religion—but by nature he was still a Gentile, not a Jew.

> Now in Christ Jesus [those Gentiles] who sometimes were far off are made nigh by the blood of Christ. For he is our peace [or has made peace between Jew and Gentile], who hath made both *one,* and hath

> broken down the middle wall of partition between [them]; Having abolished in his flesh the enmity, even the law of commandments contained in ordinances; for to make in himself of twain *one new man,* so making peace; And that he might reconcile *both* unto God in *one* body by the cross, having slain the enmity thereby: And came and preached peace to you [Gentiles] who were afar off, and to the [Jews] that were nigh. For through Him we *both* have access by one Spirit unto the Father. Now therefore ye [Gentiles] are no more strangers and foreigners, but *fellowcitizens* with the saints, and of the household of God; And are built upon the foundation of the apostles and prophets, Jesus Christ himself being the chief corner stone; In whom all the building fitly framed together groweth unto an holy temple in the Lord: In whom ye also are builded together for an habitation of God through the Spirit.
> (Ephesians 2:13–22)

One does not have to go to a commentary for an explanation of these verses. In Christ, there is absolutely *no* distinction between an ethnic Jew and an ethnic Gentile. They are now reconciled, *both* unto God, in *one* body—the Church of the living God, the Church that Christ loved and gave Himself for, the Church that He is building (Ephesians 5:25; Matthew 16:18).

Paul also spoke of a mystery that was not made known in other ages "as it is now revealed unto his holy apostles and prophets by the Spirit" (Ephesians 3:5). Paul and others received the revelation of this mystery. It was not so much that the Gentiles would be saved, for Isaiah (11:10, 62:2) and Christ (Matthew 12:18) both spoke of this. The mystery is that *both* Jew and Gentile *together* would be a whole new entity, that the Gentiles would be fellow-heirs with believing Jews and *of the same body* (Ephesians 3:2–6). The former distinction between Jew and Gentile no longer existed—it had disappeared.

GOD'S CHOSEN PEOPLE TODAY

As much as we find, especially in the Old Testament, that Jews are designated as those chosen by God (Deuteronomy 7:6), we need to constantly remind ourselves what they were chosen for. Their history reveals that, as a whole, they did not live up to their choosing in spite of God's love for His people—those whom He called the "apple of His eye" (Zechariah 2:8). In the providence of God, the Jewish lineage through which Messiah was to come was fulfilled in Christ, a Jew. But it is not the Jew who is on God's mountain peak now. It is the Church that Christ loved and gave Himself for so that anyone who trusts in Him—Jew or Gentile—would be brought into an equal relationship with any other believer. It is not the Church that is in a "valley," with Jews excelling now as God's people. It is the Church, which is comprised of *all* believers, that is to be presented to God—"a glorious church, not having spot, or wrinkle, or any such thing; but that it should be holy and without blemish" (Ephesians 5:25-27). In spite of all that we find in the Old Testament relating to Israel's future, no promise can compare with what the Church is to receive when it is presented by Christ to His Father.

Israel was chosen to be holy, special, and peculiar above all nations—a people to show others that they had been called by God's name (Deuteronomy 7:6, 14:2, 28:9–10). Her Old Testament history shows that as a nation she did not fulfill her calling. The *remnant* did, but as a nation, Israel did *not.* However, since Calvary and the Day of Pentecost (Acts 2), born-again believers from all walks of life are now God's chosen people. What Israel was called to be and do, the Church now has this calling. The apostle Peter said, "Ye are a *chosen* generation, a *royal priesthood,* an *holy nation,* a *peculiar* [special] people" (I Peter 2:9a). Acts 15:14 states that God is now calling out from the Gentiles a *people* for His name. And for what purpose? To do what Israel should have done, "to shew forth the praises of him who hath called [us] out of darkness into his marvellous light" (2:9b). Peter was addressing this verse primarily to those of Gentile origin, showing that what the Jews had in their calling in the Old Testament, Christians—both saved Jews and Gentiles—are *now* partakers thereof.

CONCLUSION

There are no strangers or foreigners in God's family. All are fellow-citizens fitly framed together on the foundation, Christ, and each one *is* God's temple, God's habitation on earth through the Holy Spirit. We are laborers together with God (I Corinthians 3:9). Believers are baptized into Christ whether they are a natural Jew or a natural Gentile. Paul adds to this truth by saying there is neither *circumcision* (Jew) nor *uncircumcision* (Gentile), neither male nor female. We are now the sons of God by faith in Christ, and also the seed of Abraham (Galatians 3:26–29; Colossians 3:10–12). Ethnically, there are Jewish Christians, Greek Christians, Indian Christians, Black Christians, Chinese Christians, and so forth.

In categorizing the human race, Paul mentions "Jews" and "Gentiles," the word *Gentile* meaning people other than Jews. Paul also mentions the Church, and there is no such thing as nationality among those who have been born again and are in the body of Christ—the Church (I Corinthians 10:32). All born-again Christians are citizens of heaven, and our nationality here on earth means nothing to the family of God. We are neither Jew nor Gentile; as Christians, we are looking for a city whose Builder and Maker is God Almighty (Philippians 3:20 NIV; Hebrews 11:10).

21

THE FALL OF JERUSALEM, DISPERSION, AND NEW SACRIFICES

There was great rejoicing in the spread of the Gospel in Jerusalem, Judea, and Samaria, in Asia Minor and Europe, and throughout countries mentioned on the Day of Pentecost (Acts 2:7–11). The teachings of believers, Philip the Evangelist, and the Apostles reveal a unity with Christ of Jews and Gentiles. In the finished work of Christ in shedding His own precious blood for all lost sinners, Jews and Gentiles were brought near God, thus breaking down the enmity between them. In spite of Satan's opposition, all this was accomplished.

After Paul's successful ministry and death, there loomed a prophecy from the days of Moses and enlarged upon by Jesus. One of the judgments that God said would fall upon His people if they disobeyed Him is found in Deuteronomy: "And it shall come to pass that the Lord rejoiced over you to do good and to multiply you; so the Lord will rejoice over you to destroy you, to bring you to naught; and you shall be plucked out from the land where you go to possess it. And the Lord shall scatter you among the people, from one end of the earth even to the other" (Deuteronomy 28:15,63,64).

Jesus endured much persecution in the many confrontations that He had with those of His own people who did evil. Before He made predictions about His second coming and events leading up to the end of the age, He levelled a barrage of accusations against His accusers and their hypocrisy (Matthew 23:1–36). Because of their disobedience and unbelief and the way in which they had treated God's servants, His heart was so grieved that He wept over Jerusalem. He announced that Moses' prophecy would definitely come to pass, that their beloved city would be destroyed, in these words: "If thou hadst known, even thou, at least in this thy day, the things which belong unto thy peace! but now they are hid from thine eyes. For the days shall come upon thee, that thine enemies shall cast a trench about thee, and compass thee round, and keep thee in on every side, And shall lay thee even with the ground, and thy children within thee; and they shall not leave in thee one stone upon another; because thou knewest not the time of thy visitation [or My time of coming to save My people from their sins]" (Luke 19:42–44).

Fig. 38. Relief on Arch of Titus in Rome showing spoils from the Temple.

Elaborating upon this coming event, He also said, "And when ye shall see Jerusalem compassed with armies, then know that the desolation thereof is nigh. . . . For these be the days of vengeance, that all things which are written may be fulfilled. But woe unto them that are with child, and to them that give suck, in those days! for there shall be great distress in the land, and wrath upon this people. And they shall fall by the edge of the sword, and shall be led away captive into all nations: and Jerusalem shall be trodden down of the Gentiles, until the times of the Gentiles be fulfilled" (Luke 21:20,22–24). Not only did Jesus predict the devastating destruction of Jerusalem, He also said that their Temple would be completely destroyed, that not one stone would be left on top of the other (Matthew 24:1,2).

About 33 years after Christ's death (A.D. 66), the Jews revolted against the Romans, triggering Rome's preparation to crush the Jews once and for all. Some Jews who rebelled went to Masada, an unusually high peak in the Judean wilderness overlooking the Dead Sea. Herod the Great had prepared a fortress there, but it was no longer occupied. In this Jewish group there were 967 men, women, and children.

Meanwhile back in Jerusalem, antagonism became so great between Jews and Romans that in A.D. 70 General Titus marched against the city. The walls were breached by battering rams, and with the aid of "siege towers," the soldiers unleashed their deadly power against the whole city. The Temple area was a scene of massacre. The entire city was plundered and burned, and more than 600,000 Jews were slaughtered. It is said that tens of thousands perished as they were thrown over the city wall into the Valley of Hinnon. According to

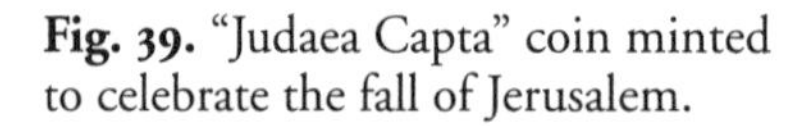

Fig. 39. "Judaea Capta" coin minted to celebrate the fall of Jerusalem.

Josephus, the soldiers plundered the Temple before they destroyed it, taking a copy of the law, the golden lampstand, the golden table of showbread, and the trumpets of the priests. The Arch of Titus, built to commemorate his victory over Judaea, still stands in Rome and depicts his soldiers crowned with laurel and carrying the seven-branched lampstand, the table of showbread, and the priests' trumpets out of the Temple. There remains even a "Judaea Capta" coin to commemorate Jerusalem's fall.

Interestingly, Christ predicted that in the destruction of the Temple, "There shall not be left here one stone upon another, that shall not be thrown down" (Matthew 24:2). In many temples or important religious buildings, stones were held together by gold or silver bars, which were bent and fitted into holes or grooves to hold the stones together. The soldiers of Titus knew of this method of construction. They also knew that "to the victor belongs the spoils." To get to this precious metal, they literally took one stone off another, thus fulfilling Christ's prophecy.

THE DISPERSION

Christ's prophecy that Jerusalem would be destroyed and Moses' prophecy that God's people would be dispersed, have both come to pass. The surviving Jews were scattered, some to Egypt, and others probably going to their relatives of the *Diaspora* who had remained in Babylon, Persia, Asia Minor, and Europe after the Northern and Southern kingdoms fell.

Those who escaped to *Masada* continued to defy Rome's order to surrender and come down. Rome established eight camps at the base of the fortress, but as soldiers attempted to scale the hillside, Jews would hurl down stones to rout them. Approach to the top seemed impossible. Finally, an earthen "dam" was constructed with slave labor to reach the wall surrounding the fort. When the Jewish leaders saw that defeat was imminent, they chose "freedom in death rather than slavery to Rome." Ten men were chosen to slaughter the people, and when the last person remained, he set fire to all the compound and then drove a sword into his body, falling dead next to his kinsmen. Two women and three children had hidden themselves, and their lives were spared by the Romans. This mass suicide took place in A.D. 73, three years after the fall of Jerusalem.

A Jewish leader named Bar-Cochba sought to win freedom from the Romans about A.D. 134, but was utterly defeated by the emperor Hadrian. What was left of Jerusalem was levelled to the ground—even foundations were plowed up. Jews were excluded from the city for the next two centuries, until the reign of Constantine. Isaiah had painted such a picture of the destruction of God's holy city, all because the people had not produced the fruit of God's vineyard as He had desired. In their producing "wild grapes," Isaiah foretold that their walls would be broken down and would be laid waste. God had looked for justice in His people but found oppression. Their sin was to bring about houses without inhabitants, and they were to be placed alone in the midst of the earth (Isaiah 5:1–9).

Moses had said that judgment would come if there was disobedience to the commandments of God, and it all came to pass. What a lesson for all of us to learn! God must always remain true to His Word, even when it involves His own in judgment. Our sin will always find us out; God will spare not, and we must always reap what we sow (Numbers 32:23; Romans 11:21; Galatians 6:7).

ISRAEL'S DILEMMA

With the destruction of Jerusalem and the Temple, the bottom dropped out for all non–Christian Jews. Although they still clung to some of their ordinances and rituals, the place of worship was no longer accessible to them. The big question for them was, Where do we go from here? Having ignored the Torah, the writings of Moses, they fell prey to the traditions of their fathers and were blind to their history and what Moses said would happen to them and their descendants if they disobeyed His commandments.

When people do not know or consider their history, they do not know where they are, and if they do not know where they are, they do not know where they are going or what their future might be. Through Moses, God had outlined the blessings that would be Israel's if she obeyed all His commandments (Deuteronomy 28:1–14). After pronouncing His love and blessings that would be theirs before all nations if they yielded to Him, He continued, "But if you do not obey the Lord your God to observe faithfully all of His laws and commandments which I give to you this day, *all* these curses [or judgments] shall come upon you and take effect [no matter where you go] (28:15). Following are a few of these judgments:

1. "Cursed shall you be in your city and in your country" (verse 16).
2. "Cursed shall you be in your comings and in your goings" (verse 19).
3. "The Lord will put you to rout before your enemies; you shall march out against them by a single road, but flee from them by many" (verse 25).
4. "You shall grope at noon as a blind man gropes in the dark; you shall not prosper in your ventures but shall be constantly abused and robbed, with none to give help" (verse 29).

5. "Your sons and daughters shall be delivered to other people while you look on, and your eyes shall strain for them constantly, but you shall be helpless" (verse 32).
6. "You shall be a consternation [become an astonishment], a proverb, and a byword among all the peoples to which the Lord your God will drive you" (verse 37). *Astonishment* means being brought into desolation, being hissed at and ridiculed, and being made the object of scornful laughter. *Byword* means a gibe, being sneered at sarcastically and taunted.
7. "The stranger in your midst shall rise above you higher and higher, while you sink lower and lower" (verse 34).
8. "You shall be left a scant few, after having been numerous as the stars in the skies, because you did not heed the command of the Lord your God" (verse 43).
9. "The Lord will scatter you among all the peoples from one end of the earth to the other. . . . Yet even among these nations ye shall find no peace, nor shall your foot find a place to rest. The Lord will give you there an anguished heart and eyes that pine and a despondent spirit" (verses 64–65).
10. "The life you face shall be precarious; you shall be in terror night and day, with no assurance of survival. In the morning you shall say, 'If only it were evening!' and in the evening you shall say, 'If only it were morning!'—because of what your heart shall dread and your eyes shall see" (verses 66–67).

"These are the terms of the covenant which the Lord commanded Moses to conclude with the Israelites in the land of Moab, in *addition* to the covenant which He made with them at Horeb [Sinai]" (Deuteronomy 28:69).

After reading about God's judgment upon His people, let us not entertain the thought that He despises them. Jeremiah often pleaded with the Israelites, as *backsliders,* to turn to God, saying that He was married to them and would give them good shepherds and heal them (Jeremiah 3:12–15,22). But in their refusal, they lost the Promised Land, the holy city of Jerusalem, and their Temple. The only place they had left to go was *out,* out into a worldwide wilderness. Their forefathers had a cloud by day and a pillar of fire by night to guide them in their wilderness journey, but after the fall of Jerusalem, Jews would have to face God's curses.

Christians believe, according to the fulfillment of Old Testament prophecies in the New Testament concerning Messiah, that His blood sacrifice at Calvary brought an end to such sacrifices for sin (Hebrews 1:3, 10:10). Since Christ was rejected by the Jews, the Temple sacrifices were continued until Titus destroyed their place of worship. Without their Temple, there was no altar for blood sacrifices. A problem arose: what can they now sacrifice? One can readily understand their dilemma—no Temple, no altar, no sacrifice for atonement. They found their answer, not in their Torah or their Scriptures, but in their oral laws, the Talmud: "The ordinances of the Written Torah were eternal and immutable; *only* when circumstances made them impossible of fulfillment—as with the sacrifices when the Temple was destroyed [by Nebuchadnezzar in 586 B.C.] and the agrarian [land] laws when the people went into captivity—were they temporarily suspended until they could be re-enacted."[35] The one blessing of the Jews in captivity was the prophecy that their captivity would only last for 70 years (II Chronicles 36:20,21); they lost their testimony and song in Babylon, but there was hope of returning to Jerusalem and rebuilding the Temple to resume the offering of sacrifices.

Now at wit's end, the Jews must have remembered that their law said, "It is the blood that makes atonement for the soul" (Leviticus 17:11). Having to suspend this observance, the rabbis saw to it that doctrines recorded in the Talmud would come to the rescue of the people in offering *several* methods of atonement. The Talmud made Jews feel that destruction of the Temple did not imply an end to their religion. They needed to be reminded that their hope for atonement was not in the least affected. Severe as their loss was, the way of approach to God was kept open, they believed.

SUBSTITUTE ATONEMENT AND SACRIFICES

1. *Repentance.* "If one repents, it is imputed to him as if he had gone up to Jerusalem, built the Temple, erected an altar and offered upon it the sacrifices enumerated in the Torah."[36] Repentance required a change for the better, else there would be no forgiveness. If it is true repentance, one's sins are forgiven immediately; in other words, the sinner atones for all his wrongdoing by being repentant.

Repentance of more serious sins remains in suspense, and the Day of Atonement brings expiation. Whenever a sin deserving capital punishment is committed, both one's repentance and the Day of Atonement remain in suspense, and his suffering will purge him. Repentance is of no avail if one profanes the name of God. Neither the Day of Atonement nor suffering has the power to purge; they all remain in suspense, and death will purge him. One Jewish scholar has suggested that an innocent child dying would atone for his generation.

The Talmud says that the atonement sacrifices as commanded in the Torah are now a thing of the past. The Synagogue Ritual for the Day of Atonement is now repentance—repentance atones.

2. *Suffering.* Atonement is secured through suffering. "There are many chastenings which purge all the iniquities of man." It is taught that just as blood sacrifices secured acceptance, so do sufferings secure acceptance. Suffering brings even greater acceptance since sacrifices cost money only, while suffering affects the body. Whatever part of the body is affected, having tasted the bitterness, the sinner becomes purified.

In a letter to a Jew who had become a Christian, a rabbi said this of chapter 53 of Isaiah: "The section known as 'Suffering Servant' is read during the Synagogue year. We Jews have taken the 'Suffering Servant' to be a symbol of the Jewish people. All Jews are suffering servants and all serve to *purify God* through their sufferings" [italics mine].[37] Since God is holy and righteous, eternal and immutable, why does He need to be purified? The implication is that He is imperfect, which would make atoning acts of repentance and suffering void.

3. *Fasting.* Religious leaders attach importance to the fast as an act of repentance, equivalent to sacrifice. A rabbi prays thus on a fast day: "Lord of the Universe! it is revealed before Thee that when the Sanctuary was in existence, a man sinned and brought an offering, of which they sacrificed only the fat and the blood, and atonement was made for him. But now, I observe a fast, and my fat and blood are diminished. May it be Thy will, that my fat and blood which have been diminished may be accounted as though I had offered them before Thee upon the altar, and do thou favor me."

4. *Prayer.* This act is declared to be even "greater than sacrifices," based on the words "We will render the calves of our lips" (Hosea 14:2). The doctrine was taught thus: "What can be a substitute for the bulls which we used to offer unto Thee? Our lips, with the prayer which we used to offer unto Thee."

5. *Wearing phylacteries.* A phylactery was a small leather case with straps containing a parchment inscribed with four Biblical passages: Exodus 13:1–10, 11-16; Deuteronomy 6:4–9, 11:13–21. This is the traditional method of fulfilling the law "Thou shalt bind them for a sign upon thine hand, and they shall be frontlets between thine eyes (Deuteronomy 6:8). By reciting "Hear, o Israel: The Lord our God is one Lord," it is as if they had built an altar and offered a sacrifice upon it.

6. *Benevolence/charity.* When someone cried out "Woe to us!" when he saw the ruins of the Temple, the place where Israel had obtained atonement for sins, he was told, "We still have atonement equally efficacious, and that is the practice of benevolence." God also announced, "More beloved by Me are the justice and righteousness which you perform than sacrifices." In other words, their kind acts and good works toward others atoned for their sins.

7. *Miscellaneous sacrifices*

Because the *Meal Offering* was bloodless, the poor person who set aside his own food was regarded as if he had sacrificed himself, "as though he had offered his own soul to God."

One's *wounds* would atone for his sins, and blood lost from a wound replaces the blood of the *olah* (offering).

The *altar* is called a "table" (Ezekiel 41:22). The table of the home has the altar's expiatory virtue because it embodies good deeds—hospitality shown to the poor. "A man's table makes atonement for him."

Humility. Evidently, this does not apply to someone who infrequently acts humble. "Humility *of the humble* is rewarded as though they offered the prescribed offering of the Law."

CONCLUSION

What is overlooked by these scholars and rabbis is that the Lord of the Scriptures gave these truths regarding repentance and contrition *in light of* the need for blood sacrifice, never *apart from* the offering.

Many Jews with whom I have conversed seem to know little about the oral laws, or Talmud, and practically nothing about their own Scriptures. They say, "We are Jews, we have our own religion, and that's good enough for us." But if asked what their religion is all about, everything revolves around their belief that they alone are God's chosen people, and that's good enough to have His favor. One told me that blood sacrifices were no longer a part of their belief, that blood sacrifices belong to the worshippers of Baal or some heathen god. One of their twelfth-century rabbis "went so far as to declare that sacrifice was archaic religion from which God had weaned Israel. The modern Jewish writers, therefore, look upon our faith in Yeshua in general, and our doctrine of vicarious atonement, as unreasonable. The idea of 'vicarious atonement' . . . the payment of penalty not by the sinner but by a substitute, is irreconcilable with Jewish ethics."[38]

A former Hebrew of the Hebrews, a firm believer in the traditions of his Jewish teachers, said this after his conversion to Christianity: "The natural man receiveth not the things of the Spirit of God: for they are foolishness unto him: neither can he know them, because they are spiritually discerned" (I Corinthians 2:14). One wonders how such rules and regulations (laws) concerning atonement can surface, when the Jewish Scriptures not only specify how atonement can be achieved, but predict through the prophet Daniel when Messiah would come and that He would "finish transgression, make an end to sins, make reconciliation for iniquity, and bring in everlasting righteousness" (Daniel 9:24). One would think that instead of concocting so many methods of atonement, the rabbis would have settled on just one and let it go at that.

The tragedy is that while all these oral laws were designed by the ancient rabbis to help the Jewish people keep God's commandments, they have prevented them from exercising "faith for righteousness" to prove that they really were God's chosen people. Blindness to the simple, understandable Scriptural method of atonement may lead them to think that there is a way acceptable for them, but sooner or later they will find out that it was a way of death (Proverbs 14:12). God said, "Look unto *Me* and be saved" (Isaiah 45:22). Jesus said, "He that heareth my word and believeth on him that sent me, hath everlasting life, and shall not come into condemnation; but is passed from death unto life" (John 5:24).

IV

THE FUTURE

22
ISRAEL'S HOPE: A NEW NATION

In spite of all the judgments and punishments that Israel inflicted upon herself because of disobedience to God's commandments, a thread of hope ran through the Scriptures. There is a much brighter hope for Israel after the tribulation period as we enter the millennial reign of Christ on earth. When the disciples asked Jesus when He would restore the kingdom again to Israel, He said it was not for them to know the times or seasons that God had put in His own power, "But ye shall receive power, after that the Holy Spirit is come upon you: and ye shall be witnesses unto me both in Jerusalem . . . and unto the uttermost part of the earth" (Acts 1:6–8). If fundamentalists would spend less time preaching on Israel's future after the rapture, and more time seeking the lost for Christ, what a revival we would have!

What is Israel's hope today, even though they are still in unbelief? God gave His people a promise that the land from the river of Egypt to the river Euphrates would be theirs to the end of time. Israel ceased to exist as a nation when the times of the Gentiles came in under Nebuchadnezzar, ca. 586 B.C., and lost it altogether when Titus caused their dispersion in A.D. 70. Not only had God made His promise of the land a perpetual one, but He often told them of His love and His desire for them to repent and live a life worthy of their calling. He also promised that one day He would bring them back into their land.

At the end of World War I in 1918, Britain was given the mandate over the land of Palestine, previously ruled by the Turks. The British had issued the Balfour Declaration the year before, giving Jews permission to return to their ancient homeland. Although some Jews returned and purchased land, most of the inhabitants were Arabs, called Palestinians. The Arabs were not happy with the Jews' presence, and there was some unrest from time to time. In the early 1940s, it appeared that certain promises that God had made were beginning to come to pass: a great number of Jews were returning by boat to enter their ancient land. Their forefathers had been told that they would be scattered among the heathens, that their land would become desolate, and that their cities would be ruined or become waste (Leviticus 26:27–33). Those scattered would be from one end of the earth to the other (Deuteronomy 28:64).

Isaiah said, "It shall come to pass in that day that the Lord will set His hand again the *second* time to recover His surviving people who are in Assyria, Egypt, Cush, Pathros, Elim, Shinar, Hamath, and the islands of the sea. They will be set up as an ensign [banner] for the nations and shall assemble the outcasts of Israel, and gather together the dispersed of Judah from the four corners of the earth" (Isaiah 11:11,12). Ezekiel also said that God would give the land back to Israel (Ezekiel 11:17).

THE UNITED NATIONS PARTITIONS THE LAND—A NEW NATION

As large numbers of Jews were leaving the four corners of the earth to fulfill Isaiah's prophecy, unrest and violence by the Arabs created an ugly scene. On November 29, 1947, the United Nations partitioned Palestine, giving a small area to the Jews and the rest to the Jordanians. The city of Jerusalem was put under international control (see Map 9). The partition plan was totally unacceptable to the Arabs and war broke out, with the Arabs vowing to drive the Jews into the sea. After a few months of fighting, a cease-fire order was drawn up after the Israelis brought the Arabs to their knees, and the new nation of Israel was established. The Israelis had gone from 586 B.C. to A.D. 1948 without being a nation—2,534 years!

Since the establishment of a new nation on May 14, 1948, many things have transpired, two of special importance. First, several battles have been fought, with Israel gaining more land each time. Egypt, Jordan, and Syria joined forces with the intention of destroying Israel, the *intruder,* once and for all. With little time for preparation, Israeli officers planned a bold strategy. Without warning, their air force flew at night and destroyed all of Egypt's planes, starting the June 1967 Six-Day War. Israeli soldiers marched on the Sinai peninsula and put the Egyptians to flight. Jordan and Syria retreated, and Israel chased the Jordanians back across the Jordan River, capturing the West Bank territory. The Syrians had been rolling stones down the hills on Israeli villages below, damaging property and killing many Jews. Israel pursued the Syrians and conquered the Golan Heights. The Arabs were beginning to realize that the Jews were in their homeland to stay! Peace talks have led to Israel returning the Sinai peninsula to Egypt. Several West Bank cities have also been returned to the Palestinians, such as Hebron, Bethlehem, and Jenin. If the Arabs and the world could only see that God's promises to Abraham and his descendants through Isaac centuries ago still hold true!

Second, as Israel took over the land under the U.N. partition, the desert territory she gained was essentially useless. With more Jews returning to Israel, more territory was required for housing. Huge pipelines were set to take water from the Jordan River to irrigate regions in the Negev Desert. Isaiah had said that they "shall build the old wastes, they shall raise up the former desolations and they shall repair the waste cities, the desolations of many generations"

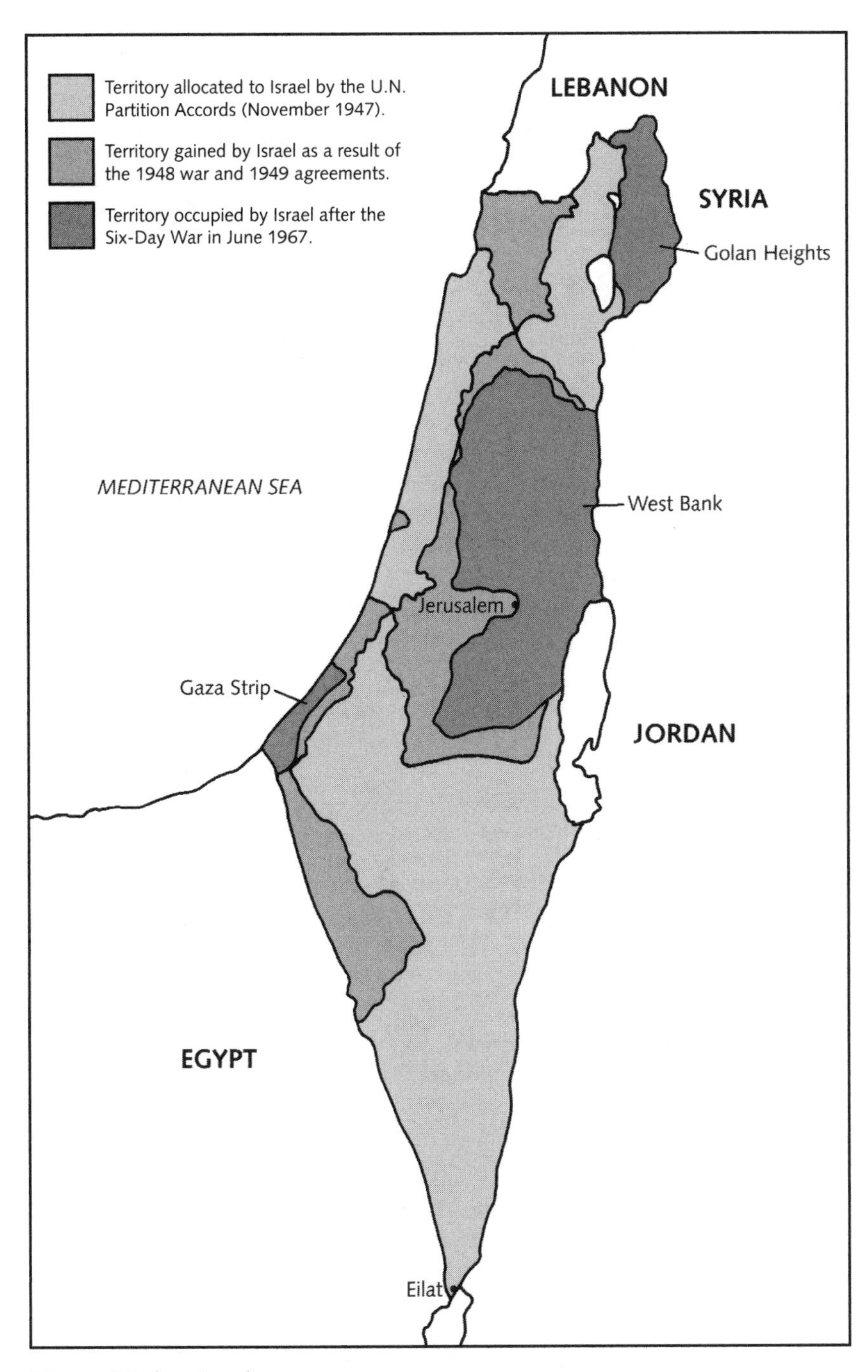

Map 9. Modern Israel.

(Isaiah 61:4). Returning refugees have gone from tents to refugee camps to rough housing to modern homes. Today the housing in Israel is just as modern as ours in America.

Isaiah also told us that trees and vineyards would be planted. "I will plant in the wilderness the cedar, the shittah tree, and the myrtle and the [olive] oil tree. I will set in the desert the fir tree, the pine tree, and the box tree together" (Isaiah 41:19). In different areas of Israel trees were planted to see which would grow fastest. The fastest-growing trees were then planted throughout the land, creating forests to help make the ground fertile.

As a result of enriching the soil, Israel has built many new cities and villages, and with new houses, vineyards have also blossomed forth (Isaiah 65:21). Jeremiah said that "houses and fields and vineyards shall be possessed in the land" (Jeremiah 32:15). Amos also gave encouraging news for Jews back in the land: "I will bring again the captivity of My people of Israel and they shall build the waste cities, and inhabit them. They shall plant vineyards and drink the juice, make gardens and eat the fruit of them" (Amos 9:14,15).

My first visit to the Holy Land was in 1951, but it wasn't until 1954 that, having visited the wastelands of Palestine, I entered Israel's territory. The coastal area seemed to be thriving, but the rest of the land was in need of repair. Having visited seven more times over a period of 30 years, everything that I wrote above about houses, trees, vineyards, and gardens has confirmed what Isaiah said: "The wilderness and the solitary place shall be glad for them, and the desert shall rejoice and blossom as the rose" (Isaiah 35:1).

LANDMARKS OF 4,000 YEARS OF JEWISH HISTORY*

B.C.

2100	Abraham settles in Canaan
1446	Exodus from Egypt
1406	Fall of Jericho
1000	David captures Jerusalem
966	Solomon begins building Temple
931	United Kingdom divided
722	Fall of Northern Kingdom (Israel)
606	Nebuchadnezzar's first siege of Jerusalem; captives taken
586	Fall of Southern Kingdom (Judah); 70-year Babylonian captivity
536	Return of captives from first siege of Jerusalem; Israel no longer a ruling nation; last captives return in 516
332	Alexander the Great conquers Palestine
285–247	Translation of Hebrew Old Testament into Greek: the Septuagint
186	Desecration of Temple by Antiochus Epiphanes

*Some dates are approximate.

165 Maccabean revolt against Greece and Greek culture
142 Hasmonean period; Jews regain land; Maccabeans assume role of priesthood and political role
63 Pompey of Rome conquers land; Jews now under Roman rule
37 Herod the Great takes over Jerusalem; Temple rebuilt
6–5 Birth of Christ
4 Death of Herod the Great

A.D.

29–30 Crucifixion of Christ by Rome
66 First Jewish revolt against Rome
70 Destruction of Rome and Temple by Titus
73 Fall of Masada
132 Second Jewish revolt against Rome
135 Fall of Jerusalem under Hadrian
500 Completion of Babylonian Talmud in two parts: the Mishna (text) and Gemara (commentary)
614 Invasion by Persians
636 Fall of Jerusalem to Mohammedans
1099 Fall of Jerusalem to Crusaders
1187 Saladin captures Jerusalem from Crusaders
1517 Ottomans conquer Jerusalem; Ottoman/Turkish period begins
1538 Sulayman rebuilds city walls, which stand today
1882 First Aliya; Jewish immigration and settlement outside city
1897 Zionist Movement founded by Theodor Herzl
1909 Tel Aviv founded; Degania Bet, first kibbutz, founded
1917 Great Britain given control over Palestine; Britain's Balfour Declaration gives Jews right to occupy land in Palestine
1921 British "white paper" states that anyone born in mandated territory is "Palestinian," the reason why the Palestine Liberation Organization (P. L.O.) claims the land
1931 "White paper" limits purchase of land by Jews and curtails their freedom
1939–1945 World War II; the Holocaust, in which 6 million Jews are slaughtered
1947 U.N. resolution to partition Palestine into Jewish and Arab states; Great Britain lifts mandate; war between Jews and Arab states
1947/48 Israel wins war; U.N. partitions land, part to Israel, part to Jordan; Israel becomes a nation
1949 Chaim Weisman is elected first president of Israel; armistice signed with Arab countries
1950 "Law of Return" is passed, giving any Jew right to "come home"
1956 Israel's Sinai campaign against Egypt

1962 Adolf Eichmann, chief Holocaust exterminator, is executed by Israel
1967 Six-Day War in June
1973 Yom Kippur War in October
1977 Egyptian President Anwar Sadat speaks to Knesset in Jerusalem
1979 Camp David accord signed by Egypt's Sadat and Israel's prime minister, Menachem Begin
1982 Israel attacks P.L.O. in Lebanon
1990/91 Gulf War; Israel is threatened by Iraq's Saddam Hussein, who launches skud missiles at several Israeli cities
1993 Peace agreement between Israel and P.L.O. leader Yasser Arafat
1996 Benjamin Netanyahu is elected prime minister; he is determined to "hold the fort" and not give territory to Arabs; eventually he agreed to turn over some territory
1999 Ehud Barak is elected prime minister; he has yielded some territory and pulled Israeli troops out of Lebanon

According to the Old Testament, the land of Palestine belongs to Israel (Genesis 15:18–21). She also owns land by right of purchase after the Balfour Declaration and by conquest since 1947; she has won every war against the Arabs since. After being given land by the United Nations, what she has won in battle since then is rightfully hers by conquest:

Israel won it from the Arabs,
The Arabs got it from Great Britain,
Great Britain from the Turks,
The Turks from the Crusaders,
The Crusaders from the Mohammedans,
The Mohammedans from the Persians,
The Persians from the Byzantines,
The Byzantines from the Romans,
The Romans from the Greeks,
The Greeks from the Persians,
The Persians from the Babylonians,
The Babylonians from Israel,
Israel from the Canaanites.

This returns us to Joshua's day (ca. 1406 B.C.), when Israel conquered Jericho. It is ironic that Israeli Prime Minister Shimon Perez, in an agreement with the P.L.O., gave it back to the Arabs.

ISRAEL'S INTERNAL PROBLEMS

Israel has probably had more external problems with enemy nations, especially the Arab states, than any other nation. Many times she has consulted her Scriptures to see how her former kings and leaders conquered their enemies, as a result she has won one war after another. But some Arabs are determined to drive Israel into the sea, completely destroying her as a nation.

Israel has numerous internal problems. For example, there has been difficulty in determining just who is a Jew: Some say that a Jew is a person born of a Jewish woman; others say that only the male is a Jew; Orthodox Jews rule out all except themselves.

Orthodox Jews are determined that Israel should be ruled not only by God's Law, but also by additional laws that the rabbis have concocted. The majority of Israeli Jews rebel against the Orthodox stand.

There are Jews who believe that Israel deserves the West Bank because of their victory in the June 1967 war. They refuse to move out, with arrests as well as unrest being the consequence. These people rebel against the leaders who are giving territory back to the Arabs.

Israel was established in 1948 as a nation for all Jews, and each has a constitutional right to a democratic government. Ultra-Orthodox Jews insist on defining what it means to be a Jew based on non-Biblical, religious standards according to the oral laws of their rabbis. The most that we as believers can do is to "pray for the peace of Jerusalem," that is, to pray for the Jews to believe that Jesus Christ is their Messiah. This alone can give them true peace (Psalm 122:6).

23

WHAT IS ISRAEL'S FUTURE?

There are a number of Old Testament promises and prophecies that have to do with Jews and Israel to the end of time, and God is not through with them yet.

In spite of all we have learned about Israel's past—her sins, rebellion, unbelief, stubbornness, and refusal to walk in the old paths of truth—God still loves the ones whom He chose centuries ago with an *everlasting* love (Jeremiah 31:3). This love contains the promise that there will come a day when the whole land that was promised to Abraham from the river of Egypt to the Euphrates River will again be theirs (Deuteronomy 30:1–4).

What must occur before Israel fully repossesses her Promised Land and in *belief* enters into peace with God? The stage has been set for three events to come to pass before the Lord's "love promise" takes effect; we are already in the first stage.

1. *Perilous times.* Jesus asked if He would find faith on earth when He returned (Luke 18:8). Before that day comes, there will be such little faith because of

- Moral and spiritual deterioration: II Timothy 3:1–7,12,13.
- Apostasy of religious leaders (modernism): II Timothy 4:3,4; II Peter 2:1,2, 3:1–4.
- Rapid increase in knowledge, communication (computers), and travel: Daniel 12:4.
- Widespread materialism and secularism: Luke 17:28–30.
- Preparation for world government and religion: II Thessalonians 2:1–3.
- False Christs, wars and rumors of wars, famines, earthquakes, and diseases: Matthew 24:3–8.

2. *The rapture of the Church.* All of the above current events point to the first stage of Christ's second coming. He promised that He would return (John 14:1–3). When He finished His earthly ministry and ascended into heaven, the disciples were told as they watched Him go up bodily that He would return *in like manner* (Luke 1:10,11). In this first stage, Christ will descend from heaven in the clouds, resurrect saints who have fallen asleep in Him, catch them up together with believers who are alive at His coming, and take them back to glory with Him (I Thessalonians 4:16,17).

3. *The tribulation period.* Immediately following the rapture of the Church, a seven-year tribulation will begin on earth. Daniel predicted that there would be a 70-week period determined upon Israel. In the Hebrew language, a *week* is seven years. Sixty-nine weeks were accomplished when Christ was crucified, and there remains this seventieth week for Israel to endure (Daniel 9:24).

This period of tribulation relates especially to Jews who have returned to their own land in unbelief. A covenant will be made with the Jews for Temple worship and their sacrifices. In the midst of this seven-year period, the prince (Antichrist) shall break the covenant, causing the sacrifice and oblation to cease, and for the overspreading of abominations he shall make it desolate. This is what Daniel called the "abomination of desolation . . . a great tribulation, such as was not since the beginning of the world to this time, nor ever shall be," according to the words of Christ (Matthew 24:15–21). Chapters 6 through 19 of Revelation give us this awful picture of the last half of Daniel's seventieth week. The period is also known as

- "Great tribulation": Matthew 24:21; Revelation 7:14.
- A "time of trouble": Daniel 12:1.
- The "time of Jacob's trouble": Jeremiah 30:7.
- The "day of the Lord's wrath": Zephaniah 1:18.

The Millennial Reign of Christ. When the three events mentioned have come to pass, Jesus will return to earth *with* His saints to rule and reign for 1,000 years. Individual Jews who look upon Him who was pierced for their sins will come to know that He *is* the true Messiah. He will be recognized as their "Great High Priest" after the order of Melchizedek, and in the millennium Temple, they will gather to worship the One who shed His blood once and for all for the sins of lost mankind—Jew and Gentile alike. In this reign of Christ, with Satan bound, they will experience the fulfillment of His promises, especially the land and His everlasting love. All ordinances of the law to which we were indebted were nailed to the cross, the veil of the Temple was torn from top to bottom, and all the blood of bulls and goats for sacrifices are null and void. What a thrill it will be for all the Jews who believe to worship the One who made salvation available for them by *faith* alone, not by their works of righteousness.

CONCLUSION

The prophet Isaiah painted a complete picture of the 1,000-year reign of Christ—the Millennium—especially as it relates to Israel.

1. Her restoration to the land: 11:10–12, 14:1,2, 35:10, 48:8–13.
2. Restoration of the land: 30:23–26, 65:21–25.
3. Blessings for Israel restored: 12, 33:24, 46:13, 59:20,21, 65:18–25.

In addition to blessings for Israel, there will be blessings for all nations: Isaiah 2:4, 27:6, 60:3–5.

The Millennium will close with Satan being loosed from the bottomless pit. He will go forth to gather people who basked in a reign of peace but refused to become believers in the King of Kings, the Lord Jesus Christ. Satan will lead these people to wage war against God, but defeat will follow and he will be cast into the lake of fire. People will face judgment at the "Great White Throne." Those not found written in "the book of life" will be cast into the lake of fire. God will then usher in a new heaven, a new earth, and a new Jerusalem (Revelation 20:11–15, 21:1–22:21).

APPENDIX A

ANTI-SEMITISM AFTER JERUSALEM'S DESTRUCTION

The word *anti-Semitism* is used by the media, and by Christians in particular, to refer to hostility toward and discrimination against the Jewish people. Today, one thinks mainly of the horror of the Holocaust during World War II, when over 6 million Jews lost their lives in Hitler's determination to wipe them off the face of the earth. The horror of this devastating catastrophe still lingers. There is still much hatred among some people throughout the world against Jewish people. This appendix will consider two things, Who are the *Semites,* and why is anti-Semitism aimed mainly at the Jewish people?

IDENTIFYING THE SEMITES

To discover the origin of the Semites, we must go back to Noah and his three sons—Shem, Ham, and Japheth. After the Great Flood, the human race remained in one location for an indefinite period of time, becoming a linguistic and racial unit (Genesis 11:1–9). Construction of the Tower of Babel represented pride in human government and a desire to build a name for themselves. God brought their work to a halt, confused their language so that they did not understand one another's speech, and scattered them in all directions to become new, separate nations.

It is commonly understood that the term Semites originates from Shem. Shem's sons occupied the Persian Gulf area and northward (Genesis 10:21–31). After 2,000 B.C., areas northwest of Babylon became a leading center of Semite culture.

Ham's sons settled in Africa, up into Assyria, along the Mediterranean coast, and eastward into Canaan (Genesis 10:6–14).

Japheth's sons settled in the vicinity of the Black and Caspian seas and extended westward through Greece into Spain (Genesis 10:2–5).

Of Noah's sons, Shem was the middle son, with Ham being the youngest and Japheth being the eldest (Genesis 10:1, 21, 8:20–24). It is interesting that Shem is mentioned *first* because of his *superiority.* A Jewish historian links this to the fact that the second-born are listed first, as in "Isaac and Ishmael" and "Jacob and Esau"—Isaac and Jacob being superior [as the promised seeds] over Ishmael and Esau (Genesis 25:9; Joshua 24:4). Shem is mentioned first because the Jews are in his lineage.[39]

Shem's Descendants. Shem was a believer in God (Genesis 9:16). He lived to be 600 years old and had five sons, plus daughters (Genesis 10:22, 11:10,11).

1. Arpachshad, his first son. Born two years after the flood (Genesis 11:10), he probably settled in the Persian Gulf area.
2. Elam, Shem's second son (Genesis 10:22). His descendants settled in Assyria and Babylon [Iraq] and Persia [Iran].
3. Asshur, Shem's third son (Genesis 10:22). His descendants settled in upper Assyria [Iraq].
4. Lud, Shem's fourth son (Genesis 10:22). His descendants founded the kingdom of Lydia in Asia Minor.

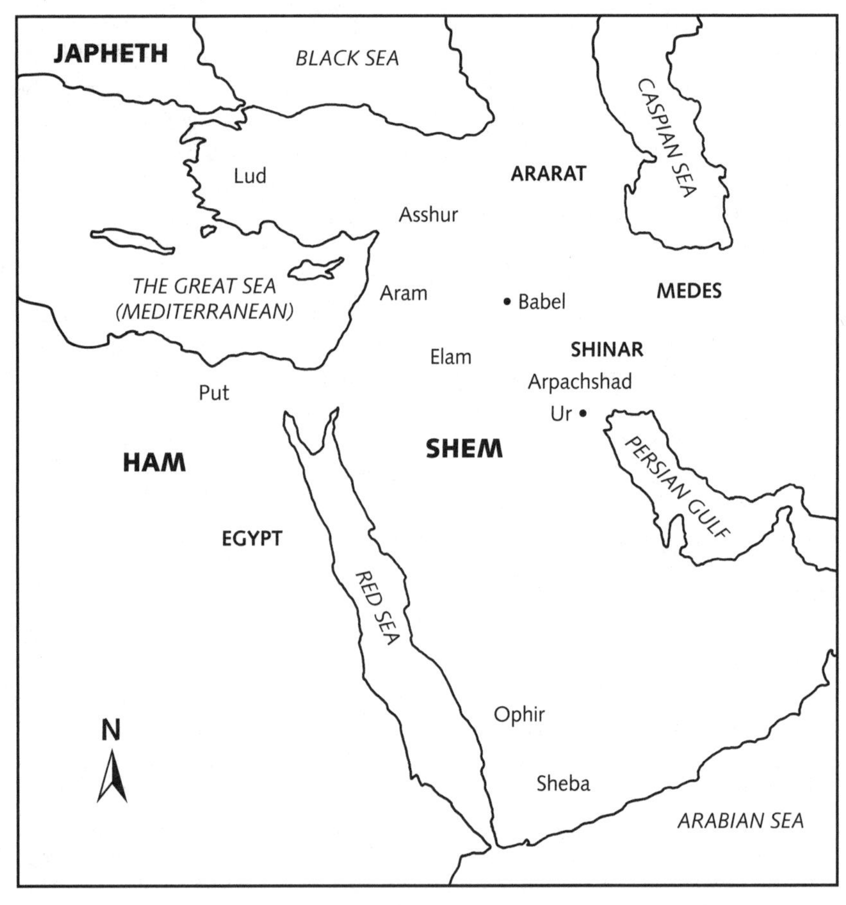

Map 10. Geographical locations of Noah's sons, Shem, Japheth, and Ham, and their descendants.

5. Aram, Shem's fifth son (Genesis 10:22,23). His descendants are called Armenians, and it is generally agreed that they settled in the north of Israel and extended eastward into Mesopotamia.

Shem's lineage through his first son, Arpachshad, is traced through Shelah, Eber, Peleg, Reu, Serug, Nahor, Terah, and then Abraham, the tenth generation from Shem (Genesis 11:10–27). It is necessary that we keep in mind that all five sons of Shem were Semites—not just the one through whom Abraham was born. We also must reckon with the fact that the Edomites, who, as descendants of Esau, go back to Shem through Jacob, Isaac, and Abraham. The Moabites and Ammonites, who were descendants of Lot, son of Abraham's brother, Haran, trace their ancestry through Lot and his daughters to Shem (Genesis 11:16,27, 19:36,38). When Israel was conquering the land of Jordan in her wilderness journey, she was forbidden to harass, provoke, or take any land from the Edomites, Moabites, and Ammonites, because they, too, were considered Semites, thus relatives of the Jews (Deuteronomy 2:5,8,9,18,19).

Map 10 shows the lands of Noah's sons divided into three areas. Shem and his sons located from Mesopotamia westward into the northern part of Israel and also southward. This area, as we know it today, includes Iraq (ancient Assyria), part of Iran (ancient Persia), Syria, Jordan, Saudi Arabia, Kuwait, and the habitable part of the southern Arabian peninsula.

For the Jews to trace their ancestry back to Abraham and from him back to Shem poses no problem. But somewhere down the line, it appears that there are others who are Semites besides the Jews. Would they be the Arabs, who claim Abraham as their father through Ishmael? They certainly cannot claim Christ's lineage, as Paul brings out in Galatians, but from the physical viewpoint the Jews are *not* the only Semites in the world. If it is argued that there have been too many mixed marriages over the centuries for others to claim that they are Semites, one must point out the mixed marriages of the Jews over the centuries, before and after Christ. Even today, in the new nation of Israel, there is a problem determining who is a *true* Jew. We definitely know the Jews are Semites, however, and the world recognizes them as such.

REASONS FOR ANTI-SEMITISM

Much has been said in this book that could be interpreted as anti-Semitic, but it is the *Jewish* Scripture that has been telling us what the majority of these people did, and it is God Himself who told the writers what to record. Speaking the truth hurts at times, but I believe that God's Word has set forth the reason why there has been so much antagonism against the people chosen by Him centuries ago to represent Him on earth. These people were to be known as those who were called by the name of the Lord to be the *head, above* other nations, and not *below* them as the *tail* (Deuteronomy 28:9,10,13). No other nation has ever had this calling, nor ever will. Why, then, is there such an anti-Semitic attitude toward these people worldwide?

A spirit of bitterness arose in the hearts of the Israelites when Pharaoh put them in bondage. The severity of the whiplash of the taskmasters produced a hatred and bitterness second to none. Once God freed them and they began their exodus to the land promised to Abraham and his seed, very little satisfied them. Out in a barren land, free to express their opinions, bitterness seemed to be the norm. When Moses gave his farewell speech, charging Joshua with the responsibility to take Israel into the Promised Land, he said this of the people: "When you get into the land you are going to break God's covenant and serve other gods for I know your rebellion and your stiff neck. While I am alive and with you this day, you have been rebellious against the Lord, *how much more after my death?*" (Deuteronomy 31:16,20,27). Tragically, Israel took their feelings out on God and Moses by "setting themselves on mischief" (Exodus 32:22b).

Self had become their biggest enemy, their besetting sin. One generation after another seems to have inherited this trait, recalling for us Moses' words, "how much more after my death?"

We have seen how the Jews persecuted the remnant and their prophets (Hebrews 11:32–40). We admire them for standing against Antiochus Epiphanes, who forbade them to conduct their Jewish rites, and finally overthrowing him and his demands. But in putting more emphasis on political matters instead of spiritual ones, they slaughtered and banished many true priests. We see their selfish bitterness during Christ's ministry, during His trials and crucifixion, and during the Acts of the Apostles.

When they rebelled against Rome, the empire vowed to put an end to their existence in their homeland; Titus and his army destroyed their city and Temple, and expelled the survivors. They were without a place to worship and offer their sacrifices, which intensified their bitterness. Little did they realize that the nations in which they must find a place to live knew a lot about their selfish pride, their way of life, their characteristics, and therefore would be hostile toward them. It is a pity when one group of humans pits their anger against another group, but it seems that the world in general has done just this against the Jews.

With most Jews being known as *anti-truth* during Old Testament days in their worship of Baal, and as anti-Christian during the New Testament period, we note that a few years after Jerusalem's fall, a policy was formed in synagogues to single out Jews who believed in Jesus, called "Nazarenes." The policy suggested that those who believed in Messiah be blotted out of the book of life, with their names never to be recorded with the righteous.

In A.D. 135, the remaining Jews sought to throw off their Roman yoke. Rabbi Bar Kochba rallied the Jews to fight against the Romans, but more than half a million Jewish men, women, and children perished. Crushing the Jewish revolt, Roman soldiers levelled Jerusalem by plowing it under. Death threatened any Jew who entered the city, renamed Aelia Capitolina. The land was called Syria Philistia, from which we get the name "Palestine."

As Jews scattered, more settled in Europe than in the Near East and Middle East. Beginning with the period of Constantine the Great, about A.D. 315, Christianity was embraced as a national religion. From that point through the Dark Ages and up to the time of Hitler in World War II, bitter, untold anti-Semitic persecution befell the Jews.

There are good Christians who love the Jewish people, even though they believe that the Jews instigated the crucifixion, as was predetermined by God (Acts 2:22,23). Are there any good Jews? Of course there are, but when it comes to the propagation of the Gospel, the majority oppose it. Even today, in the new nation of Israel, the law forbids a Christian to publicly witness to a Jew.

In a recent letter, the president of the *Chosen People Ministries* brought out that the spirit of "Saul of Tarsus" (a persecutor of the early Church) is alive today. "Yes, that same spirit exists in 1993 [and today] . . . among the dedicated 'anti-missionaries' who work very hard to undermine and destroy our Gospel among Jewish people in many major cities. They are trained and committed to stop the Gospel! I would not go so far as to say our missionaries live under continual death threats, but violence is certainly not out of the question. It took dozens of police officers to hold back an angry crowd of up to 400 Hasidic Jews who besieged a Passover Seder [feast] conducted by our New York staff for Russian Jews. Following the dinner, those in attendance had to be escorted to their cars by the police, right through the pushing, shouting mob who reached between the officers to grab our workers. Despite the tremendous disruption and the demonstration of hatred against our staff, twelve Russian Jews indicated they received Jesus as their Messiah during the Seder."[40]

COMBATTING ANTI-SEMITISM

The apostle Paul handled anti-Semitism well and eloquently. In a portion of Scripture dealing with irregularities at the Lord's Table and eating meat sacrificed to idols, Paul gave some marvellous principles to both Jews and Gentiles regarding anti-Semitism. "Whether therefore ye eat, or drink, or whatsoever ye do [even speaking], do all to the glory of God. Give none offence, neither to the Jews, nor to the Gentiles, nor to the church of God: Even as I please all men in all things, not seeking mine own profit, but the profit of many, that they may be saved" (I Corinthians 10:31–33). Two things in particular stand out in this passage. First, Paul told these Corinthians that whatever they did, it was to be done "to the glory of God." Second, they were not to be an offence to each other. This includes Gentile with Jew, Jew with Jew, and Gentile with Gentile, whether Christian or not.

> We should heed Paul's admonition in this dynamic passage of Scripture. We often offend other believers by words and actions. Many Christians no longer fellowship with God's people because they are wounded spirits, as it were, having been offended by other Christians. Further,

> many non-Christian Gentiles who are referred to as Greeks in this passage, want nothing to do with Christ because of the words or actions of believers. And finally, Paul taught that we are not to offend the Jews, rather, we should love them. Jewish people the world over are looking for genuine love. Let's follow Paul's advice and show Jewish people the kind of love Christ has for them and for all mankind.[41]

These encouraging words from Dr. Fred Hartman, a converted Jew, should challenge every believer, young and old, to really love *every* Jew for his own soul's sake, just as God loves us and everyone for their own soul's sake.

CONCLUSION

Jews have suffered through a long history of anti-Semitism, often inspired or poured out in the name of Christianity. Is it any wonder that they say, "We don't need any dialogue with Christians. The best they have to offer has been demonstrated by 2,000 years of Church persecution."

This statement is only partially true. Not all Christians are to blame. Not all believers have entered into acts of persecution, verbal or physical abuse. Our Jewish friends need to understand that those who are true Christians do not harbor evil in their hearts against them. It is wrong for anyone, whether sinner or saint, to be guilty of anti-Semitism.

A Modern Jew Looks at Jesus. An article written by a Jew, Henry Einspruch, giving his opinion of Jesus, states:

> For more than nineteen centuries the Jews have been living in a world fired by a religion that was cradled to them. After all, Jesus was a Jew. His followers were Jews. The New Testament was written mostly by Jews, and Palestine, the land of the Jews, was a place from which sprang forth faith in Him of over 600 million people today. Do the Jews assert that all these people are demented and that they, the six million Jews, are sane?
>
> Does it not strike the Jews rather strange that a Jew, Jesus of Nazareth, should have surpassed the national heroes of every civilized land? Towering over Washington or Abraham Lincoln looms Jesus, the Jew, in the estimation of the people of America. Greater than Shakespeare or Darwin is the significance of Jesus to the people of England. Higher than Zola or Clemenceau rises Jesus in the veneration of the French people.[42]

APPENDIX B

THE JEWS—A CHALLENGE TO THE CHURCH

Despite all that we have learned about the majority of the Jews from *their* Old Testament and *our* New Testament, the world, and especially the Church, is indebted to these people. When Jesus was speaking with the Samaritan woman at the well, He said to her, "Salvation is *from* the Jews" (John 4:22). Some translators of the Bible say "*of* the Jews," but the literal translation is "*from the Jews.*" *From* indicates that *salvation,* who is Jesus Christ, Messiah, is by birth *from* Jewish lineage. When Jesus called Zacchaeus down from the sycamore tree, He said to him, "This day is salvation come to this house," which means that He, who is *Salvation,* is come to his house that day (Luke 19:1–10).

Since salvation has been revealed in and through the Person of Jesus Christ, and since the Jews are blinded in part for having rejected Him, God is calling out from among the Gentiles a people for His name (Acts 15:14). Those who trust in Him have been given truth, which is called the "Gospel," the one and only message to be preached to the whole world. There is no other name given under heaven but Jesus for one to be saved (Acts 15:14). "This is a faithful saying, and worthy of all acceptation, that Christ Jesus came into the world to save sinners," which includes Jews as well as every other person (I Timothy 1:15).

Having reviewed Israel's history and seeing them still in unbelief today in their new homeland, I have to ask the question, How concerned are Christians today, even in fundamental Churches, for the salvation of the Jewish people? I find very little concern. I hardly ever hear any discussion of their spiritual need. Paul's argument in the first five chapters of Romans is that Jews are as much sinners as anyone else and that their only hope for salvation is Jesus Christ, their Messiah. Christ has already fulfilled the Old Testament prophecy in being led to the slaughter as the sinner's sacrifice for sin. We are very much concerned about our unsaved loved ones, and rightly so since we all want to be together in eternity, but God doesn't love our family members any more than He loves the lowest sinner, simply because He is no respecter of persons.

I heard a great message, titled "Where are the Jews in the Pews?" The pews are empty of Jews mainly because many "New Testament" Church pastors have left the Jewish ministry to Christian-Hebrew organizations. This message on "empty pews" by a missionary to the Jews was very enlightening, and from it I ask the question, What has it cost the Church to withhold the Gospel from the Jews?[43] Here is the answer:

1. The Church has lost her balance. The Gospel is for *all.*
2. The Church has lost the blessing of God. We are not doing a *full* job; consequently we are losing blessings.
3. The Church has lost spiritual health and vigor. Her weakness is such that very few Gentiles are able to influence Jews.
4. The Church has lost her doctrinal unity. Never was Truth intended for one class of people to the exclusion of another.
5. The Church has lost her zeal. Since the Church's failure to obey the command to "go," the lost are *outside* the Church because Christians are on the *inside.*
6. The Church has lost the respect and friendship of the Jew himself.
7. The Church has lost a blessed fellowship
   - With the Father, who loves the Jew with an everlasting love (Jeremiah 31:3).
   - With the Holy Spirit, who first came upon the Jew.
   - With Christ, who came as the Seed of David.
   - With Christian Jews, because we do not seek them out.
   - In intercession, because we do not burden ourselves to pray for them (I Samuel 12:23a).

TO THE JEW FIRST

Romans 1:16 hits the nail on the head in the matter of Jewish evangelism. "The gospel . . . is the power of God unto salvation . . . to the Jew *first,* and also to the Greek [or other nationalities]." In New Testament days it was to the Jew first. It must break the heart of God as He looks down on the Church today and sees that the Jew has been put *last.* When believers remember that they have been purged from their old sins and that God saved them to serve, there will be a total dedication of self and a desire to be a *fisher of men,* including *all* men, Jew and Gentile alike. We need, as the hymn writer, a passion for souls.

Give Me a Passion for Souls, Dear Lord[44]

Give me a passion for souls, dear Lord,
A passion to save the lost;
O that thy love were by all adored,
And welcomed at any cost.
Jesus, I long, I long to be winning
Men who are lost and constantly sinning;
O may this hour be one of beginning
The story of pardon to tell.

May I suggest that you spend some time in prayer for the Lord to empower you to assume your responsibility to be a good soul winner? Just think, if believers in the past generation had not been faithful to the Lord in telling others of God's saving grace, where would you, or I, be today?

If you would like information about how best to witness to Jews, contact the organizations listed below; they will gladly send you helpful information.

The Friends of Israel Gospel Ministry Inc.
P.O. Box 908
Bellmawr, NJ 08099-0908

Immanuel Ministries International, Inc.
Message to Israel
P.O. Box 100052
Brooklyn, NY 11210-0052

The Chosen People Ministries, Inc.
1300 Cross Beam Drive
Charlotte, NC 28217-2800

Zion's Hope
P.O. Box 690909
Orlando, FL 32869

Jews for Jesus
60 Haight Street
San Francisco, CA 94102-5895

Global Outreach Mission
℅ Dr. Fred Hartman
P.O. Box 2010
Buffalo, NY 14231-2010

APPENDIX C

THE NEW COVENANT AND HOPE FOR THE JEWS

GOD'S COVENANT OF GRACE

The Scriptures speak of an old covenant and a new covenant—the dispensation of the law that was written on stone, and the dispensation of the law that is written in the heart. "Stone" refers to the Old Testament, "heart" to the New Testament. A generally accepted term combines these into "dispensations of law and grace." The old covenant dealt with the Jew prior to Christ's coming; the new, or Gospel, dispensation deals with those who, when Christ came, recognized and accepted Him as Messiah. It should be made clear that ever since Adam sinned and sin was passed upon *all* men, God, from the beginning, has had but *one* plan of salvation (Romans 5:12, 10:8–13).

In dealing with Israel, God prepared the way for the New Testament plan of salvation. He gave the law, which had several aspects: civil, moral, ceremonial, and religious. Perhaps the greatest thing in this revelation of His will was the giving of the moral law—the Ten Commandments, which are really an expression of what God is and what we must be in order to have His favor resting upon us. It should be understood, however, that God did not give the law so that, by the keeping of it, man should be saved, for the man has never lived who kept it. The law implied that one cannot save himself, because he has no merit of his own. It spelled out in black and white what sin is, and was to be in effect until the "Seed" should come who would fulfill the law. It was the "schoolmaster" to lead all who had sinned to Christ (Galatians 3:19, 24). The Gospel of John states, "For the law was given by Moses, but grace and truth came by Jesus Christ" (John 1:17). The purpose of Christ's coming was to defeat Satan, solve the sin problem, and be Lord both of the living and the dead (I John 3:8; I Peter 3:18; Romans 14:9).

When the Old Testament prophecies relating to the full ministry of Messiah were fulfilled, something devastating happened to the Jews' religion. Christ was the fulfillment of the Law and all the types and shadows of the sacrifices relating to the atonement for sin. "For the law having a shadow of good things to come, and not the very image of the things, can never with those sacrifices which they offered year by year continually make the comers thereunto perfect." If these sacrifices could make them perfect, cleansed once and for all, why offer them annually?

> For then would they not have ceased to be offered? Because the worshippers once purged should have had no more conscience of sins. But in those sacrifices there is a remembrance again made of sins every year. For it is not possible that the blood of bulls and of goats should take away sins. Wherefore when [Christ] cometh into the world, he saith, Sacrifice and offering thou wouldest not, but a body hast thou prepared me: In burnt offerings and sacrifices for sin thou hast had no pleasure. Then said I, Lo, I come (in the volume of the book it is written of me,) to do thy will, O God. Above when he said, Sacrifice and offering and burnt offerings and offering for sin thou wouldest not, neither hadst pleasure therein; which are offered by the law; Then said he, Lo, I come to do thy will, O God. He taketh away the first [covenant], that he may establish the second [covenant]. By the which will we are sanctified through the offering of the body of Jesus Christ once for all. . . . But this man, after he had offered one sacrifice for sins for ever, sat down on the right hand of God" (Hebrews 10:1–10, 12). See also Hebrews 1:3 and Psalm 40:6–8.

Truth in these verses is simple: Christ "taketh away the first [covenant], that he may establish the [new covenant]" (Hebrews 10:9). The old came to an end at Calvary when Christ, "blotting out the handwriting of ordinances that was against us, and took it out of the way, nailing it to his cross" (Colossians 2:14). Paul mentioned that there was the first, which was *natural,* afterward that which is *spiritual* (I Corinthians 15:46).

The old covenant, written on tablets of stone, is likened to "a letter that killeth," but the new covenant or testament is of the spirit that "giveth life" and writes the law in their hearts, as prophesied by Jeremiah (33:31–33; II Corinthians 3:3,6). The writer of Hebrews confirmed this by saying, "This is the covenant that I will make with them after those days, saith the Lord, I will put my laws into their hearts, and in their minds will I write them; And their sins and iniquities will I remember no more. . . . Now that which decayeth and waxeth old is ready to vanish away (Hebrews 10:16,17, 8:13). Jesus is now the surety of a better testament or covenant, and the valid confirmation of this covenant is that it is *everlasting* (Hebrews 7:22, 13:20).

The question is often asked, What about believing Jews, whose act of faith was counted for righteousness in Old Testament days—where do they stand in light of the old covenant having passed away and the new established? That there was a remnant of believing Jews in that period, none will deny. What effect does the establishment of the new have upon them? God gives the answer: through the offering of the blood of Christ without spot to God, "He is the mediator of the new testament [covenant], that by means of death, for the redemption of the transgressions that were under the first testament, they which are called might receive the promise of eternal inheritance" (Hebrews 9:14–15). This verse assures us that the remnant was made up of Abraham's spiritual seed, having expressed faith to declare righteousness.

THE JEWISH PEOPLE AFTER CHRIST

What about the Jewish people since Messiah's establishment of the new covenant? There are two questions that we need to consider: Who is a Jew? and What is the spiritual status of an unbelieving Jew?

Who is a Jew? We define a Jew as a person who can trace his natural ancestry back to Abraham, Isaac, and Jacob. There are some who say that they are Jews, but their identity is misleading—they have fair skin, blue eyes, and blond hair. Intermarriage with others besides Jews over the centuries has made some to look otherwise. Some have the Jewish identity, and some do not. The Chinese people, for example, have for centuries before Christ had a unifying identity, but to say that one is a Jew by identity is not always true.

A related question, What is a Jew?, has been discussed often, especially in recent years because of the many changes that have engulfed the Jewish people as a nation and as individuals. Judaism, as a religion, is practiced in many different forms: Orthodox, Conservative, and Reform. With various degrees of "faith" among the Hebrew people, with one congregation voting to retain a Rabbi who affirmed that he is an atheist, with some Reform groups stating that in the years ahead it may be that Judaism will find no value in the word "God," one wonders: What is a Jew?

A public opinion survey of 1,500 Jewish families, conducted by the National Religious Party, on the "Who is a Jew?" question, yielded the following results:

12% declared that a Jew is a person whose father or mother was Jewish or who has a Jewish spouse.
23% claimed that a Jew is a person who considers himself a Jew.
19% upheld religious law, that is, that a man born to a Jewish mother or who converts to Judaism is a Jew.
13% said that a Jew is one who lives in Israel or who identifies himself or herself with the Jewish state.
13% said that a Jew is one who observes Jewish religious practices.
11% answered that a Jew is one who is raised and educated as a Jew.
9% said that they could not define the term.

When Israel became a nation, it was created as a safe haven for *all* Jews.

Regardless of these varied definitions of a Jew, he is a Hebrew who can trace his lineage to Shem through father Abraham. Strictly speaking, Jews belong to an ethnic group, the same as an African, Italian, Chinese, or German.

The Spiritual Status of a Jew. When Paul wrote to the Church at Corinth, he listed three classes of people (I Corinthians 10:32), making a distinction between the first two (Jews and Gentiles) and the third (the Church of

God). The first two groups were unbelieving Jews and pagans/heathens, those of other nationalities. The Church of God included converts to Christ made up of national Jews and peoples of other nations. Those in the Church were distinguished from lost sinners, whether they were of the Jewish race or other nationalities.

Since the old covenant has passed away, Jews who are of the natural seed of Abraham have no spiritual hope or claim to anything pertaining to the Law. Sacrifices are no longer valid, since the veil of the Temple was rent in twain at Christ's death and a new and living way was established or opened for *anyone* to come boldly to God through Christ, no matter what their national origin is. Christ is *now* the Way, the Truth, and the Life (Hebrews 10:19–22; John 14:6). Before God, all Jews, all Caucasians, all those who are black, yellow, brown, or red, are lost without Christ—period. Every human being is of one blood (Acts 17:26), and when God looks at the human race, He sees only two classes of people—saved and lost. He does not see a Jew or any other ethnic group. All are precious in His sight, but each, without Christ, is under condemnation and under God's wrath (John 3:18, 36; Romans 3:9). With the establishment of the new covenant, all human beings have equal standing. God has commanded *man everywhere* to repent, and it is appointed unto man once to die, and after that, the judgment (Acts 17:30–31; Hebrews 9:27).

The Gospel of John states that "the law was given by Moses, but grace and truth came by Jesus Christ" (1:17,18). In a note on this verse, the 1917 *Scofield Reference Bible* says, "As a dispensation, grace began with the death and resurrection of Christ. *The point of testing is no longer legal obedience as the condition of salvation.*[45] From this note it appears that God had two plans of salvation—legal obedience to the law under the old covenant and a crucified Christ in the new. One is saved *only* "by grace . . . *through* faith; and . . . not of works"; "a man is justified by faith without the deeds of the law" (Ephesians 2:8,9; Romans 3:28).

Are Jews God's Favored People Today? God chose Jews, not because He loved them more than He loved all peoples that He created, but because He used them in giving the world His will and His plan for the redemption of the human race. "Salvation is *from* the Jews" (John 4:24). From the blood sacrifice that provided "coats of skin" for Adam and Eve to give them standing again before God to the blood sacrifice of Christ to cleanse us from sin, God has had only one plan of salvation. With the inauguration of "grace" coming by Jesus Christ and acceptance of Him as Saviour, God now becomes their God and they become His people, or children (John 1:12; Romans 8:16).

In reviewing the standing of Jewish people in his epistle to the Romans, the Apostle Paul made note of the following:

1. God is no respecter of persons: 2:11.
2. Those who have sinned—Jew or Gentile—will all be judged by Christ: 2:12,16.

3. A hypocritical Jew causes God's name to be blasphemed among the peoples of the world: 2:17–24.
4. One is not a Jew unless his circumcision is of the heart: 1:28,29 with Jeremiah 4:4.
5. Jews have the advantage of truth because the "oracles of God" (the Scriptures) were entrusted to them, but they are no better than others because all have sinned and come short of God's glory: 3:1–2,9,23.
6. God is the God of both Jews and Gentiles: 3:29.
7. One receives righteousness by faith, whether circumcised or not: 4:1–9.
8. They are lost: 9:1–3, 10:1.
9. One is not of *spiritual* Israel who is *natural* Israel: 9:6.
10. Israelites who follow the law of righteousness have not attained righteousness, because they seek it not by faith: 9:30–32.
11. They stumble at the stumbling Stone (Christ): 9:32,33; I Peter 2:6–8.
12. They are ignorant of God's righteousness because they seek to establish their own: 10:3.
13. There is no difference between them and the Gentiles: 10:12.
14. Whom God foreknew would believe on Christ (Messiah), He selected. God has not cast off His people whom He foreknew. There is a remnant according to the election of grace. Only those Jews in the election of His foreknowledge have or will obtain salvation: 11:1,2,5,7.
15. All people—Jews and Gentiles—are in unbelief without Christ: 11:32.

In reviewing any man's standing before God without Christ, we conclude the following:

1. Both Jew and Gentile, *all* are under sin: Romans 3:9; Jeremiah 9:25.
2. Christ Jesus came unto the world to save sinners: I Timothy 1:15.
3. Neither is there salvation in any other (than Jesus Christ), "for there is none other name under heaven given among men whereby we must be saved" (Acts 4:10–12).
4. Jews may be saved on the same terms as anyone else: Acts 16:31, 20:20,21; Romans 10:123,13.
5. Never mind the future, *today* is the day of salvation for all mankind: now is the accepted time: II Corinthians 6:2.

Jews may be saved today in the same way that all others may be saved, by repenting of their sins and exercising faith in Jesus, the only Saviour of men (Luke 13:3; Galatians 2:16). By so doing, they are "justified freely by his grace through the redemption that is in Christ Jesus: Whom God hath set forth to be a propitiation through faith in his blood, to declare his righteousness for the remission of sins that are past, through the forbearance of God; To declare, I say, at this time his righteousness: that he might be just, and the justifier of him which believeth in Jesus. . . . Therefore we conclude that a *man* is justified by faith without the deeds of the law" (Romans 3:24–26,28).

It is tragic for any person to be ill- or misinformed as to God's purpose in redemption for the whole human race. What every individual must learn from both the Old and New testaments is that one's faith is counted for righteousness, that salvation is "free," and that the wages of sin is death, but the gift of God is eternal life through our Lord Jesus Christ (James 2:23; Romans 6:23).

CONCLUSION

God does not recognize anyone in Christ as a "national" or "ethnic" Christian. He sees them as new creatures in Christ, having been baptized into the body of Christ, the Church. "There is neither Greek [foreigner] nor Jew, circumcision nor uncircumcision, Barbarian, Scythian, bond nor free . . . neither male nor female: for ye are all *one* in Christ Jesus . . . who is all, and in all (Colossians 3:11; Galatians 3:28). As stated previously, all believers in Christ have become God's *chosen* generation, His royal priesthood, His holy nation, and His peculiar people (I Peter 2:9). Under the old covenant, the Jews only were God's chosen nation, His peculiar people. Now, under the new covenant, *all believers* are His chosen ones.

Some Jews who receive Christ as Messiah make much of the fact that they are "Hebrew Christians" or "Messianic Jews." They are Jews who are saved, and although they are in Christ, they do not lose their ethnic background. If one is born a Jew, he will die a Jew. One who is born of another race will die his racial origin. No one is born a Christian, but anyone who is born again, Jew or foreigner, is positionally sanctified forever and is *complete* in Christ (Hebrews 10:14; Colossians 2:10). Many converted Jews will boast that they are "completed" Jews, but this is true of *every* believer. It is wonderful to know that in this dispensation of the new covenant or testament, *all* believers are *equal*—we are heirs of God and joint heirs with Jesus Christ (Romans 8: 16–17). We can all thank God that when Christ died, he died for all lost mankind, no matter what their national or ethnic origin is.

If anyone, regardless of nationality, ever has Scripture fulfilled in his or her life, it has to be done on the basis of Abraham's decision: "And the scripture was fulfilled which saith, Abraham believed God, and it was imputed unto him for righteousness [righteousness put to his account, making him likewise]: and he was called the Friend of God" (James 2:23). Such a decision makes one a child of God *by faith* in Christ Jesus, and if we are Christ's, we are Abraham's seed and heirs according to the promise. This eliminates nationality, for in Christ there is no such thing—we are one in Him (Galatians 3:26–29).

APPENDIX D
JEWISH EVANGELISM

There is much to-do in Christian circles today concerning what is in store for Jews in the future—much unfulfilled prophecy that awaits them either in the tribulation period or the millennium. Just before Christ ascended, His disciples were concerned about the future, saying, "Lord, wilt thou at this time restore again the kingdom to Israel? And He said unto them, It is not for you to know the times or the seasons, which the Father hath put in his own power. But ye shall receive power, after that the Holy Ghost is come upon you: and ye shall be witnesses unto me . . . unto the uttermost part of the earth" (Acts 1:6–8). In what we call the "Great Commission," Christ told His disciples to "go ye into all the world, and preach the gospel to every creature." They obeyed and "went forth, and preached every where" (Mark 16:15, 20). It is apparent that the responsibility of believers is to "arise and go" anywhere, everywhere to reach the lost with the Gospel. "Today is the day of salvation," not tomorrow. "Only one life 'twill soon be past, only what's done for Christ will last." And if Jesus told His disciples not to be so much concerned with the future, but recognize the present need, who are we to do otherwise?

Every believer is to be a soul-winner. "Let the redeemed of the Lord say so" (Psalm 107:2). Not only are believers to witness individually, but a church's ministry in evangelism is not complete unless the pastor has encouraged and adopted a strong missionary program. This, of necessity, would include *Jewish evangelism.* Most fundamental and missionary-minded churches in America claim to be "New Testament" churches: they adhere to Biblical truths, usually with the statement, "We preach Jesus Christ crucified, risen, and coming again." In examining their method of reaching the lost, however, we find that the vast majority *exclude* any evangelism for the Jews. Their programs simply are not geared to reaching them. In New Testament days, Jews were surprised if any Gentiles were saved. Today it is news if a Jew becomes a Christian. That the Christian Church in general ignores the Jews, none will deny. It seems that sharing Christ with them is a taboo. We talk about reaching the lost, but *which* lost?

A quick look at the Book of Acts convinces us that Peter used the Jews' own Scripture to reach Jewish people who had gathered at Jerusalem, and almost 3,000 were saved (Acts 2:22–36). Later, under the preaching of the Word, almost 5,000 men were saved, with no mention of the women and children who experienced the joy of God's salvation (Acts 3:12–4:4). What we see here is that at the beginning of New Testament evangelism, Jews reached Jews. But when it came time to "branch out" to reach Gentiles, God had a battle with the key Jewish evangelist, Peter, in getting him to witness to one (Acts 10). True, the early New Testament Church was Jewish oriented, but the converted Saul (Paul) was anointed to preach to "Gentiles . . . and the children of Israel" (Acts 9:15). We note from his missionary journeys that both Jew and Greek (Gentile) were saved under his ministry.

Once Christianity began to take hold on both the Asian and European continents, this pattern of Paul's has been God's will all along. Why, then, are not the so-called "New Testament" churches of our day seeking to reach all—Jew and Gentile—who are lost? Did not Isaiah the Prophet say that "*all* we like sheep have gone astray . . . and the Lord hath laid on Him [Messiah] the iniquity of us *all*" (Isaiah 53:6), and did not the Jewish apostle say that Christ died for us *all* (Romans 5:6,8; II Corinthians 5:14,15)? Can a church that has an extensive missionary program but does not support Jewish evangelism really claim that it is fulfilling God's "Great Commission"?

The reasons why we are failing to evangelize the Jews are, I believe, only *excuses.*

Excuse No. 1. Could it be the stigma that down through the centuries we have blamed the Jew for crucifying Christ and called them Christ-killers?

Certainly, Jews have hated Christians for calling them that. Peter himself accused the Jews of doing just that (Acts 2:22,23), but in reality it was the Romans who did the actual killing. Peter, I believe, was blaming the Jews for their instigating the crucifixion through false trials, but he let them know in no uncertain terms that Christ's death was in God's plan from before the foundation of the world (Revelation 13:8). Why, then, should we blame the Jews, when we, too, are guilty? Everyone's sins were nailed to the tree (I Peter 2:24), and we have no excuse for blaming them alone.

Excuse No. 2. The Church has been taught that the Jewish people were condemned of God—cut off—and could not be saved.

Today, some are even teaching that the Jewish people do not need to be saved, but rather that they are saved under a different covenant, or in a future dispensation, forgetting that they are lost *today.* There has been so much prophetic teaching of a glorious future for the Jew and a Temple in the millennium after they look upon Him whom they have pierced, that there is no concern for them now. Some believe that because Jews are God's chosen people, none are in need of Christ. We forget Paul's teaching that "they are not all Israel, which are of Israel" (Romans 9:6b). Yes, there was a "remnant" who believed, but only the individual Jew who believed by faith was counted righteous. It took "faith" for righteousness then, the same as it does today (Romans 4:1–8; Ephesians 2:8,9). If a Jew without Christ is as hell bound as any Gentile without Christ, why try to reach one and not the other? God is no respecter of persons, so who are we to be? (Acts 10:34). We have no business hoarding the Gospel—we must *share* it with *all* sinners.

Excuse No. 3. "Blindness in part is happened to Israel" (Romans 11:25).

It is quite possible that many Gentile believers are "blinded in part" to the need of reaching Jews for Jesus. They seem to think that because God is "calling out from the Gentiles a people for His name," this is the "Gentile dispensation," and only Gentiles are called by God (Acts 15:13–18). When we look at Israel's history, we can understand why "God spared not the natural branches" (Romans 11:21a). Going all the way back to their disobedience to God and His judgment upon a thousand generations, we can see the fulfillment of this portion of Scripture upon this race of people (Deuteronomy 28:15–68). Their blindness is due to their own substitution of "tradition" for Scriptures (Matthew 15:3,6; I Peter 1:18). This unbelief in God's Word led to their rejection of Christ as their own Messiah as He came to his own people (John 1:11), and ultimately to their demand that Pilate crucify Him. As Moses said, they would become a hated people, a "byword," a "proverb" among all nations. But they are not blinded *completely,* only *in part.* We have no right to "write them off." They are still loved by God, who loves *all* sinners, and if He loves them, we have no excuse for not doing the same and seeking to win them.

It makes no difference whether a Jew lived in the Old Testament period or in the New, or might be alive during the tribulation period or the millennium reign of Christ: *he is a sinner before God.* God has only *one* plan of salvation—faith through blood, either looking forward to Christ's sacrifice or looking back to His finished work once and for all at Calvary. This same plan will apply to anyone, after the rapture of the Church, whose robes will be washed white in the blood of the Lamb (Revelation 7:9–14). If any Jew or Gentile has not, or will not, obtain God's righteousness in Christ by faith, he is on the broad road leading to destruction (Matthew 7:19; Isaiah 14:9).

Excuse No. 4. They might not listen to us as we proclaim the Gospel.

Paul reminds us that people do not hear because those who are sent do not go to inform them about the Gospel: "How shall they hear without a preacher? And how shall they preach, except they be sent?" (Romans 10:14–17).

Excuse No. 5. Only one with a Jewish background can effectively witness to Jewish people.

Titus, a Gentile, had many occasions to witness to Jews in his travels with Paul and in the churches on the island of Crete. Luke was a Gentile, and he, too, witnessed to many Jews. Any Gentile who has a changed life as a Christian and is neighborly without prejudice, can be an effective witness to anyone, including *Jews.* "If ye have respect to persons, ye commit sin" (James 2:1,9).

Excuse No. 6. We simply don't know how to witness to Jewish people.

What about other religions that do not recognize Christ? When Elijah had his contest with the prophets of Baal on Mount Carmel, he knew enough about what they believed to combat them with truth. We need to know what another believes and then use Scripture to show truth. If all are saved by grace through faith, it isn't a matter of going to one with one plan of salvation and to another with a different one. When Paul preached, he gave the Gospel in a nutshell in I Corinthians 15:3,4, and he got the Gospel from the Old Testament. We need to familiarize ourselves with what the other fellow believes. If one feels inadequate in how to witness, especially to a Jew, he may write for assistance to any organization interested in the salvation of Jews. See page 219 for a list of such organizations.

SUGGESTIONS FOR WITNESSING TO JEWS

1. You must realize that all unsaved Jews are lost (Romans 10:1).
2. You must love them as God loves you (Acts 10:34; John 3:16).
3. You must make the first move, being friendly and willing to converse with them, and win their confidence (Leviticus 19:18; James 2:8).
4. You must let them see that Christ is a reality in your own heart and life (II Corinthians 5:17).
5. You must use *their* Old Testament Scriptures to show what they say about their coming Messiah. Isaiah 53 and Daniel 9:24–27 are good portions to use. Isaiah refers to a *person* who bears sin (and not the nation Israel), and Daniel pinpoints the time of Messiah's first appearance. You need an historical background for this portion to know when the command was given to rebuild Jerusalem (see the time of Messiah's coming in the index). Be familiar with verses that show that an Israelite was accepted as being righteous by God through faith, and not by *works* of righteousness.

There are many things that God wants the Jew to know from his Old Testament, but here are a few promises for them if they receive Messiah:

- "A new heart also will I give you, and a new spirit will I put within you: and I will take away the stony heart out of your flesh and will give you a heart of flesh. I will put My Spirit within you and cause you to walk in My statutes, and ye shall keep My judgments and do them" (Ezekiel 36:26,27).
- "I will ransom them from the power of the grave; I will redeem them from death: o death, I will be thy plagues; o grave, I will be thy destruction" (Hosea 13:14).
- "And many of them that sleep in the dust of the earth shall awake, some to everlasting life" (Daniel 12:2).
- "For I know that my Redeemer liveth, and that He shall stand in the latter day upon the earth: and though after my skin worms destroy this body, yet in my flesh I shall see God, Whom I shall see for myself, and mine eyes shall behold, and not another, though my reins be consumed within me" (Job 19:25–27).

These promises and blessings must be appropriated to be effective. Just as Ezekiel said that we must give warnings, such verses as "Today if you will hear His voice, harden not your heart," and "Boast not thyself of tomorrow, for thou knowest not what a day might bring forth" should be used wisely (Ezekiel 3:18,19; Psalm 95:7,8; Proverbs 27:1).

6. Having familiarized yourself with the literature made available by the organizations listed on page 219, literature that lists prophecies fulfilled in Christ and verses that relate to the Trinity, present copies of the literature to those to whom you witness.
7. Get your church involved in Jewish evangelism. Plan to have a special evangelistic ministry for them.
8. *Never* give up in your pursuit to win them. Jews are "tough to crack," but all things are possible with God. They are steeped in tradition and oral laws; for them to accept Christ means that they must forsake all the teachings of their parents and rabbis.

I Did Not Know They Wanted Me[46]

A Jewish girl learned Christ was God and for her sins had died,
And in a Gentile place of prayer, she came, and wept, and cried.
"I did not know you wanted us, my heart was grieved and sore.
If I had known you wanted us, I would have come before."
She failed, within the Law, to find a pardon for her sins.
And did not know the Church of Christ would gladly let her in.
And many more of Israel would seek the Savior's face,
If they were sure within His Church they'd find a welcome place.
Let every Christian Church awake in this auspicious day,
And offer life to every man, till not one soul can say:
"I did not know you wanted us, my heart was grieved and sore.
If I had known you wanted us, I would have come before.

APPENDIX E
CUSTOMS

This is a survey of the offerings and feasts instituted by God for Israel while on her wilderness journey, their purpose, and the period of their validity, as well as feasts that the Israelites adopted later in response to certain circumstances and events.

MOSAIC OFFERINGS AND SACRIFICES

Prior to sacrificial laws and instructions given at Mount Sinai and during Israel's journey to the Promised Land, the practice of sacrifices was familiar to God's people from their knowledge of Cain, Abel, Noah, and the patriarchs. On behalf of Israel, Moses received special instructions for various kinds of offerings, four of them involving the shedding of blood.

1. *Burnt offering.* The entire animal sacrifice was consumed on the altar (Leviticus 1:5–17, 6:8–13). A lamb was offered each morning and evening to remind Israel of her devotion to God. The apostle Paul gave a good spiritual application by reminding believers to "present your bodies a *living* sacrifice" (Romans 12:1).
2. *Peace offering* (Leviticus 3:1–17, 7:11–34). This voluntary offering represented communion and companionship between man and God. It involved the sprinkling of blood to make atonement for sin. See also Leviticus 19:5–8, 22:21–25.
3. *Sin offering.* This was required for sins committed ignorantly and sins committed knowingly (Leviticus 5:1–35, 6:24–30). Many other reasons for the offering are listed throughout Leviticus.
4. *Trespass offering* (Leviticus 5:14–6:7, 7:1–7). This offering related to the legal rights of a person, his property, and his responsibility for bringing to God the first fruits, tithe, and other required offerings. By paying his dues, one was always aware of the price of sin.
5. *Grain offering* (Leviticus 2:1–16, 6:14–23). This offering required no animal sacrifice, but the presentation of the fruit of one's labor, indicating the dedication of his gifts to God.

FEASTS AND SEASONS

Mosaic Festivals

1. *The Sabbath,* Israel's day of rest (Exodus 20:8–11). This day was to be a reminder that God rested from His creative works on the seventh day and that God had freed them—giving them "rest" from Egyptian bondage to become His holy people (Exodus 31:13; Deuteronomy 5:12–15). This day of rest was not only for them personally, but for their hired help and animals.
2. *New Moon and Feast of Trumpets,* the announcement of the beginning of the new month (Numbers 10:10). With the blast of the Trumpets, the New Moon feast was observed by appropriate food and by sin- and burnt-offering sacrifices (Numbers 28:11–15).
3. *Sabbatical Year* (Leviticus 25:1–7). The purpose of this year was to let the land rest every seventh year with the fields not sown and the vineyards not pruned. Debts were cancelled and slaves were freed (Deuteronomy 15:1–18). It was due to Israel's failure to keep the Sabbatical Year for 490 years that caused her to be taken into Babylonian captivity for 70 years (Leviticus 26: 34–43; II Chronicles 36:20,21).
4. *Year of Jubilee.* Occurring every fiftieth year or every seven observances of the Sabbatical Year, this was a time to proclaim liberty throughout the land (Leviticus 25:8–55). Family inheritance was restored if it had been lost.
5. *Passover,* or *Feast of Unleavened Bread.* These two formed a double festival: to commemorate deliverance from Egyptian bondage and the establishment of God's redemptive act—"When I see the blood I will pass over you" (Leviticus 23:4–8; Exodus 12:12).
6. *Feast of Weeks,* or *Feast of Pentecost.* This feast was observed 50 days after the wheat harvest, by offering two loaves of unleavened bread to the Lord in the Tabernacle, to thank Him for supplying daily bread and to remind Israel how He had supplied her with manna in the wilderness (Exodus 16:15; Leviticus 23:15–20; Deuteronomy 16:9).
7. *Feast of Tabernacles,* or *Booths.* This was the last of the sacred festivals under the old covenant. It was a time when the Israelites lived in tents to remind them how their ancestors wandered in the wilderness and lived in tents or booths (Leviticus 12:33–43).
8. *Day of Atonement.* This is the Jews' highest holy day. It was the day that the high priest sprinkled the blood of two sacrificial animals, one for his own sins and the other for the sins of the people (Leviticus 16; 23:26–32; Numbers 29:7–11). In this way he made an atonement for the holy place because of the uncleanness of the children of Israel (Leviticus 16:16). This yearly event showed God's hatred for sin and revealed to Israel how infectious sin is, reminding them of death. Its annual observance pointed to their Messiah as the One upon whom God would lay all sin (Isaiah 53:6; Hebrews 10:10; I Peter 2:24).

Post-Mosaic Festivals

Besides the festivals in the Law of Moses, others were observed to perpetuate the memory either of great national deliverances or of great national calamities. There were four fasts and three feasts.

Fasts

The only Divinely ordained public fast was to be held on the Day of Atonement. Beginning with the Babylonian captivity, the Jews added what may be called "memorial feasts" on the anniversaries of the occurrence of specific events.

1. The *Fast of the Fourth Month* (Tammus—June-July), in memory of the taking of Jerusalem by Nebuchadnezzar and the interruption of the daily sacrifice.
2. The *Fast of the Fifth Month* (Ab—July-August), in memory of the destruction of the first Temple and desecration of the second Temple.
3. The *Fast of the Seventh Month* (Tishri—September-October), in memory of the slaughter of Governor Gedaliah at Mizpah (Jeremiah 41:1,2).
4. The *Fast of the Tenth Month* (Tebeth—December-January), when Nebuchadnezzar began his siege of Jerusalem.

Feasts

1. The *Feast of the Wood Offering.* This feast commemorated the last of the nine occasions on which offerings of wood were brought for use in construction of the Temple after Israel's Babylonian captivity. It was a time when the people, notably the priests and Levites, brought wood in the best of condition.
2. The *Feast of Purim,* also called the *Feast of Esther,* and sometimes called *The Day of Mordecai.* The word *Purim* is derived from "the lot" that Haman cast to determine the best time to have all the Jews in the kingdom of Ahasuerus slain. The Jews were spared, Haman was hanged on the gallows that he built to hang Mordecai, and Purim is celebrated in the month of Adar (February-March) to commemorate the Jews' being spared. See Esther and the Laws of the Medes and Persians in the index.
3. The *Feast of Dedication,* or *Feast of Lights.* This feast was instituted after the Maccabees won back independence from the Greek Antiochus Epiphanes in 164 B.C. In cleansing the Temple to rededicate it, there was just enough oil in the sacred candlestick to keep it burning for one day. Miraculously, it burned for eight days. Today, the feast is called *Hanukkah* and is celebrated on the twenty-fifth day of Kislev (November-December).

CONCLUSION

Jews today, by custom, still observe many of the sacrifices, offerings, and feasts found in the Old Testament Scriptures, plus those added in later years.

The Mosaic offerings of the Torah all foreshadowed Messiah—His coming, His ministry, and His blood sacrifice for sin as the Lamb of God, foreordained by God as mentioned by Peter (Acts 2:22,23). If these Old Testament types and shadows of Christ are a part of God's holy Word, *and they are,* they were a part of the old covenant that is now obsolete—done away with—all nailed to the Cross with atonement for sin having been provided by the Son of God—Messiah—*once and for all!* All that is left for any Jew today—or anyone else for that matter—is what was accomplished by Messiah at Calvary (Romans 5: 6–8).

NOTES

1. Robert T. Boyd, "Joseph in Egypt," *World's Bible Handbook* (Iowa Falls, Ia.: World Bible Publishers, 1991), 99.
2. George B. Fletcher, Bible Institute of Pennsylvania, Pa., from lecture, October 1940. Used by permission.
3. Boyd, "The 'I Wills' of God," *World's Bible Handbook*, 71.
4. Ibid., "Answer to Moses' Prayer," 87.
5. Ibid., "Manna," 55.
6. Adam Clarke, *Adam Clarke's Commentary,* vol. 1 (Nashville: Abingdon-Cokesbury Press, n.d.), 468.
7. Boyd, "The Brazen Serpent," *World's Bible Handbook*, 83.
8. J. Vernon McGee, *Briefing the Bible* (Wheaton, Ill.: Van Kampen, 1949), 14.
9. M.M.B. *The Seven Nations of Canaan* (Pittsburgh: Bethany House, 1946), 24.
10. Robert T. Boyd, *Baal Worship in Old Testament Days* (Hagerstown, Pa.: Hagerstown Printing, 1960), 2.
11. Boyd, "Conditions for Success," *World's Bible Handbook*, 125.
12. Bishop Pillai, Indian Orthodox Church, "Rahab," from message, 1946. Used by permission.
13. The lyrics from the song "Rolled Away," written by W. D. Kallenbach, are used by permission from Encore Publications, © 1972.
14. Clarke, "Gilgal," *Adam Clarke's Commentary,* vol. 2 (Nashville: Abingdon-Cokesbury Press, n.d.), 19.
15. Harry Rimmer, *The Harmony of Science and Scripture* (Grand Rapids: Eerdmans, 1942), 273.
16. Stephen Bly, "Little Did Joshua Know," *Moody Monthly* (April 1978): 106.
17. The lyrics from the song "Turn Your Eyes Upon Jesus," written by Helen H. Lemmel, are used by permission from Encore Publications, © 1972.
18. Boyd, "Cities of Refuge," *World's Bible Handbook*, 83.
19. Ibid., 195.
20. Clarke, *Adam Clarke's Commentary,* vol. 2, 676.
21. Joseph P. Free, *Archeology and Bible History* (Wheaton, Ill.: Van Kampen, 1950), 211.
22. C. I. Scofield, ed., *Scofield Reference Edition of the Bible* (New York: Oxford University Press, 1945), 1,323.
23. Robert T. Boyd, "God's Job for Me," *Clip 'N Save* (Scranton, Pa.: Bob Boyd, 1961), 26.
24. Sam Nadler, "A Fence Around the Law," *The Chosen People* (November 1990): 7.
25. Arnold Fruchtenbaum, *Jewishness and the Trinity* (San Francisco: Jews for Jesus, n.d.), 3.
26. J. I. Packer, Merrill C. Tenney, and William White, Jr., *The Bible Almanac* (Nashville: Thomas Nelson, 1980), 511.

27. Michael Grant, *Tacitus: The Annals of Imperial Rome* (New York: Dorset Press, 1984), 364.
28. W. D. Mahan, "Pontius Pilate's Letter to Caesar," *The Archko Volume* (Philadelphia: Antiquarian, 1896), 129.
29. Scofield, *Scofield Reference Edition of the Bible,* 1,132.
30. Merrill F. Unger, *Unger's Bible Handbook* (Chicago: Moody Press, 1966), 462.
31. Boyd, "Save Me from This Hour," *World's Bible Handbook*, 439.
32. Allen Clark, "The Court Trials of Jesus—Illegal," *Faith for the Family* (March-April 1976): 14.
33. Wyatt H. Heard, "A Judge Looks at the Trial of Jesus," *Harvester* (n.d.), 7.
34. Boyd, *World's Bible Handbook*, 461.
35. Marv Rosenthal, "Not Without Design," *Forsaken* (n.d.), 17.
36. Sam Nadler, "Cheap Sacrifices," *The Chosen People* (December 1990): 12.
37. Steve Schwartz, *Dear Rabbi* (Orangeburg, N.Y.: Chosen People Ministries, 1980), 11.
38. Nadler, *The Chosen People* (December 1990): 12.
39. Eliezer Shulman, *The Sequence of Events in the Old Testament* (Jerusalem: Ministry of Defense Publishing House, 1978), 17.
40. Sam Nadler, from letter. Used by permission.
41. Fred Hartman, Friends of Israel Gospel Ministry. Used by permission.
42. Henry Einspruch, *A Modern Jew Looks at Jesus* (Baltimore: Lederer Messianic, 1964), n.p.
43. Charles Stevens, *What It Has Cost the Church to Withhold Christ from the Jews* (New York: American Board of Missions to the Jews), 13.
44. The lyrics from the song "A Passion for Souls," written by Herbert G. Tovey, are used by permission from Encore Publications, © 1972.
45. Scofield, *Scofield Reference Edition of the Bible,* 1,115.
46. *I Did Not Know You Wanted Us* (Independence, Mo.: Gospel Tract Society, n.d.).

BIBLIOGRAPHY

"Anti-semitism." *Israel My Glory* (April/May 1993): n.p.

Armerding, Carl. *The Fight for Palestine in the Days of Joshua.* Wheaton, Ill.: Van Kampen, 1945.

Baseman, Bob. *Masada: Pictorial Guide and Souvenir.* Jerusalem: Palphot, n.d.

Boyd, Robert T. *Baal Worship in Old Testament Days.* Hagerstown, Pa.: Hagerstown Printing, 1960.

———. *World's Bible Handbook.* Iowa Falls, Ia.: World Bible Publishers, 1991.

———. *Tells, Tombs, and Treasure: A Pictorial Guide to Biblical Archaeology.* Eugene, Ore.: Harvest House, 1981.

Brickner, Al. "The Jewishness of the New Testament," *Issues: A Messianic Perspective.* San Francisco: Jews for Jesus (n.d.): 1:2.

Ceperley, Gordon G. *A Promised Land for a Chosen People.* Bellmawr, N.J.: Friends of Israel, 1979.

Chappell, Clovis G. *When the Church Was Young.* Nashville: Abingdon-Cokesbury, 1950.

Dimont, Max I. *Jews, God and History.* New York: New American Library, 1962.

Douglas, J. D., and Merrill C. Tenney, eds. *The New International Dictionary of the Bible.* Grand Rapids: Zondervan, 1987.

Edersheim, Alfred. *The Temple, Its Ministry and Services As They Were at the Time of Jesus Christ.* Boston: A. I. Bradley, 1874.

Eerdmans' Atlas of the Bible. Grand Rapids: Eerdmans, 1978.

Einspruch, Henry. *A Modern Jew Looks at Jesus.* Baltimore: Lederer Messianic, 1964.

The New Encyclopædia Britannica, ed. 15, vol. 8. Chicago: Encyclopædia Britannica, 1995.

Fleischer, Jerome. *Recognizing the Messiah.* Bellmawr, N.J.: Friends of Israel, n.d.

Free, Joseph P. *Archaeology and Bible History.* Wheaton, Ill.: Van Kampen, 1950.

Fruchtenbaum, Arnold. *Jewishness and Hebrew Christianity.* Orangeburg, N.J.: Sar Shalom, n.d.

Gardner, Joseph L. *Reader's Digest Atlas of the Bible.* Pleasantville, N.Y.: Reader's Digest, 1981.

Gartenhaus, Jacob. *The Virgin Birth of the Messiah.* Atlanta: Southern Baptist Home Mission Board, n.d.

Goldberg, Daniel. "To the Jew Last," *The Chosen People* (n.d.).

Grant, Michael. *Tacitus: The Annals of Imperial Rome.* New York: Penguin, 1956.

Haldeman, I. M. *The Tabernacle, Priesthood and Offerings.* New York: Revell, 1925.

Hartman, Fred. "Combating Anti-Semitism in the Church," *Israel My Glory* (April/May 1993): n.p.

———. "Where is the Jew in the Pew?" n.d., n.p.

Hauck, Gary L. *Equipped for Service.* Schaumburg, Ill.: Regular Baptist, 1993.

Hertzberg, Arthur. *Judaism.* New York: George Braziller, 1961.
Hill, Gary. *The Discovery Bible (New Testament).* Chicago: Moody Press, 1987.
The Holy Scriptures. New York: Hebrew Publications, 1936.
The Holy Scriptures According to the Masoretic Text. Philadelphia: Jewish Publications Society, 1945.
"How Would You Recognize the Messiah?" *Israel My Glory* (April/May 1993): n.p.
"Jewishness and Hebrew Christianity," *The Chosen People* (November 1990): n.p.
"Jewishness and the Trinity," *Issues: A Messianic Perspective.* San Francisco: Jews for Jesus (n.d.): 1:8.
Josephus, Flavius. *The Jewish War,* translated by G. A. Williamson. Harmondsworth: Penguin Books, 1959.
Levy, David M. "Anti-Semitism in the Middle Ages," *Israel My Glory* (April/May 1993): n.p.
M.M.B. *The Seven Nations of Canaan.* Pittsburgh: Bethany House, 1946.
McQuaid, Elwood. "A Portrait of the Messiah," *Israel My Glory* (November 1992): n.p.
Mahan, W. D. "Pontius Pilate's Letter to Caesar," in *The Archko Volume,* translated by M. McIntosh and T. H. Twyman. Philadelphia: Antiquarian, 1896.
Maier, Paul L. *Pontius Pilate.* Wheaton, Ill.: Tyndale, 1981.
Mawson, C. O. Sylvester. *Roget's Thesaurus.* Garden City, N.Y.: Garden City, 1936.
May, Herbert Gordon. *Oxford Bible Atlas.* London: Oxford University Press, 1974.
Meldau, Fred John. *The Prophets Still Speak: Messiah in Both Testaments.* Denver: Christian Victory, 1988.
Midnight Call, West Columbia, S.C. (October 1993): 12.
Nadler, Sam. "Cheap Sacrifices," *The Chosen People* (December 1990): n.p.
———. "A Fence Around the Law," *The Chosen People* (November 1990): 7.
"Of Whom Does Isaiah 53 Speak?" *The Chosen People.* n.d., n.p.
Owen, G. Frederick. *Jerusalem.* Grand Rapids: Baker, 1972.
Packer, James I., Merrill C. Tenney, and William White, Jr. *The Bible Almanac.* Nashville: Thomas Nelson, 1980.
Papini, Giovanni. *Life of Christ,* translated by Dorothy Canfield Fisher. New York: Harcourt, Brace, 1923.
Peritz, Ismar J. *Old Testament History.* New York: Abingdon, 1915.
Pfeiffer, Charles F., ed. *The Biblical World.* Grand Rapids: Baker, 1966.
Prager, Dennis, and Joseph Telushkin. *Eight Questions People Ask about Judaism.* Whitestone, N.Y.: Tze Ulmad, 1975.
The Revell Bible Dictionary. Old Tappan, N.J.: Revell, 1990.
Rimmer, Harry. *The Harmony of Science and Scripture.* Grand Rapids: Eerdmans, 1936.
———. *Outline Studies of the Trial and Death of Christ.* Los Angeles: Research Science, 1928.
———. *A Scientist's Viewpoint of the Virgin Birth.* 1925.
Rosenthal, Stanley. *One God or Three?* West Collingswood, N.J.: Friends of Israel, 1978.
Roux, Georges. *Ancient Iraq.* Cleveland: World, 1964.
Ryrie, Charles Caldwell. *The Ryrie Study Bible: Epistles of Paul and Hebrews.* Chicago: Moody Press, 1976.
"Sabbath Laws," *Midnight Call.* n.d., n.p.
Sanders, J. Oswald. *The Incomparable Christ.* Chicago: Moody Press, 1971.
Schultz, Samuel J. *The Old Testament Speaks.* New York: Harper & Row, 1960.

Schwartz, Steve. *Dear Rabbi*. Orangeburg, N.Y.: Chosen People, 1980.
Scofield, C. I., ed. *The Scofield Reference Bible*. New York: Oxford University Press, 1945.
Shepherd, Coulson. *The Genealogy of Israel's Messiah*. Brooklyn: Message to Israel, n.d.
Showers, Renald. "Why Anti-Semitism?" *Israel My Glory* (April/May 1993). n.p.
Shulman, Eliezer. *The Sequence of Events in the Old Testament*, translated by Sarah Lederhendler. Jerusalem: Ministry of Defense Pub. House, 1987.
Stevens, Charles. *What It Has Cost the Church to Withhold Christ from the Jews*. New York: American Board of Missions to the Jews, n.d.
Strauss, Lehman. *From Sinai to Calvary*. New York: Loizeaux, 1946.
Tanakh, A New Translation of the Holy Scriptures According to the Traditional Hebrew Text. Philadelphia: Jewish Publication Society, 1985.
Unger, Merrill F. *Unger's Bible Handbook*. Chicago: Moody Press, 1966.
Vine, W. E. *The Expanded Vine's Expository Dictionary of New Testament Words*, edited by John R. Kohlenberger III. Minneapolis: Bethany House, 1984.
Walton, Arthur B. *Tarnished Glory*. Schaumburg, Ill.: Regular Baptist, 1991.
Wilson, William. *New Wilson's Old Testament Word Studies*. Grand Rapids: Kregel, 1987.
Wright, George Ernest, and Floyd Vivian Filson, eds. *The Westminster Historical Atlas to the Bible*. Philadelphia: Westminster, 1945.

INDEX